Katharine Whitney Curtis

Katharine Whitney Curtis
Mother of Synchronized Swimming

Jordan Whitney-Wei

McFarland & Company, Inc., Publishers
Jefferson, North Carolina

All photographs are from the author's collection
unless otherwise indicated.

Library of Congress Cataloguing-in-Publication Data

Names: Whitney-Wei, Jordan, 1992– author. | McFarland & Company.
Title: Katharine Whitney Curtis : mother of synchronized swimming / Jordan Whitney-Wei.
Other titles: Synchronized swimming
Description: Jefferson, North Carolina : McFarland & Company, Inc., Publishers, 2020. | Includes bibliographical references and index.
Identifiers: LCCN 2019053972 | ISBN 9781476664583 (paperback : acid free paper) ∞
ISBN 9781476638232 (eBook)
Subjects: LCSH: Curtis, Katharine Whitney. | Synchronized swimmers—United States—Biography. | Women swimmers—United States—Biography. | Swimmers—United States—Biography. | Synchronized swimming—United States—History.
Classification: LCC GV838.C87 W55 2020 | DDC 797.2/17092 [B]—dc23
LC record available at https://lccn.loc.gov/2019053972

British Library cataloguing data are available

ISBN (print) 978-1-4766-6458-3
ISBN (ebook) 978-1-4766-3823-2

© 2020 Jordan Whitney-Wei. All rights reserved

No part of this book may be reproduced or transmitted in any form or by any means, electronic or mechanical, including photocopying or recording, or by any information storage and retrieval system, without permission in writing from the publisher.

Front cover images: Katharine Whitney Curtis
in Madison, Wisconsin—"First Wool Suit" (1915);
inset The Kay Curtis Modern Mermaids—publicity photo
for the 1934 Chicago World's Fair.

Printed in the United States of America

McFarland & Company, Inc., Publishers
Box 611, Jefferson, North Carolina 28640
www.mcfarlandpub.com

To Gaylord Lee Whitney, my mother's father,
who kept our family story alive,
and who inspired me to share it with the world

Acknowledgments

It's impossible to itemize every source of encouragement and support for a five-year project, but I should certainly begin with my family. They have all witnessed my awkward growth as a writer, and their optimistic patience has challenged me to bring one of my more "goofy" ideas into reality.

I want to specifically recognize my enterprising mother, Andrea Whitney Wei, for inspiring me to develop my own sense of creativity. And my younger brother, Derek, should also be warmly thanked, for strengthening my resolve through both good times and bad. I'm a lucky beneficiary of Grandma Caroline Whitney's uncompromising "red pen," and I shall be eternally grateful to Grandpa Gaylord Whitney, not only for our many words shared in confidence, but especially for his unconditional confidence in me.

Furthermore, I would like to inscribe a smothering hug for each of the following morale-builders: Nancy Parsons, Lisi & Cameron Cuckler, Viktor Karakay, Teresa Brammer, Alex Berrier, Ryan Coolidge, Latearia Jones, Alex Baumann, John Michael & Meredith Honaker, Isaac Rhoades, Jake Schaeffer, Aric French, Spencer Mattix, Melanie Creed, Meredith Ward, Garrett Mahoney, John McCambridge, Eddie Mowery, Kevin Alexander Lankford, Carmen Smith, Ryan Donovan, David McCreary, Joel Kovacs, Tyler Joseph and Clancy.

Finally, this project is indebted to the generous efforts and contributions by Bob Duenkel, Elizabeth Wright, Paul Carvalho, Carl Hardee, Donna Dorn, Bert Hubbard, and the entire Goodwin family: Jamie, Amy & Cathy Goodwin. "Coach Cathy" has been an invaluable ambassador for the Whitney family in Chicago, and she's certainly the only other person whose passion for the history of Katharine Whitney Curtis has rivaled my own. *Soli Deo gloria.*

Table of Contents

Acknowledgments vi
Preface 1

The First Diversion: Beauty (1897–1942)

1. Noble Diversions — 5
2. Out of Madison — 16
3. Making History — 26
4. A Change of Plans — 40

The Second Diversion: Hope (1942–1946)

5. She's Over There — 53
6. Lifting Morale — 66
7. Victory Lap — 79
8. Loved and Lost — 96

The Third Diversion: Harmony (1946–1980)

9. Rebuilding — 115
10. Passing the Torch — 136
11. A Rolling Stone — 165

Chapter Notes 187
Bibliography 192
Index 197

Preface

The story behind the following pages began when my grandfather first revealed and explained the significance of his family's legacy. He was an only child, with not even a cousin to share the burden of keeping this legacy alive, and now it has been entrusted to me. For this reason (among many), this project has been the center of my endeavors for nearly five years.

There has been no full-length biography of my grandfather's "Aunt Kate" until now. And there is little more by way of publications that even mention her role as the originator of synchronized swimming. My comprehensive research on the life of Katharine Whitney Curtis has included the first of several tasks: I have digitized, indexed, "translated" and analyzed over 2,000 pages of (mostly hand-scribbled) correspondence archived at the Chicago History Museum. I have interviewed the very few remaining individuals who knew Curtis throughout her lifetime, and I have therefore gained a rare level of combined insight. And after discovering many other important historical resources, I have now compiled them for academic reference and further inquiry.

But after more than 40 years since her death, the boundaries of this exposition can only extend to whatever time and the personal discretion of my subject have allowed. There were several areas of Curtis's life that she never wished to make known in private, and especially not "on stage." So it would seem that the ideal nature of biography, like poetry or music, is the subtle composition of true and fitting notes, with enough silence to facilitate a deep and affective resonance. I will only provide informed speculation regarding these areas, with a trust that the audience will recognize the most likely truth when they hear it.

Finally, it's not only my job to state the facts, but also to explain their historical context for drawing basic conclusions. And one of the most overarching themes that I've observed and will seek to emphasize is that, despite the chaos and darkness of great challenges across the world, there is a nobility to be found in focusing (at least for a moment) on the beauty, hopes, and harmony of life. I would therefore open my book with the same poetic words that Katharine Whitney Curtis composed to open hers:

> For rhythmic sense of action free,
> We swim.
> To make life what it ought to be,
> We swim.
> We swim to bring us sweet release
> From cares of day and our troubles ease.

The First Diversion
Beauty (1897–1942)

In the beginning, there was water...
And from the water came music.

1

Noble Diversions

True nobility is not achieved by being better than other people—or better than your former self—but by choosing to help other people for the better. And sometimes, the best method is to help them forget their suffering with a reminder of what life ought to be. Beauty can inspire hope, and hope can lead anyone from chaos toward harmony. So, to distract people from their troubles temporarily is to help them recover themselves and move forward in life whenever they're ready. These were the noble diversions of Katharine Whitney Curtis, and this story is meant to remind the world of how she forever changed people's lives for the better.

* * *

In more recent days, an old man with a strange name was clearing the summer storm debris from a remote graveyard. He was on an island among the Great Lakes of the American Midwest for his annual visit to a childhood retreat, about 30 minutes from shore. It was expected to be a casual and uneventful afternoon like most others on Washington Island, which, while beautifully idyllic, was never an ideal location for anyone wholly discontent with peace and quiet. Its population always increased with the temporary return of summer homeowners from the mainland, but far fewer individuals were ever left behind to greet the heavy winter snows that form an icy tundra over the waves. Many of these hardy folk are proud descendants of that region's Nordic pioneers, who, after initially crossing the Atlantic, were naturally drawn to these sturgeon-filled waters. Unsurprisingly, Washington Island's natives are still regarded as starkly independent, resourceful, and traditionally isolated (by choice).

This was the general impression of things for Gaylord Lee Whitney, just another "fair-weather" summer visitor, as he tended the grave of his Grandma Anne. She always called herself "the old woman who lives under the hill," and was also from the mainland originally, but Mrs. Whitney was uniquely respected as an invaluable force of nature. In her time, she lived (all year round) at a well-established homestead, and was particularly renowned as the writer-researcher of *Let's Talk About Washington Island*, a small book that devotedly chronicled the centennial history of this special community—a veritable Hobbiton for Wisconsin, that is, if hobbits looked more like Vikings.

Just beyond the verge of his grandmother's plot, Gaylord cleared an overgrowth of green and white lily-of-the-valley, which was shrouding the sight of a marble-carved Madonna and Child. This travel relic was once salvaged from the ruins of an Italian battlefield, and was now fittingly planted to watch over its adventurous savior (also interred nearby). As Gaylord finished his reverential task, he noticed a young woman wandering across the graveyard. She seemed to be showing great curiosity in everything around her, and, after greeting the only other pilgrim in view, it was soon revealed that she had spontaneously boarded the local ferry to explore the unknown vistas across the water. The old man praised her adventurous spirit, and then pointed her toward another gravestone for a surprising discovery. Little did she know, there—carved in stone, and countersunk among the grass—the name of Katharine Whitney Curtis was curiously misspelled. But the hiker was delighted by the mere happenstance of this unexpected roadside distraction, and she made sure to take a couple photos before departing again.

Katharine Whitney Curtis's gravestone, with her first name misspelled, in Washington Island's cemetery.

Gaylord returned to Ohio and gave his unofficial report to the Whitney family's current writer-in-training, who had remained equally delighted ever since his own moment of offhand revelation. The premise of this story once began as a baffling enigma to Gaylord's most distractible grandson, who had somehow failed to appreciate (or even comprehend) previous remarks like, "My Aunt Kate was the creator of synchronized swimming." But by one fine day of chance, this phrase ignited into a source of pure fascination with a magical reordering of all former childhood impressions—especially from Disney's *Beauty and the Beast* (1991), with its enchanted flatware diving to music in splashes of punch. With surprising nonchalance, the old man seemed to personally summon this prominent star down from the sky, and just for the sake of educating a boy of his secret heritage among the world. This process matured into a simple devotion for the truth, and with an eager hope that this story might likewise inspire the imagination of future stargazers. It was shortly after my grandfather's 2015 trip to Washington Island that I signed a publishing contract with McFarland, and so my own journey officially began.

This Is Your Life

About 50 years before, in West Germany, a radio microphone was positioned on stage by the upright piano, and a crowd of local military personnel was getting ready for the big surprise. Director Kay Curtis was a longtime compatriot for everyone now gathered, and today was going to be their attempt to recreate a popular TV show and recognize her many accomplishments. She had first arrived decades ago with the armies that stood against fascism in Europe. And only a year since Berlin was partitioned by communists to keep their war-torn citizens in captivity, the woman with many stories was now setting sail toward retirement and her journey's end. Everyone was affected by the extreme global tensions that would very soon lead to the Cuban Missile Crisis, but, despite all of this political discord, brief moments of levity always seemed ready to insulate local morale from the pervasive frostbite of the Cold War. So, as the emcee finalized some last-minute notes among the official script in her binder, Curtis was being pulled aside from her work to attend one last diversion between friends.

Curtis (*center*) celebrating her retirement in West Germany (1962).

The event began with a young woman drifting toward center stage with a lost expression. She was carrying a well-traveled suitcase and wearing the formal dress uniform of the Special Services, an entertainment branch of the U.S. military. The room was silent until the emcee made her first announcement: "This is a familiar sight in Europe today, because … Kay Curtis … this is your life!"

A different woman, waiting for the cue, began to play the piano as a soldier led Curtis up some stairs to an armchair beside the title card. The music faded, and the emcee continued:

"On January 4 (1897) in Milwaukee, Wisconsin—before Special Services was special, or even a service—a girl was born who was to change the mind, manners and memories of over a million US citizens. We are here this afternoon to reconstruct some of the events that brought this young lady to the position she now holds."

There was some commotion behind a screen, and the voice of an elderly woman addressed the room:

"Kay, you don't remember me, but I was the first draft-typist for your book on synchronized swimming!"

The woman revealed herself with a smile.

"Gee, Kay, do you remember me? It's Gladys Gouch! It was a swell book, Kay. Are they still using it?"

In fact, *Rhythmic Swimming* had been published in several editions by this time, and the audience was soon informed of its various followers, including the American Red Cross and numerous colleges back home.

"Gee, Kay, when I worked on your book, I lived, lived, lived. It was great working with you, Kay. But, you know, you couldn't spell worth a damn!"

"Please, Miss Gouch, we are on the air! Please take your seat with Miss Curtis. You'll have a chance to visit later. Kay, while teaching swimming at the University of Chicago [in 1923], you synchronized body movements in the water with rhythm of music, and you are credited with giving birth to a sport which has become popular throughout the world. Kay, do you remember the show that you had at the Chicago World's Fair of 1934, the Kay Curtis Modern Mermaids?"

With that announcement came three young women dressed in period bathing suits as the piano introduced a theme. The girls danced in a circle on the main floor below the stage, and what followed was the debut performance of a special song, "Katie":

> Katie, do you remember when we swam at the Chicago Fair?
> My, wasn't it pretty there?
> Honors, why we won a whole pool full
> The judges gave us the eye
> It was great to be a mermaid and swim the ballet leg—down,
> Deep, under the water blue—the dolphin we swam, just me and you
> Katie, do you remember the submarine we started there?
> It was Chicago ... yes, Chicago
> A short twenty-eight years ago.

The mermaids sat with Gladys down in front of the stage while the audience gave their applause.

"Kay, while you were working on grace and beauty, the world was moving in the opposite direction. World War II was in the making. You gave up your place beside the pool and took your place at the front. You landed alongside Ike [Eisenhower] and worked as a Red Cross recreation director in North Africa and Italy. Someone was needed to direct a rest home near Casablanca—you were that gal! Someone was needed to open and operate a rest center for aviation pilots in Capri—you were that gal! And from 1944 to 1946 you supervised all the American Red Cross clubs in Southern France. At the close of World War II, when both the economy of Europe and GI morale needed a boost, the army established its Leave Activities Office."

"Kay Curtis, you were the one who knew the needs of the GI traveler: Private's Pay, The Long Weekend, and The Three-Day Pass. Your dream and plans have taken American servicemen and their families on jaunts to the nearest castle, to the world's best music festivals, from across the snow-capped mountains to the desert plains, and across Iron Curtains. But good travel plans are not made in a day; because of your interest, a GI can walk into any one of two-hundred service clubs or libraries and find reams of tour material, country books, recreation area information, hop-schedules and up-to-date documents on where and with whom to travel ... a GI today can take a trip—a three-day trip—to Paris!"

The background music suddenly began to swell for a grand announcement by another voice behind the screen:

> Nuremberg, Germany—October 2 (1959)—Mrs. Kay Curtis, chief of the Leave Activities Office [...for the] United States Army, Europe, has been elected to the Helms Athletic Hall of Fame in Los Angeles for early and noteworthy contributions to synchronized swimming. Together with Annette Kellerman—a famous swimmer of the early 1900s who introduced the one-piece bathing suit and solo water ballets—Mrs. Curtis recently was selected by the national American Athletic Association for an initial niche in the newly established synchronized swimming honor roll at Helms Hall.

The last of Curtis's surprise guests emerged to join the cheering section, and the emcee started to conclude the event:

"Kay, you have been a very busy person. There is no end to your work. You have made the world smaller, and enlightened the hearts of many. We understand from your friends that you will continue your travels instead of returning directly home. So we have collected money from all the tours funds from all over [our] service clubs! And we would like to present you with tickets to your destinations."

Some corresponding travel posters were walked out for the crowd to recite, and the last of these was revealed to be Hawaii.

"Since you will probably have a chance to dress formally on the islands, we would like to present to you this lei, designed especially for you. This last memento is a symbol of your work in Europe, and of all the good times that we have had in working with the tours program."

The first woman, in the Special Services uniform, wrapped a commemorative bracelet around Curtis's wrist, and the hall was filled with the chorus of a final farewell.

"So, to you, Kay Curtis … '*Auf wiedersehen und gute Fahrt!*'"[1]

Family Traditions

A few more decades back, in December of 1923, a man by the name of Lee Rankin Whitney was on his way home from his meeting with the president of the United States, Calvin Coolidge. Lee was visiting Washington, D.C., as a vice president of the National Federation of Federal Employees (NFFE), a labor union embroiled with concerns surrounding the recent Salary Reclassification Act. He was in attendance with other officials when Coolidge personally gave assurance of "fair play," and that the federal employees in Wisconsin were expected to receive their full benefits. A week later, this encouraging news was happily reported in the newspaper back home, when Lee was already back to work at the Milwaukee Bureau of Marine Inspection and Navigation (also known as the Steamboat Office).[2]

Lee had risen to the rank of vice president in the NFFE after only a year of membership, and was a frequent subject of interest for local newspapers. Readers were treated to various stories about his unique experiences, both comical and heartfelt, which he always knew how to transform into an anecdote for the right occasion. One such example was found among other clippings:

> Another son of the sea has come forth to prove the adage of the sailors, that they always "square a debt." Six months ago, a sailor went to the office of Lee R. Whitney, clerk in the United States steamboat inspection office. He was looking for work, he said. He had not eaten since the night before. Whitney pressed a dollar into the man's hand, told him to get a good meal, and promptly forgot the incident. Yesterday, the sailor came back. He walked to Mr. Whitney's desk. Mr. Whitney did not recognize the youth until he pulled a dollar bill from his pocket, handed it to the clerk, and walked out. After he had gone, Mr. Whitney realized he had not learned the name of the ship or the sailor.[3]

Lee was also featured in a brief advertisement concerning his loyalty to a straight Jimmy pipe, which he regarded as "just the thing to give one a nautical air." The ad-spot continued boasting, "Wherever Lee goes, the pipe goes with him. Such fidelity must be deserved."[4]

Lee was widely known as a generous man who always stood by noble ideals, such as in one particular instance, "The good citizen in thought and deed embodies loyal service to enrich the common life." He was active with the local Masons (like his father before him), and Lee was also a principal founder of the Wisconsin Archaeological Society. It was hard to not be impressed by either his many accomplishments or his overall bearing as a gentleman, and he undoubtedly served as a grand figure of inspiration for his eldest child, Katharine, whenever it came to stepping up as needed in the public light. But, by the time Lee returned home from DC that winter, it was to the Milwaukee residence of his mother, Jane Rankin Whitney. She always kept a spare room prepared for him, even as early as 1911, when another lighthearted anecdote was printed:

> That night, [Lee] was invited out and started for his mother's home at about 10:00 in the evening. His room is at the head of the stairs, and, as he silently crept up the winding steps (without a light), he slid his hand into his back pocket for his latchkey. He had just reached the top landing and started for his door when suddenly he lurched off into space, and, before he could get his hand out of his pocket and his arms into action, he found himself halfway through the floor, dangling by one leg and one arm to a rafter. Unbeknown to Whitney, his mother had ordered the house wired for the installation of electric light, and the electricians had pulled up the entire floor in the hallway. Lee stepped through the plaster ceiling of the room below. He avows flight through space and plaster was the worst drop he ever experienced, and intimates that he will teach those wire experts a lesson if he ever gets a chance.[5]

Sometime between this (less dignified) evening and his visit with President Coolidge, Lee had separated from his wife and moved in temporarily with his mother. By the 1920 Census, Lee was recorded as being "single," while the former Mrs. Whitney saw fit to report that, unfortunately, she happened to be "widowed." This apparent animosity may be related to the 1930 Census, which later revealed that Lee was already living within the household of his second wife, who also happened to be 18 years younger than him. But despite all this romantic drama, the love never waned between Lee and his children, especially Katharine, who would always regard his paternal support as her "anchor to the wind."

Katharine was one of five siblings, although one had died very young in 1904. Little is known about this sister (Edna), but her loss was certainly a strain on the newly established family, and perhaps a driving wedge between Lee and his formidable wife. Mrs. Whitney would ultimately move the remaining children to Madison, Wisconsin, about 80 miles away from their early home in Delafield. And by Lee's D.C. trip in 1923, everyone else had already moved 90 miles south to Chicago, Illinois. So, while the chief clerk at the Steamboat Office would always make an effort to support and encourage his children, he would remain otherwise committed to both his second wife (Pearle) and his Irish-born mother (Jane) in Milwaukee.

Lee was very proud of his family heritage, and would often promote its unique history to fascinate and encourage those around him. The Whitney name is of English origin, and can be traced back confidently to the early Massachusetts Bay Colony, before the Revolutionary War in America. Lee Rankin Whitney's father was Leroy Chester Whitney (1846–1910), another public servant who likewise managed to appear in various newspaper articles, including one such public encounter (around 1902) with President Theodore Roosevelt.[6] Overall, this family line can be linked back to the original John Whitney (1592–1673), who traveled from England in 1635, fifteen years after the historic *Mayflower* landing at Plymouth.[7] In this sense, the family could not be more "American" without having any specific aboriginal birthright. But, in contrast to Lee's paternal lineage, his mother's family was entirely new to the United States, and would come to fully embody the classical immigrant archetype.

Lee's mother, Jane Whitney (née Rankin), was born across the Atlantic to a privileged household amid the infamous devastation of the Irish Potato Famine. Her family had been long established in Ireland with roles of esteem in their community, including a line of protestant ministers, and some respectable marriages into the "landed gentry" (land-owning commoners). Jane's maternal grandfather was the vicar of Rathcline in County Longford, and resided at the beautiful estate of Drummond Park. Jane's (2X) great-grandfather was the venerable archdeacon, Daniel Hearn of Cashel (1693–1766), who was the private chaplain to Lionel Cranfield Sackville, the first duke of Dorset and lord lieutenant of Ireland.[8] Jane also happened to share Daniel Hearn as an ancestor with a famous third-cousin, Lafcadio Hearn, an expatriate writer who achieved some cultural notoriety in Japan. Overall, there was much to revere about their family traditions, and especially the lives of two other remarkable individuals, whose adventurous tale of struggle and noble contribution would inspire generations to come. These individuals were Jane's mother and father.

Arabella Rankin (née Hearn) was born in 1819 and married Francis Hamilton Rankin on September 8, 1843, in Dublin. Arabella had grown up at Drummond Park as a clever and high-spirited girl who showed great promise toward a variety of interests, and Francis was a well-educated widower who worked as a government employee in the Dublin Custom House. For five years, they lived an exciting life surrounded by interesting people, including the famous writer William Carleton, who is credited with first depicting in literature the stereotypical "Irishman." It was during this period of prosperity that Jane was born, in 1846.

By the end of 1847, the Rankin family's condition was drastically upturned after Francis discovered and exposed an embezzlement scheme by his immediate superior. The resulting legal trial swiftly concluded with a guilty verdict on February 18, 1848, but, by the very next day, Francis was forced to resign because of his mere association with the public scandal. He regretfully recounted in his journal, "I was now to be cast off, without the discovery of any new fault against me. Went home and told Arabella our misfortune, which she bore like a Trojan, [and we] determined on immediately disposing of all our available goods, and going to America."[9] By March 14, they arranged for their children to be looked after temporarily by Arabella's sister. And, after saying their difficult goodbyes, they boarded the good ship *Infanta*, bound for New York.

Francis and Arabella suffered stormy weather, extreme sea-sickness, and delays that amounted in a month-long voyage. When they arrived on April 22, 1848, the ship was met with the brashness of the American revenue officers, who, after boarding from a steamer at 6:00 a.m., made their cursory inspections and proceeded to transfer the luggage "with such roughness that many chests were literally smashed, and some went overboard." Luckily, the Rankin couple's own luggage was spared any damage, which allowed them to more fully appreciate their final approach, as further described by Francis:

> New York looks magnificent coming in from the harbor: her broad river on which a thousand ships are floating—ferry steamers of beautiful build, flitting every moment between NY and Brooklyn—and the spires and domes of fine buildings catching the eye on every side. We were soon landed in the country of our adoption, and had no sooner set foot on the quay [loading dock] than we were surrounded by runners from low boarding houses—enticing us with flattering promises—to prefer the house each was employed by. Having been already warned of these people, I dreaded going with them; however, being entirely ignorant of where else to go, a party of the passengers agreed to go together to the house of an Irishman in Washington St. named Nixon.

Meanwhile, Francis and Arabella just sat there in the hot sun, unsure of what to do next. They managed to buy some fresh cheese and white bread, which provided a welcome break from the lengthy salt-diet of their venture, but their troubles quickly resumed after reluctantly deciding to follow a runner.

> Between the quay and the lodging house, the luggage tumbled off the cart at least half a dozen times. Then, such a house as we got into—the table not supplied with half enough of food, and that of the most inferior description—the beds were filthy and literally alive with bugs. About sixteen of us sleeping in one room! "Sleeping" it could not be called, for poor Arabella was obliged to get up and sit all night on her box, being able to lie no longer when she found the pillow absolutely speckled with bugs and lice.

A few days later, they arranged to leave New York on an evening steamer for Albany, but only after dramatically quarrelling over their housing bill. The landlord had deceived them about their daily rate, but Francis had the ingenuity to petition the local Irish Emigration Society, which armed him the legal knowledge that this landlord could be arrested for refusing to release their luggage. Francis later recounted that, in addition to resolving his own situation, "[I] settled for all our party, to the discomfiture of all the bullies who had amusingly gotten off their high horses." He then bought two tickets with an extra fee for Arabella to sleep in a narrow bed, and one of the last notable details recorded for this day was, that, after all was settled, "[I] roughed it myself all night on a chair."

They traveled up the Hudson River to Albany, and boarded a train going west to Buffalo. They were joined by great crowds of other Irish and Dutch immigrants going by the same passenger cars, "Which were merely baggage wagons without seats or springs, [and] our trunks and boxes being converted into the only seats we had." They admired the scenery in the open air during the day, and they "suffered dreadfully all night from the cold, without any place to lie down." And by the morning of May 5, they took an old railway car up through the woods to Pontiac, Michigan, "Where we had been told [Francis' cousin] lived—our principal inducement to come here—[but] great was our disappointment to find he had left this a few months ago." So after traveling over 800 miles, with the modest hopes of seeing their only family in America, they sat there weary and alone once again, wondering what to do next.

Their money was nearly spent by this point, so on May 6, 1848, they found a house for rent, and were fortunately met with the "greatest possible kindness" by their new neighbors. "In short, all seemed vying with each other in serving the stranger." On May 8, Francis wrote his cousin a long letter that both announced their arrival and requested advice on how to get involved in the local newspaper industry. Meanwhile, Francis got some work as a house painter in the town of Lapeer (30 miles north), after the local clergyman of Pontiac invited Arabella to live with his family temporarily. So the couple parted reluctantly for over two weeks as Francis worked tirelessly to establish their life in America. He made sure to correspond regularly with Arabella, who was particularly distressed at their being separated. And on June 28, while not being able to otherwise find a ride back south, Francis received some news so critical that it compelled him to walk those 30 miles all day in the heat. After finding Arabella blissful and well-attended in Pontiac, he nearly collapsed and "went to bed almost immediately."

The reason for his urgency was revealed two weeks later on August 11, 1848, when Francis finally wrote about something he'd not mentioned so far in his diary:

> A day to be remembered! Poor Arabella [was] complaining going to bed, though she walked a good deal in the evening. About 3:00 in the morning, she got so ill [...that] I found it necessary to go for Doctor Paddock. [...] And, about 5:00, a young American came into the world, in safety to both mother and son, thank God!

Arabella had been pregnant for the whole journey, ever since Ireland, and the "seasickness" she suffered—along with any other general discomfort—can be easily understood by her condition. This also explains the extra measures taken by Francis to accommodate his wife during their difficult journey. But the struggles of their tale were not to lessen, for, only a month later, the child contracted cholera—a bacterial disease spread by water contamination—and Francis mournfully recounted on September 15, 1848, "I was startled into wakefulness by Arabella's crying to me: 'Francis, our baby's dead!'"

In the days that followed, Francis threw himself back into his work, pursuing a job at Pontiac's local paper after connecting with his cousin. And, by September of 1849, Arabella gave birth to another child, who would thrive for years to come. Francis proved determined to learn everything about the printing trade, and his own big opportunity arrived at the start of the next year, when a managing position became available in the town of Flint, Michigan. They moved there in February 1850, and were later joined by Francis' eldest son, Charley, who came from Ireland to assist them with the reporting and other newspaper operations. These four Rankins began to prosper and establish a respectable position in that society, especially Arabella, who became a founding member of many local organizations. The next decade provided a flurry of activity, with Arabella giving birth to three more children, and while also arranging for Jane and her brother to come over from Ireland.

It was upon this new decade that Francis considered stepping into public service. He had already become political by the activities of his newspaper, which was starting to support a promising new candidate, Abraham Lincoln, who would win the national election just before Charley went off to college. Francis had well earned the respect of many local politicians, and would himself be elected to represent Genesee County in the Michigan State House by his first journal entry for January of 1861:

> Another new year opens upon me, and I thank God with better hopes, less anxieties, and in a prouder position than any I have yet occupied. Today, I leave my family to take my seat among the legislators of my adopted state—a position I could not have dared to hope for ten years ago. Although my embarrassments are by no means at an end, the prospect looks better for overcoming them, and especially if Arabella proves equal to the task of attending well to the business in my absence.

Indeed, Arabella would prove just as successful throughout Francis' tenure at the Michigan state capi-

A photograph with four generations: (*clockwise*) Katharine Whitney Curtis (three months old), Arabella Rankin, Lee Rankin Whitney, Jane Whitney (née Rankin).

tal of Lansing, which was more than 50 miles away. She not only supervised the children, but also managed to correspond daily with Francis, fold newspapers, collect debts, sell advertising, and balance their bookkeeping. Her eldest son would help with all the physical labor for a time, but he would eventually join the Union Army by July 1861, only a couple months after the start of the American Civil War.

Charley volunteered with the Second Michigan Infantry (Company F), known as the "Flint Union Greys." They arrived in Virginia by July 21, 1861, for the Civil War's first major engagement, the Battle of Bull Run, and were initially posted in Washington, D.C., when the rebels arrived at the railroad crossing of Manassas Junction. The Union troops advanced on the Confederates, who, after various skirmishes, made a victorious last stand on Henry Hill. It was here that their famously statuesque general acquired his nickname, Stonewall Jackson, and Charley Rankin would provide first-hand reporting of this historic event for his father's newspaper back home.

Charley soon died of disease on September 20, 1861, like so many others in his regiment, due to both poor living conditions and substandard medical practices. This period was dominated by a heavy silence in Francis' journal until the first day of 1862.

> I resume my diary, after another break and hiatus since September [1861]. In that month, I was summoned to Virginia to see my brave boy, Charley, before he died. Alas! I arrived there to find his body was on its way home for interment. I will pass over the pain of that time. Suffice it to say, I lost my talented son, and wrote no journal since until today.

Francis devotedly returned to Lansing and the responsibilities of his elected office, while Arabella continued her own rapid pace of activities, being further inspired by this tragedy to somehow improve conditions for the common soldier. She volunteered for the Soldier's Aid Society, became associated with the Chicago branch of the U.S. Sanitary Commission, and was chosen by 1863 to serve on their executive committee.

More than 80 years later, toward the end of World War II, Arabella's side of the story was more effectively described by her grandson, Lee, who sought to inspire his fellow Americans by arranging this feature in *The Milwaukee Journal*:

> When the Civil War broke out, Arabella helped her husband write bristling headlines for their weekly newspaper, *The Wolverine Citizen*, in addition to superintending the education of their seven children. These tasks were not enough for this forceful woman, however. Her dark brown eyes flashed with fanatic fire as she wrote, with painstakingly beautiful handwriting in her diary, "I feel I must do something, even in a secondary way, for those who have done so much for us. There must be some way to express thanks."
>
> A little later, when her eldest [stepson] died in service, she didn't take to her bed. Not Arabella! She tied her diminutive bonnet (of straw and green velvet) firmly under her chin, removed the hoops from her skirt, and got busy turning the local Lady's Aid Society into the Soldier's Aid society, and then into the US Sanitary Commission.
>
> At first, Arabella and her daughters merely stayed at home and sewed. She was president of the group in Flint. They outfitted entire regiments with uniforms. [...But] soon, these women decided to do more than sew. Under Arabella's direction, they appeared at railroad stations whenever trains bearing soldiers arrived. Many of these expert homemakers brought loaves of homemade bread, jam, meat, eggs, and pots of hot coffee to feed the hungry, blue-clad men. Others of the group stood in long lines with basins of hot water, soap, and clean towels, so that the travel-worn soldiers could wash. Whenever a wretchedly ill soldier was found, he was taken home by Arabella and put to bed in the family's best four-poster. "Angels of mercy," Lincoln called these women, when he approved their organization in 1861.
>
> [While also establishing many important] kitchens, canteens, hospitals and clubs, the purpose of the US Sanitary Commission was to see that the troops were made sanitary. The doctors willing to affiliate

themselves with the group received two dollars a day for inspecting. The women received no recompense but letters like this one, which Arabella Rankin received:

Headquarters, Tenth Regiment
Michigan Infantry
Nashville, Tennessee
June 15, 1863

Mrs. F. H. Rankin:

We send you this chart embracing a short history of our regiment, thinking that perhaps it may prove acceptable to you, as you have shown yourself truly a friend to the soldiers. Our regiment is indebted to you for many substantial proofs of your friendship, and we can never forget yourself and your lady friends of Flint for the many kindnesses received at your hands. We ask you to please accept with this our sincere wishes for your future happiness and that you may soon see our once happy country again united.[10]

The U.S. Sanitary Commission involved many other impressive women, including Clara Barton, who would keep this organization's objectives alive by founding the American Red Cross (ARC) in 1881. And by the time Lee was sharing the Rankin family documents for this article in 1945, his eldest daughter was already overseas as a recreational director in the ARC, establishing many important kitchens, canteens, hospitals and clubs. Curtis would likewise meet the American soldiers of her day with a loving smile and a tender mindset—no doubt, thinking about the many noble examples preceding her own efforts to make a positive difference in people's lives.

2

Out of Madison

A week before D-Day, June 6, 1944, and the start of the Normandy Landings—the largest seaborne invasion in history—there was an impressive Memorial Day parade along Michigan Avenue, back home in Chicago. Over 400,000 citizens were in attendance, including a diverse representation of America's veterans, both past and present. And while many more GIs were secretly preparing to begin a desperate fight for the liberation of Europe, Chicago was celebrating every ribbon, medal and bandage-clad hero all the same. But somewhere among the parade's 30,000 participants, marching to inspiring music and hopeful ovations, there was an open-top car with four very old men. They were some of the last surviving veterans from the American Civil War, and the youngest of these was a former drummer boy—James Crugom (Jr.)—who, at 94 years old, was often referred to as "the baby" amongst his peers. He was a retired piano teacher who first came to Chicago from Wisconsin in 1888, and he also happened to be the brother of Katharine Whitney Curtis's (maternal) grandmother.

The night before the parade, "Uncle Jim" was interviewed for *The Chicago Sun* newspaper by a local writer, Paul T. Gilbert, who was known for featuring more public figures, such as Albert Einstein or Eleanor Roosevelt. But Gilbert would have been just as fascinated by this small and modest character, who would reminisce upon request about running bandages as a child through ranks of Yankee muskets, and with a stout memory of thunderous mortar shells bursting overhead. Jim's life would ultimately span from the days of slavery in America to the dawn of the Nuclear Age, and he was now gladly offering Gilbert some personal reflections to help bolster Chicago's wartime morale when it was most needed.

At his home, [James (Jr.)] produced from among his souvenirs a faded daguerreotype [photograph], in which he is portrayed in the uniform of the "Boys in Blue" at the age of eleven, and with his father, Major James Crugom (Sr.), staff surgeon.

"One of the duties of the drummer boys," [James (Jr.)] said, "was to aid the army surgeons at the base hospital. The artillery, firing grape and canister caused wounds comparable to those made by shrapnel today. […] Hideous operations had to be performed without anesthetic, and, as you can imagine, I was scared to death. But, eventually, I outgrew my fears and could look on unmoved at the torture of the wounded soldiers."

[James (Sr.)], a widower, […first] took his eldest son, Joseph, with him into the Army. Joseph was fifteen years old, and a drum major. "'Why can't I go, too?' I demanded," Crugom (Jr.) recalls. […] "So, Dad, maybe because he wanted to keep me under his wing, took me along. I carried his instrument case for him on the field. And, part of the time, he kept me in the guardhouse so that I wouldn't wander off and get into trouble."

Crugom (Jr.) saw action in Kentucky at the Battle of Perryville, where the Rebels charged, "Yelling like wild Indians. We couldn't load our Springfield rifles fast enough, […] and our men were fighting with their gun stocks and bayonets. Our regiment was decimated, but we had the Johnnies on the run. The hospital was in shambles after that engagement."

[…And], at the age of ninety-four, Crugom (Jr.) is not only the youngest GAR [Grand Army of the Republic] man in Chicago, but probably [one of the youngest] in the United States. He was born in 1850 in Paris, France, of English parents, [before moving to Wisconsin].

[…] The First Wisconsin [Infantry] was attached to General Grant's "Army of the West." Of Grant, Crugom (Jr.) says, "He was beloved by all his men. He put on no airs, and there was no style about him."[1]

Katharine Whitney Curtis would have been raised with similar tales of adventure throughout her entire childhood, especially with Uncle Jim acting as storyteller for each and every Memorial Day celebration until the day he died on May 30, 1948—remarkably, the eightieth anniversary for the very first U.S. Memorial Day.

The full measure of Uncle Jim's patriotism and nostalgia can be appreciated by opening his scrapbook of clippings and photographs that showcase his many public appearances. And, as depicted through its final pages, the growing number of empty chairs at each annual reunion would have only underscored the solemnity of his final years. But Jim remained energetic and cheerful to the very end, walking a mile every day, and playing (just as impressively) the piano songs that he wrote as a much younger man. He was always determined to celebrate the intrinsic beauty of life, and, by faithfully respecting and remembering the past, he so inspired those around him to make their own mark on the future.

Uncle Jim's father, Dr. James Crugom (Sr.), was born in London (1822), and obtained his medical license from the Royal College of Surgeons in 1841. After avoiding some debt and the "sponging houses" by moving to Paris, he eventually moved to Milwaukee in 1852 to conduct his own medical practice (before and after the Civil War) until 1870. He then returned to Europe, "To give his children the advantage of a musical education at Leipzig, Germany." This would be his final provision as a parent, for, after "returning to Milwaukee, his career was suddenly terminated by an accident, being run over [by a horse carriage in 1874]."[2] James (Jr.) was 24 years old at the time, and thus began his adult life without either of his parents to guide him further. It was shortly after this tragedy that he began to compose music. And just after the release of Thomas Edison's first commercial light-bulb patent in 1879, James (Jr.) contributed to the atmosphere of public fascination by composing a lively and optimistic polka, "Electric Light." His sister, Ellen, would be the only sibling of their immediate generation to have children, one of which would be Katharine Whitney Curtis's mother, and therefore this story's next important character.

Anne Townsend Whitney

Anne Townsend Whitney was born Anne Ellen Townsend in Milwaukee, December of 1875, during the economic flurry of the Black Hills Gold Rush, which was drawing hopeful prospectors and pioneers west to the Dakota Territory. Her father, Akerly Townsend, would eventually run the PX (postal exchange) for the now famous Fort Abraham Lincoln in North Dakota. It was from this outpost in 1876 that George Armstrong Custer departed with 700 U.S. cavalry toward the Montana river valley of the Little Bighorn. This fateful venture led to shocking headlines around the world, reporting the tragic climax of their "Last Stand." Custer and 267 of his men were annihilated by the Lakota Sioux (and other local tribes), who were resisting unchecked relocation efforts by the American government.

Fort Abraham Lincoln would eventually be made redundant after the building of a new railroad line to Montana in 1883, but subsequent letters to Akerly and Ellen Townsend still survive from this transition period with the handwriting of a young "Annie," who was being raised by other family members (just west of Milwaukee) in Waukesha, Wisconsin. Among other details, Anne wrote about receiving her Christmas presents by mail, which generally suggests that this period was indeed when her parents were initially posted on the western frontier.[3] Their family was ultimately reunited for the context of a special story that has since been passed down. But, in order to frame the exact timeline of this family's oral history, it must also be stated that the fort was fully abandoned by 1891, scrapped for materials and rebuilt by 1895—after which, it would have been much safer (and much more likely) for Anne to join her parents out west.

Regardless of when, it was here (or someplace nearby) that "Buffalo" Bill Cody showed up for one of his iconic "Wild West" productions. Whitney would later recall how Cody so characteristically arrived at their local barn dance, dressed up with his big hat, and looking to join arms with the most beautiful girl around. In retrospect, her own grandson would freely remark that she was probably "too good-looking for her own good," so it was only inevitable that Buffalo Bill picked "Grandma Anne" to match his own charm, confidence and charisma. They danced as equals under the twinkling strands of (newly installed) electric light, while everyone else just marveled in the blurry sidelines around them. And it was obvious that Anne Townsend Whitney retained this power to intrigue anyone throughout her lifetime, with an alluring smile that always implied she knew how to dance with legends.

Whitney evolved as a self-taught and self-motivated student of the world, with an insatiable curiosity that was often seen as being either delightfully contagious or just plain exhausting. She was never shy at quoting Shakespeare, as in one particular instance, that "all the world's a stage, and all the men and women merely players; they have their exits and their entrances, and one man in his time plays many parts." Her literacy in this regard developed from her undying love of theater, which eventually led her to establish and preside over a relatively successful troop, "The Fine Arts Players." It always seemed that she was finding a creative way to research, kickstart and sustain some new endeavor, with a uniquely effective tenacity for any woman born in the nineteenth century.

It was to this passionate tempest that a 25-year-old Lee Rankin

Anne and Katharine (c. 1898).

Whitney pledged himself on January 30, 1896. They were married among all their family at the Episcopal St. James Church in Milwaukee, and their first child was conceived only a few months later. Meanwhile—in Athens, Greece—the first modern Olympics Games were also being brought into reality, by April 6. This renewed institution was curiously destined to mature as a slightly older sibling for someone who would help change it forever. And thus, the future mother of synchronized swimming was born, on January 4, 1897. The new parents chose the name of Katharine Townsend Whitney.

Her siblings quickly followed. Robert Lee Whitney was born on December 13, 1898, and Edna Whitney was born sometime around August of 1899. Katharine once explained, "Because of a growing family of children, [my mother eventually] moved from Milwaukee to a small Wisconsin village, in order to raise us in the wide-open spaces."[4] This village was Delafield, and Jane Ellen Whitney was born on April 26, 1903, with George Whitney being the last to arrive, on March 13, 1906. Curtis continued describing her childhood in what she creatively titled, "The Saga of an Untrained Recreation Worker," a speech about the history of her early inspirations:

> The seed started in my mother, who had the spirit but no training. [...] She soon became the character who introduced the [Delafield] villagers to St. Nicholas with an annual St. Nick's parade for the children in the hall above the grocery store, where we haltingly spoke our pieces in order to secure a bag of penny candies. It was in our yard that the July 4 social was laboriously created, with prayers that it would not rain and ruin the crêpe paper streamers.
>
> In the old post office building, [Anne Townsend Whitney] established a small library, the first in [Delafield], which is still living. She helped the teacher of the consolidated school to teach the participants in the graduation maypole dance, at which my petticoat fell off in the midst of the winding. As I dashed in tears to the schoolhouse to button it on again, in my opinion, I might as well have been naked.
>
> Mother entered the dramatic field with a group of the village children, playing "Florinda: A Fairy Play," with all of us in long underwear, slippers (made of old sheets), and stiff tutus. We even toured neighboring villages with our horse and [carriage]. I can still remember how crushed I was the night my youngest sister lost her slipper and sat down in the footlights, [with her] back to the audience to replace it, while the whole dance had to stop. But we started up again at the signal of the piano accompanist in the wings. Mother also dragged us out on horse-cart camping trips, on one of which, a cow turned our storage tent into shambles and scared us all to pieces.

These happy memories were eventually darkened by the death of Edna in 1904, and also by the shroud of Lee's growing impatience with Anne's domineering personality. And while it cannot be overlooked that Lee was probably the one to initiate the split (with an extramarital affair), the requisite friction leading them to divorce was ultimately mutual.

Another important historical detail about this period was mentioned by Curtis: "I began my swimming career, long before I could swim on the surface of the water, by diving for pennies thrown into the millpond by summer visitors." Overall, this time in Delafield was a crucial step in her childhood, and it also allowed her mother to strategically prepare for their future. "With an eye on all of us attending the university, my mother moved the family to Madison," the capital of Wisconsin, and "during my high-school career I was very active in sports." She quickly became proficient in speed swimming, while also showing promise in hockey, ice skating, track and field, horseback riding, basketball, and various other offerings at the school clubs or summer camps in between. Curtis wrote that she was inspired to get further involved in these activities when "an article appeared in the Madison paper about a new project called a 'Recreation Program.' [...The administrators] needed a volunteer assistant [...which] began my long career in the recreation field."

Curtis swimming at Camp Pinemere.

Anne Townsend Whitney was perpetually encouraging her daughter's many interests and endeavors, with a small example of this creative support also being mentioned in Curtis's later speech:

> My first speech on recreation was given during my freshman year in high school, at the request of the son of the chairman, [...] in a nearby rural area. With the help of what books on recreation we could find in our local library, Mother and I worked out a speech, titled, "Recreation Is Re-Creation," which I rehearsed while we washed dishes. I delivered it nobly in a little, one-room schoolhouse filled with farm folks.
>
> Because of these experiences, during my sophomore year, I was waited on in the principal's office by members of the city recreation department, and offered a summer playground job at ten dollars per week—a royal stipend at my age, [and] in that period—and my career was launched.

Katharine was already making a name for herself as the 15-year-old playground assistant of Tenney Park when a greater such opportunity arose during her sophomore year. This would prove to be the first major landmark of her swimming career.

Lake Mendota

The city of Madison, Wisconsin, resides among the boundaries of four freshwater lakes, and, by 1912, the largest of which had never been swum across by a woman. Katharine naturally considered this a surmountable challenge, and soon began practicing with a shorter swim between University Pier and Picnic Point. "After this [practice] swim, Miss Whitney declared her belief that she could make the [full] journey across Lake Mendota."[5] It was only a few weeks later, on August 4, 1912, that she splashed into the cold water with a man's "skimpy swimsuit," which consisted of a basic jersey, instead of the typical female attire of bloomers, long stockings, and a sailor blouse. The next day's papers reported what happened next:

> Madison has a youthful Annette Kellerman.
> She is Miss Katherine T. Whitney [...] who yesterday performed the feat of swimming across Lake

Mendota—a feat that has never before been accomplished by a woman, and only a few times by a man.

She made the journey from the University Pier to Governor's Island, a distance of three and one-half miles, in three hours and forty minutes. Three men (all expert swimmers), who started out to swim across the lake with Miss Whitney, were forced to give up before half of the distance was traveled.

What makes Miss Whitney's performance all the more remarkable was the fact that, before the two-mile point was reached, whitecaps [caused by headwinds] were encountered, making the headway doubly hard. But she kept on, completing the journey without taking a rest. When Governor's Island was reached, Miss Whitney was tired out, but a short rest revived her.[6]

Governor's Island was also the location of The Mendota Mental Health Institute, an "insane asylum," whose employees offered Katharine a towel before humorously asking why she didn't want to stay there permanently. Despite three days of confined bedrest from "lobster-red" sunburns, and also despite being admonished by the local dean of women for her choice in swimwear, the overwhelming swell of public recognition was her first taste of glory, and the kind which inspires a young mind to dream even bigger. Twenty-nine years later, she'd modestly refer to this childhood record, of three hours and 40 minutes (using the breast-stroke), as a "terrible [swim] time," which had long since improved with her growth as an athlete.[7]

Annette Kellerman, the woman to whom Katharine was compared in the Madison article, was a famous Australian swimmer who performed solo water ballet in a glass tank with her trademark (and revolutionary) one-piece swimsuit. In 1959, Kellerman and Curtis would be inducted together into the Helms Hall of Fame, which credited them as co-contributors in the wider timeline of synchronized swimming's early development. With this longstanding parallel always existing between them, Curtis would have been particularly inspired by Kellerman, who might otherwise be referred to as synchronized swimming's "Aussie grandmother."

Katharine continued working as a playground instructor for the Madison Board of Education through 1913, after which time, she graduated from high school and enrolled at the University of Wisconsin by autumn of 1914. It was during this summer interim, on June 28, that the archduke of Austria, Franz Ferdinand, was assassinated by Serbian nationalists in the occupied city of Sarajevo. A month later, the empire of Austria-Hungary declared war on Serbia, triggering a series of reactionary declarations that is officially regarded as the beginning of World War I. The United States would not join the conflict until 1917, when all efforts to remain neutral failed because of continued German aggressions. Many young Americans would then be drawn overseas, including Katharine's brother Robert—all of whom would become intimately acquainted with extreme and generation-defining experiences.

While chaos broke out in Europe, and as every young man in Madison started wondering about his own immediate future, Katharine joined the student body at the University of Wisconsin with an initial major in home economics. This was a natural starting point for all other female students, but her own interests gradually shifted toward declaring a physical education major, while retaining home economics as her minor. It was rare enough for women to attend college whatsoever at the turn of the century, making them all the more popular among their male counterparts. Katharine was no exception, and some revealing details were recorded by a Wisconsin reporter in 1977:

"I just came back from my sixtieth class reunion," [Kay] told me with a broad grin. "I don't know if you realize it or not, but the University of Wisconsin really turned out some kooks back in 1917."

Whitney family: (*clockwise*) **Katharine** (*center front*), **George, Anne, Robert, Jane, Ellen Crugom Townsend (c. 1917).**

> One of the kooks—an eighty-year-old classmate she hardly remembers—cornered her in the elevator of the Madison hotel, and asked if he could kiss her. "I've wanted to do it ever since our college days," he said wistfully. "Would you mind just one little kiss?"
>
> Kay, still attractive, athletic, and remarkably youthful, was delighted. She's had her share of suitors in her day, but this unabashed homage meant something special. "He still remembered me," she exclaimed. "Can you imagine someone wanting to kiss you for sixty years?"[8]

She was never one to kiss and tell, so little more is known about her "share of suitors" during this period, beyond what was implied with a characteristic wink and a smile.

Katharine had every advantage in school, being "blessed with super-strength, verve, supreme self-confidence, and her mother's gregarious nature."[9] Undoubtedly an extrovert, she always seemed to be instinctually striving for greater breadth in life, with telling evidence of this appearing in the *Wisconsin State Journal*, under the "University Happenings of Interest" section:

> Katharine Whitney is the candidate for [student] vice-president. She is [already] president of Red Gauntlet, the sophomore girl's organization. Last year, she played on all the freshman athletic teams, being captain of the baseball team. This year, she played on the varsity hockey team and is, at present, a member of the varsity basketball quintet.[10]

She was also a strong intuitive thinker, proving successful in many classes outside of physical education, including physics, philosophy, chemistry, bacteriology, physiology, zoology, history, French and German. But her preferred element never changed from that of her childhood, and despite every interesting class or exam requiring her to climb out of the pool, she would always be seen diving back in afterwards.

By 1915, Katharine was proving predictably rebellious in her choice of swimwear, with a consistent disregard for the period norms. Dean Lois Kimball Mathews was reported to have hauled her out of the water (perhaps more than once) and "lectured her severely" about her lack of modesty.¹¹ It wasn't long before this impressive young student was noticed by a local athletic trainer, Joe C. Steinauer, who was known as the "shepherd of the little red gym" (on Langdon Street), for if "he spotted someone with a special aptitude in a particular sport, he would send the individual to the proper coach as a 'good prospect.'"¹²

Before arriving at the University of Wisconsin, Steinauer had gained early experience as a vaudeville acrobat, and this background influenced his later brainstorming sessions with Curtis, for what they called "stunt swimming." Curtis explained in her book, "I was a graceful versatile swimmer, but had neither the speed nor the interest necessary for competitive swimming. Stunts, however, were a challenge to me."¹³ This idea would prove essential for evolving a finer hybrid of water ballet, and, although these rudimentary elements would still have to be "synchronized" to music, Steinauer's encouragement and ideas were undoubtedly inspirational. "In other words," Curtis later joked, "I stole his routines. Whatever he did in the air, I taught my students to do in the water."¹⁴

On December 3, 1916, "A Page of Sports for Women" in *The Sunday State Journal* provided some details of Katharine's final year in college:

"College graduation" photograph (c. 1917).

> Madison Girl near to the "New Woman." She plays nearly everything the Madison boy does, and, at the same time, is a Home Lover. Miss Whitney well deserves the title of the greatest all-around athlete in the university. [...] She has been judged the best woman skater in the school, and also was picked as forward for the all-university hockey team. She is a member of the senior basketball team and is also active in track events.¹⁵

It was on April 6, 1917, during Curtis's final semester at the University of Wisconsin, that the United States finally declared war against Germany. A later interview in *The Wisconsin Alumnus* (1941) explained that "Kate didn't take her degree at Wisconsin. She was right at the brink, with the diploma almost in her hand, when a technicality interfered."¹⁶

She was then offered a job as a swimming instructor for a (three-month) "summer session" at the University of Chicago in June of 1917, and, after completing this session, she traveled 700 miles for a nine-month opportunity to teach both elementary and high school PE in Tulsa, Oklahoma. She was 21 years old at the time.

Many friends and family members had joined the war effort by this time, and one particular soldier—whose words survive, but not his exact identity—wrote on June 2, 1918, from "somewhere in France," while on active duty with the American Expeditionary Force. What follows is an extensive, but worthwhile, excerpt from a much longer letter. When first received, it would have provided another captivating window into the noble lifestyle of service and adventure that Katharine would eventually pursue for herself. One can immediately observe just how much her correspondence meant to this young sergeant, whose only diversion from war and discipline could be expected to arrive (after much delay) in satchels packed with small, precious envelopes:

Dear Kate,

Well, I haven't time, but I'm making off that I have, so that I might drop you a few lines tonight. You know, I'm easily convinced, sometimes. Our delayed and accumulated mail has apparently found us [...and] we will no doubt hereafter receive our ever-welcome missives as soon as our friends can write them, and as soon as they are then given a ride across the "Deep Blue."

[...] Believe me, I greatly appreciate your thoughtful and kind attitude in regard to writing me. You know me well enough to know that I want to write to you as often as I possibly can. However, I can plainly see that the "US Drill Regulations" did not take this fact into consideration, for no time was prescribed for the letters which I'd like to write to you. Father Time never gives me any encouragement, and so I slip in a few lines here and there, when his back is turned. He generally stares me in the face however.

I'd like to carry out my original intentions of acquainting you, in full, regarding the facts in detail connected with our voyage and our early days and experiences in France. It however, now seems unwise for me to refer to such ancient history—for, even at that, the most interesting parts could not be stated. Nevertheless, I'll not slight the past entirely. I'm going to flatter it a bit now by talking about it. Ho!

Though we lined-up to be a motorized or tractor-drawn outfit, we were again issued horses at our previous camp, and we are now a horse-drawn outfit again. Our battery drew about two-hundred horses, all French horses. Yes, I have my own single-mount. Our battery was one of the two batteries of our regiment (of six batteries) to be picked to move into the "Zone of Advance," and consequently, we are now drawing service stripes here—one stripe every six months. I hope I don't look like a jail-bird when I come back.

Picture our outfit moving thru France. [...] We had quite a circus train, winding in and out, thru the villages, and so on. It was about a forty-six hour run. The trip was an agreeable one, for we traveled in comfort. The scenery in some places was quite wonderful. However, it was easily apparent that the country was quite inactive—no doubt, due to the fact that the colors have called the men. The country really seems to be at a standstill, awaiting the end of this bitter argument. Women are doing men's work. Everyone seems to have a father or a brother or a husband, or a husband "to be," at war; it is a universal happening, in common with all. The visible male members are either too young, extremely old, or already crippled. France is in the argument in no half-hearted manner. Armless men are quite numerous, and it really is no surprise, for, this war at the very outset must have been little short of slaughter. Circumstances and conditions however are now changed. The inhuman and merciless slaughters are over, let's hope.

[...] We are in a fine, old, big building—a chateau or mansion. The people who own the building occupy the other half of it. They are quite old, very agreeable and congenial, and seem rather glad to have us here.

[...] I have been long-winded, haven't I, Kate? But, then, I am glad to have been enabled to write to you, so I'll disregard a little other work I still have to do tonight—at least, for a few more minutes.

[...] I believe I already advised you that, a week ago today, I saw and spoke with our honorable leader, General Pershing. He sure is a wonderful man—good looking, tanned, stately—and a real man. It just seems to stick onto him everywhere. We were engaged in battle-imitation warfare, in accordance with the [GI] school's program, and I was stationed at an OP (observation post) when General Pershing came down to inspect the work of the schools. The general was within fifteen feet of me for about a half hour, and I greatly appreciated the privilege of his presence.

It is late at night, Kate, and every little while I am picking my head up off of my table, so I suppose I had better tear another sheet off the calendar and go to bunk—congratulating myself on the fact that I really did succeed in finally writing that letter. Write often, Katie-dear. Letters are all we have to look forward to here. Receiving letters is the height of pleasure, so make me happy. [...] With the best of all good wishes to you, continue to remember me as being—always [and] sincerely—your loving "soldier man," Over Here.[17]

"The Great War" ended only five months after this letter was written, and one hopes that the celebrations back home included this "loving soldier man," whom Katharine most likely befriended and went to school with in Madison.

The entire World War I generation was forced to grow up faster than any before, while many of its veterans would be tested further in the years to come. Decades later, after the start of another world war, Curtis would visit French mansions and chateaus of her very own, and within the same privileged proximity to both enlisted men and famous generals alike. But as she left her childhood behind in Madison, "setting sail" toward many new and exciting possibilities, that golden horizon was truly destined for her determined exploration. The wind of change was at her back, and the skies were clear—for now.

3

Making History

During the final months of World War I, the young and unanchored "Katie" Whitney continued to travel wherever work could be found. After school let out in Tulsa, Oklahoma, she moved to California in order to teach physical education (PE) at Chico State Teachers College for a few months in 1918 (June–August). Afterwards, she returned to the University of Chicago as a swimming instructor for their (August–September) summer session. And then she went up to St. Paul, Minnesota, where she taught girls' PE at the Summit School for the next nine months, from September 1918 until June 1919. There was another brief summer session in Chicago (June–September) before she moved to St. Louis, Missouri, where she was "endowed with the title 'Sports-Mistress' at Principia," an all-girls private school. It was here that "Kay introduced her girls to field hockey, basketball, and, of course, her favorite of all sports, swimming."[1] She stayed there until June of 1921, and during that 21-month period, she also worked as a generic sports coach at Camp Chocoroa in Tamworth, New Hampshire. After this, she was hired as a swim coach for three months (June–September) at Camp Minewonka in Three Lakes, Wisconsin, before returning to Chicago more permanently.

Anne Townsend Whitney had moved the younger siblings of the Whitney family to Chicago by this point, and was herself employed by Armour & Company, the prominent meatpacking industry. She had risen to become the director of "Personal Services," and, like her daughter, was particularly keen on promoting general health and wellness. In February of 1920, just as women all across America were about to gain the historic right to vote, a sports magazine featured her in this article, titled "Physical Fitness for Business Girls":

> When we want to know about any industrial situation in Chicago, our interest immediately turns to our oldest and most famous industry, the stockyards—what are they doing out there? In the line of physical culture for business girls, they are doing extremely well, and they have as healthy and Junoesque a force of office girls as could be imagined anywhere. Perhaps, just because the stockyards are externally unlovely, […] a great deal is done to give the girls some imaginative work that can go along with their everyday life. At least, this would seem to be the ideal of the Personal Service department of Armour & Company.
>
> […] The head of this department, Mrs. Anne T. Whitney, is an ardent physical culturist, but she believes that work of this sort should do much more than develop the girls along health lines. "Physical education," she says, "especially when conducted in classes, develops a degree of good sportsmanship, which is essential in business, and a characteristic which is becoming more and more pronounced in women in the world of commerce today." Mrs. Whitney believes also that the esthetic side of exercise and bodily development should be taken in to account, and that it is possible to combine this with a good deal of cultural training.
>
> About five years ago, Armour & Company built a model gymnasium adjoining their stockyard offices for the benefit of the office employees. The women have the use of this, with instructors three nights a week, and the time will be extended if demand warrants it. Two evenings are given up to

gymnastic work, and the third to esthetic and folk dancing, in which many of the girls are becoming experts. They also have the use of the tank with a swimming instructor, and the services of an osteopath, who is present on these evenings. Costumes are furnished, and, on class nights, supper is provided by the firm in the company restaurant.[2]

The local work environment was steadily improving for women in Chicago, and this positive trend would only continue after the success of the Women's Suffrage movement in America. Katharine would have naturally advised her mother on the general strategy behind Armour & Company's expanding recreational activities for women, and might have been involved even more directly between jobs.

From the start of September 1921, Katharine worked for three months at a department store in Chicago, selling swimwear, and then taught elementary-level PE for six months until June of 1922. She spent another summer at Camp Minewonka in Wisconsin (June–September) before returning to the University of Chicago on a much steadier job offer, renewing for the next five years. That first school year (1922–1923) began her official university career, teaching PE, while she also continued to serve as swimming instructor during the month-long summer sessions. By September of 1923, she enrolled herself in part-time classes, and would finally graduate with a bachelor's degree on June 16, 1925.

The year of 1923 was even more significant because of Katharine's renewed focus on stunt swimming. She started "one of the first […] college women's swimming clubs [in America], the Tarpon Club." She was further quoted about this beginning in a later interview:

"The beautiful Ida Noyes Hall had just been built [in 1916], and when I took one look at the women's gym and pool, I knew I'd be spending a lot of time there," Kay recollects. "The fact that a nickelodeon [record player] stood near the pool tempted me to combine swimming with swing."

Kay had the nickelodeon fixed so it would only respond to slugs [tokens], and then hid the slugs. "I didn't want the other teachers hogging the machine," she explained. When the girls became upset because they couldn't hear the music underwater, she advised them to hum.

"The only song they all knew was the 'Merry Widow Waltz.' I don't know how many dance routines were performed to that old faithful."[3]

Curtis also mentioned the Tarpon Club in her book, *Rhythmic Swimming*, which was first published in 1936, and then later updated with an historical summary:

While working with this group, the ballet, or synchronized, type of performance was developed. Our programs were no longer composed of isolated tricks, such as the "Monte Cristo" sack trick, or swimming with one's hands and feet tied, but we added music to group swimming. At first, the music was merely an accompaniment, but later the movements in the water were synchronized exactly with the beat and measure of the music, just as one would synchronize dance steps.

This new form of rhythmic swimming requires endurance, not speed; versatility in the use of all strokes, not specialization in one; a keen sense of rhythm; the specific development of the ability to adapt one's strokes to the average strokes of the group. The team is only as strong, as finished, as its weakest performer. In this type of swimming, however, is the opportunity for the swimmers of middle ability. The degree of difficulty in any performance can be adjusted to the individual's ability; she can progress at her own rate of speed; her success depends not upon her strength, but upon her skill; her creative interest finds a wide field in the development of routines; and there is a strong carry-over value, not only to the participant, but to her family and friends.[4]

It was during Katharine's tenure at the University of Chicago that she became acquainted with David Clark Leach, a fellow swimming instructor, who would become an important ally as the later chairman of the Central Amateur Athletic Union's swimming committee. He greatly appreciated her developing ideas, and would include her in various athletic programs and local exhibitions. In one such instance, 6,000 people were entertained by two boxing bouts, a demonstration in human pyramid-building, a championship volleyball game, and some fancy diving. But, as also advertised, there was the equally intriguing promise that "Mrs. Katharine Whitney Curtis [...] will show the crowd how she swims with her hands and feet securely tied, besides doing her 'walking on the water' feat."[5]

This is one of the first mentions of her married name—the earliest being from the spring of 1925, just before she graduated from college—and while there are barely any surviving details of her marriage with George W. Curtis, it would seem (according to a few photos) that they went on a honeymoon in December of 1928 to the Atlantic City boardwalk in New Jersey. The husband's only "presence" is merely implied by the photos themselves, which were taken of Katharine standing alone by the ocean, and dressed in expensive-looking garments. By separate oral accounts, she was only married for "a few weeks," or at least that was how she later described it to friends and family. The only (known) documentation regarding her divorce comes not in the form of an actual certificate, but a letter from her lawyer, "Enclosing herewith a certified copy [of that divorce certificate]," in January of 1937. The time gap of these differing narratives may be reconciled by the tentative theory that the couple was indeed separated after a relatively short period—perhaps longer than a few weeks—with the official divorce proceedings being postponed a number of years.

"Honeymoon" in Atlantic City, New Jersey (December 1928).

The only questions that remain are why Curtis both kept her married name and continued to wear a wedding ring for the rest of her life. This apparent facade may be explained by a desire to avoid the considerable stigma of divorce, and also to be taken more seriously at work. However, it would be later assumed by isolated sources—including some members of her own family—that Curtis was simply a lesbian. It was a natural thing to wonder about, even though the subject was never openly discussed with her personally. This speculative theory usually cites the fact that she never had any children, in addition to the unavoidable stereotypes regarding short-haired, athletic women. Furthermore, this line of questioning is expandable to Curtis's diverse circle of friends, several of whom have been confirmed as

Curtis standing noticeably alone.

members of the LGBT community. However, it must also be foreshadowed here that Curtis would become genuinely involved with a handsome soldier (or two) throughout the Second World War. Nothing more definitive can be said at this time, except with a wary conclusion that her life was more complicated than what labels can generically ascribe.

There was another early mention of Curtis with her married name on August 20, 1926, within the article, "Record Swim by Pinemere Lady":

> A most successful swimming feat was accomplished Wednesday when Mrs. George W. Curtis, swimming instructor for Camp Pinemere, [...] swam lake Kawaguesaga from the camp to Bosacki's boat house in Minocqua, a distance of three miles in one hour and twenty-nine minutes. The contestant used the same stroke, known as the Trudgeon Crawl, for the entire distance, averaging twenty-two strokes to the minute. She reached her destination in fine physical condition, and partook of a hearty meal following the swim. It is the first effort of any individual to attempt such a venture, and to Camp Pinemere belongs the record for the long-distance swimming. Conditions for the event were ideal. Mrs. Curtis is to be congratulated for her excellent showing, a fine example of physical endurance.[6]

Curtis had been serving as the swimming instructor for Camp Pinemere during the summer break of 1925 (June–September), before returning to the University of Chicago for the 1925–1926 school year. She was the summer swim coach for the University of Michigan in June (1926), after which time she returned to Camp Pinemere in Wisconsin for the aforementioned swimming event in August.

Curtis's last year of teaching PE at the University of Chicago (1926–1927) was followed by another summer month away, this time, at the University of Alabama in Tuscaloosa. She returned to Sturgeon Bay, Wisconsin, by September 1, 1927, which was the date of the following article:

> Miss Whitney Curtis, professional swimmer, in the near future will attempt to cross the threshold of Death's Door between the tip of the mainland peninsula and Washington Island. The waters of Green Bay and Lake Michigan, at what is known as Death's Door, is considered as the most treacherous place

on the lake. If Miss Curtis is successful in her attempt, she will be the only woman known to accomplish the feat. Miss Curtis [...] has been training for a [twenty-one-mile swim] at Toronto this fall and has been swimming five miles each day.[7]

By autumn of 1927, Curtis began teaching at a variety of Chicago public schools, the first of which was Chicago Normal College, later renamed Chicago Teachers College (1938) and then Chicago State University (1971). It was here that she arranged a grand swimming pageant that contained 23 original sketches, and each was reported "to be a positive mirth provoker." Santa Claus was portrayed as a floating cut-out, and drawn across the water by four swimmers in a line (wearing reindeer antlers). The program also included "a most cunning, bright-green speckled frog, and a rickety-rackety old man," with progressively funnier appearances.[8]

Ever since working at the University of Chicago, Curtis had been tangentially involved with swimmer's first-aid training, which continued into 1928. On February 13, her American Red Cross demonstration was quoted in this article:

> "Women don't know enough about lifesaving," said Miss Curtis. "Some of them think the first thing to do after pulling a drowning girl out of the water is to dry her face and powder her nose. This is what you should do."
>
> And Miss Curtis, with [a volunteer] lying as though [she was] just taken from the water, demonstrated artificial respiration methods. It's very simple: Just push downward on the person's midsection as if you were working a pump handle, and presto! Out rushes the water, and in comes the air.[9]

Notably, Curtis was attending a local convention for midwestern field secretaries, and she would continue to be closely associated with the ARC for years to come.

By February 14, 1928, Curtis was also planning a "Lake Marathon" simulation, "In which all the swimming will be done in our tank," as further described in this local bulletin:

> The large map in the tank-room shows that the distance is five miles, extending from Municipal Pier to Thirty-Ninth Street Beach. The distance marked on the map will be city blocks, and it takes eleven lengths of the tank to make one block. The entire five miles can be made by swimming 889 lengths. It is not necessary for all the lengths to be made at once, but the number may be spread out over the semester. The purpose of the contest is to see who will make the five miles first.[10]

Despite this realistic goal for her students, Curtis also would have reminded them that the whole five-mile length could be accomplished in one attempt, as she was used to repeating on a daily basis.

Her organizational ambition continued to build that year in Chicago where, from May 23 to May 26, she organized a "Mammoth Pageant" for local students. It was advertised that "over a hundred girls are participating in the pageant," while "any advanced swimmers desiring to participate may [also] do so." By May 28, this "aquatic playlet" was reported as a grand success:

> We went fishing last week in our pool and, really, we found the queerest creatures imaginable. We were under the impression that the college pool contained no fish, frogs, etc., but we were sadly disillusioned. What we really did was to witness the water pageant, and if you didn't see it, you missed an unusual and very artistic event.
>
> The story of the pageant is that of a little boy [played by a girl] who goes fishing. Soon, old Mister Frog comes to the pool and tells Jack not to give up, but to wait and see what will happen. Jack does so, and is amazed to see tadpoles, starfish, frogs, water-birds, seals, etc., come to life before his eyes. The animals jump, dive and splash in the water, and altogether have a very merry time. Of course, there is a dangerous-looking swordfish, and a whale that spouts water out of his mouth. The lobsters in red grease-paint already perform in the water, and the water-lilies and mermaids swim and dive to perfec-

tion. The flying-fish use the spring-board as their medium, and all sort of difficult dives were done by them. The final act is the "moth parade," when everyone swims [while] carrying a moth on a stick.

It is to Mrs. Curtis that the water pageant owes its great success, for she [with her assistants] worked for many weeks planning the carnival.[11]

This performance involved many creative elements that would later resurface with Curtis's "Modern Mermaids" at the 1933–1934 Chicago World's Fair, which was already starting to be planned (as early as 1927).

Toward the end of 1928, Curtis began exploring a more competitive application for water pageantry. She arranged a swimming meet between her (speed) swimmers at Normal College and their local rival, Crane College, who were soundly defeated on December 17. Beforehand, it was thus advertised: "Splash, splash! Normal College's mermaids are all ready to show what they can do in the line of swimming, at the Crane College pool. Because of the great number of students with a wonderful ability to swim, Mrs. Curtis, the judge in picking those that will represent Normal College, is having one grand time."[12]

This growing enthusiasm for competition prompted Curtis to brainstorm further, and she wrote this statement for the (1928) Amateur Athletic Union's "Official Aquatics Guide":

> Why must our competitive swimming be primarily speed, with diving the only recognized form event? Why not center our interest on grace and ease of movement in the water, developing the aesthetic values of swimming? Why not a figures swimming contest? Canada began the summer season in 1926 with such an event in Toronto. Let's not let the United States fall behind.[13]

In the same year as this Toronto event, there was also an important championship being held in Montreal to demonstrate "The Art of Graceful and Scientific Swimming." Dawn Pawson Bean, the foremost historian on synchronized swimming, concluded that "while the Canadian competition was not synchronized swimming as we know it today, it was certainly the first recognized national event in a related form of swimming. Canada must get the credit for starting the technical or figures competition. […] But the more characteristic combination of strokes, figures and floats, synchronized to the musical rhythms and tempos, was evolving in the United States with Kay Curtis."[14]

After Curtis returned from her honeymoon in Atlantic City, she returned to Chicago Normal College for the start of the 1929 school year. Her experimentations in water pageantry continued with another creative playlet, "The Pirate's Plunder," wherein Neptune was forced to walk the springboard plank in front of a "scurvy" crew of swimmers wearing black bandanas and eye-patches.[15] But it's also important to remember that, aside from these lighthearted pool parties and costume changes in Chicago, Al Capone was waging war with local gangsters in the Prohibition underworld, and the summer stock exchange was ballooning dangerously high from easy credit access (and other factors). Curtis's younger brother, George, had only just graduated with a philosophy degree on June 24, four months before the markets crashed on "Black Thursday," the start of the Great Depression.

While economic pressures were felt across all demographics, the middle class suffered the starkest lifestyle changes over the next 12 years. Expectations for long-term job security virtually disappeared for the average American, and George Whitney was particularly affected. Sarcastically nicknamed "Speed" by his family for his general lack of pace, George was quickly disillusioned, and found little work beyond what his mother eventually provided him at the Armour & Company stockyard offices. He reluctantly submitted himself to performing every menial task, but was soon revitalized by a budding courtship with a "devastating, tantalizing, and divine person," named Marion Baker. She was raised in relative affluence before her father's untimely death, and, despite being reduced in financial status, Marion retained her sense of cultural sophistication for the rest of her life.

George wrote to Marion with repeated overtures of marriage (on borrowed stationary), while intensely lamenting ever having to be apart. And on one such occasion, after some family drama in December of 1932, he vented to Marion with particular flare: "I treat you terribly. I wish I didn't feel so indebted to my family—they'll never interfere with us again. But this way I won't feel so funny about not going up there [to Wisconsin] over Christmas."[16] Despite the fact that he'd never make her rich again, George eventually convinced Marion into matrimony, and he never took it for granted. Their relationship would be prioritized above everything and everyone else in life—except, one day, their only son (with a strange name).

While George was shedding lover's tears, Katharine was holding down her job at Chicago Normal College through 1930. She had befriended one of her more talented swimming students, Victoria Vacha, and they were soon planning a cathartic road trip to Mexico, where alcohol was alluringly unprohibited. Curtis obtained her master's degree in education after a year at DePaul University. And, by March 17, 1932, she had transitioned to Chicago Normal College's friendly rival, Crane College, while she was also appointed to the "Woman's Division on Swimming" (sports committee) for the upcoming world's fair. Meanwhile, the Japanese Empire had already begun its invasion of Manchuria in northeastern China, and the Nazi Party in Germany was rising to become the dominant political power under Adolf Hitler. The world was swelling with the elements of future conflict when Curtis departed with Victoria Vacha on Saturday morning, July 2, from Oak Park near Chicago—heading toward the adventurous unknown for one of the first times, but not the last.

Learning to Wander

Their journey was planned to cover 1,647 miles south along U.S. Route 66, which was recently established as one of America's first interstate highways. Katharine and Victoria had affectionately nicknamed their Ford motorcar, "Pansy," which was only a model or two removed from the original (Model T). They took one of their first diversions on July 3, 1932, after noticing several signs for "Fisher Cave," which they discovered at the end of a hazardous red-clay path that curved along the hills near Sullivan, Missouri. Details of this were recorded in their combined travel notes:

> [We] then followed an exciting hour and a half of tunnels, underground rooms, stalactites and stalagmites, all revealed to us in the flickering lights of kerosene lanterns, which each of us carried [that made] our party look like fireflies in the eerie darkness of the cave. But lo and behold, our exit from the cave revealed the fact that, although "it never rains at this season," it had been raining for some time—and the clay road looked like mud pies! Lord! What a prospect for an inexperienced flat Illinois driver![17]

After separating from the chaos of all the other motorcars honking and sliding in the mud, the two women were confronted by the natural beauty of the Ozarks, where they spent the night in a rustic cabin.

On Tuesday, July 5, they were passing through Oklahoma when they happened across another noteworthy sight:

> We continued, passing carts and wagons of all sorts, pulled by tiny ponies and lazy mules, loaded down with families, both white and colored, [with] children by the millions! And the original

cover-wagons, real ones, with barefooted boys, half-asleep on the front of the cart, [and] holding the reins as the mules plodded along; a couple of hound dogs tied on to the rear, all their worldly belongings, and all the rest of the family under the dirty dust cover.

Astonishingly, this was a genuine firsthand encounter of the iconic Oklahoma migrants, or "Okies," who were later depicted by John Steinbeck in his novel *The Grapes of Wrath* (1939). This was the beginning of the "Dust Bowl" period, which consisted of devastating prairie droughts, crop failures, and massive clouds of unanchored dust, or "Black Blizzards," that swept across the country. Many of these economic refugees that Curtis passed along Route 66 would have been pursuing false hopes of a better life in California, where an overabundance of unregulated labor culminated in many heartbreaking stories of exploitation, violence and starvation.

The two women continued through "desolate Oklahoma," and found themselves (in stark contrast) at a relatively expensive cabin in Texas, "Where even an icebox and a fan are provided, [...] with good food just across the road." They took advantage of the local attractions in Austin and San Antonio, before traveling to the southerly town of Pharr, where the local postmistress had been looking for them all week. They had prearranged a month-long visit with some friends at a citrus farm nearby, where they could work the orchards to save up for a greater excursion south, into Mexico. They wrote back to their families in Chicago about that previous week in early July 1932, and, all the while, peering over the Mexican border toward their next point of exploration.

On August 3, 1932, they obtained their tourist passports from the Mexican consulate in McAllen, and they picked up an old friend named Ross, who agreed to serve as their translator in exchange for the opportunity to sketch some landscapes. They continued to the border town of Laredo, Texas, where they purchased a sketch pad for Ross, changed their money, and entered Mexico (via Nuevo Laredo) across the Rio Grande. It wasn't long before they sought out the forbidden fruit of the Prohibition era:

Curtis in Texas (1932).

> Stopping frequently for beer, the miles of level, hot and arid Mexico slipped by until we saw the peaks of the Sierra Madre on the horizon. Then, although we had stopped frequently for water, [...] because Pansy boiled like a steaming kettle [whenever] we ran out of *agua*, [...] we sat in the middle of nowhere until she cooled off enough to put in the remainder of our drinking water from the thermos. We lunched on prickly pears from the nearby cactus, and chugged up through Mamulique Pass (a rise of one-thousand feet in less than four miles). Pansy suffered terribly from this sudden rise, and chugged, hiccoughed and dragged like an old Model T. [And we] thought she would turn over and gasp her last, any minute.[18]

Later that evening, they arrived in Monterrey, Mexico, and decided to treat themselves to a luxurious night at the Continental Hotel on Zaragoza Plaza, before stopping by "Karl's Place," a German bar with a diverse selection of liquor that they "tippled" until 2:00 a.m.

The next day, they brought Pansy in for some minor repairs, and were on the road again to the nearby *Palacio del Obispado*, or "Bishop's Palace," where they discovered bullet holes from the 1914 revolution. They returned to the city by sundown, watched a massive dancing circle for local youths in the plaza, before Katharine and Victoria went back to Karl's Place for some more drinks. Ross then suggested that they go to a swanky nightclub called "The Terpsichore," with beautiful gardens and lampshades of ornate stained glass.

> Between two gardens, our path led through a huge formal ballroom. Since the orchestra sounded like an American one, Vic and I danced the length of the floor on the way out. At the door, we were met by an American [named Mount] who asked Vic to dance with him, and then attached himself to our party. At his invitation, we returned to Karl's for a few more drinks.
>
> We sat until closing time (3:00 a.m.), during which time, an American couple who had been drinking all day had a knock-down, drag-out fight, making us wish we were anything but American. Then, [Mount] had a fight with the waiter, since he had no cash to pay the bill. When the waiter suggested calling the police, we fell over each other, trying to get the money out to foot the bill. We even giggled to think that we had been like regular tourists on the "bar fly game."

Katharine and Victoria covered most of the tab, while "Ross stayed with Mount until he parted with one American dollar." Despite the chaotic expense, this "drinking culture" would have seemed terribly exciting to these temporary rebels, who later recorded being "somewhat wiser for the experience."

On Friday, August 5, 1932, Pansy was having more mechanical problems, so the group wired their banks in Chicago for some extra cash. They were able to drive to a liquor wholesaler by nightfall, and had returned to the hotel for dinner when "Mount had the nerve to put in his appearance—having taken a decided shine to Vic, [who] was appreciative!" This evening also proved eventful when Ross was driving Pansy around town and she spontaneously caught fire, owing to "something wrong with the wiring, and, as a result, the floorboard burned through in spots." This pattern of activities repeated on Saturday, with Curtis remarking, "All we seem to do is sleep, eat, and drink [...] and we aren't the least bit sad about it either!"

On Sunday, August 7, the group was preoccupied again with "getting that damn car fixed," before departing 50 miles south of Monterrey to explore Horsetail Falls, "Which is heaven for artists—too lovely and picturesque for our description." They set out walking through "a beautiful tropical gorge with a dashing mountain stream and covered with huge elephant ears, [where we] suddenly came out at the marvelous falls—which were gloriously cool. Vic and I hiked to the top and [were surprised to find] there a corn field!" Curtis then took the time to marvel at that ambient paradise of misted color, appreciating the harmonious balance of beauty and hard work before returning home to prepare for the Chicago World's Fair.

On Monday, August 8 (1932), Pansy was treated to some more repairs before rolling everyone back to Nuevo Laredo, "[Where we] had our last gin fizz and proceeded to the American side [of Laredo]." The trio only had $5.14 when they tried to cross the border.

> [The inspection officers] searched the car and found nothing, but they also searched our purses, and in Kate's found a sample bottle of habanero which [we were falsely assured that] we could carry over. The bottle reposed peacefully in an envelope that the officer told us advertised the lottery [also prohibited in 1932], and did he raise hell! In the first place, there was a five-dollar fine on the bottle, and a threatened five-dollar fine on the envelope, [so] there went our last five dollars, and Kate was booked for "petty smuggling." Since Vic had the duplicate to Kate's bottle (undiscovered) in her purse, and Ross was smuggling fruit seeds in his handkerchief, we just sobbed, "How will we ever get home?" And the officer said, "Move on."

Curtis was 35 years old at the time, and, according to a later article, "That slight penetration of Mexico was all Kate needed to set her permanently agog. Every year [through 1941], she has gone back in the summer or during the holidays, or both."[19] And, at the conclusion of their combined travel notes for 1932, either Ross or Victoria thought of a lighthearted postscript to revel in their recent misadventures, boasting, "Kay's pedigree now reads: Kay Curtis, [BS], MA, PS—(Petty Smuggler)."

The Modern Mermaids

One hundred years after the founding of Chicago in 1833, and 40 years since that city's first international exhibition in 1893, "The Chicago World's Fair: A Century of Progress" began on May 27, 1933, with a grand lightshow in the evening sky. This was triggered by an electrical signal dispatched concurrently from four remote observatories aimed at Arcturus, a relatively bright star, which just happened to be about 40 light years away from Earth. And so, with an otherwise insignificant sparkle, Chicago's anniversary celebration of scientific and cultural progress commenced, with a symbolic greeting of some light that first emanated around the time of the previous international exhibition (40 years ago).

The buildings were glowing with color to create a "Rainbow City," and some showy search lights were dancing with each other in between. There was an underwater halo shimmering around the "World's Largest Fountain" in the center of an artificial lagoon next to Soldier Field. And this (North) lagoon was divided from the South Lagoon by the "Sky Ride," which rose 628 feet and would catch the glance of over 48 million visitors. "The Avenue of Flags" ran perpendicular to the Sky Ride, just behind a stage area on the western bank of the North Lagoon, and this stage area was flanked by several restaurants with swarms of patrons from the main thoroughfare. Little did these people know in 1933, this performance marina would soon host the "Kay Curtis Modern Mermaids" (1934), which history would ultimately remember as the international debut of something called "synchronized swimming."

A month into that first year of the world's fair, Curtis was just returning from a two-week summer sport session at the University of Michigan. Their February (1933) brochure listed her current credentials and associations:

> Mrs. Katharine Curtis of Crane Junior College, Chicago, will assist [...] in the teaching of swimming. Mrs. Curtis has been a member of the staff of the Water Institute of American Red Cross in Chicago for a number of years, and holds a special examiner's certificate. She has taught swimming at De Paul University and at the University of Chicago. At the present time, she is chairman of competitive swim-

Katharine Whitney Curtis (*wearing black*) and her Modern Mermaids, in front of the (1933-1934) Chicago World's Fair "Sky Ride."

ming for the World's Fair of 1933, and also chairman of swimming for the Central Amateur Athletic Union.[20]

According to this, it would seem that Curtis was not initially tasked with demonstrating her water pageantry at the world's fair, but soon enough, "The authorities were searching for something to emphasize the underwater lights in the lagoon and Mrs. Curtis was asked to present a water ballet which would be effective over lights. Thus, The Kay Curtis Modern Mermaids were born."[21]

By 1934, Curtis had recruited a core group of over 30 swimmers from the Tarpon Club and other past affiliations, while each "mermaid" was also assigned an alternate, in order to accommodate their three daily performances. One of those substitutes was Curtis's young friend, Victoria Vacha, who had since graduated from college after their (1932) trip to Mexico.[22] When asked about the group's physical dimensions and cultural diversity, Curtis responded that "the girls represent American, German, Russian, English, Swedish, Irish, and Bohemian parentage."[23] It's also been remarked that there were some potential sponsorship deals, such as with the U.S. Rubber Company:

> Perhaps the first commercial sponsor for the sport, [...] they were asked to partly underwrite the costs of continuing the Aquacade, [...] but declined saying, "We appreciate very much the interest these suits have attracted ... but it will be out of the question for us to pay any money for their use."
>
> Perhaps they still needed to work on those suits. [A former Modern Mermaid] recalls, "We were given rubber bathing suits, (the newest thing at the time) for the shows. When we dove in, the suits split. It was fortunate that it happened at dress rehearsal."[24]

Ultimately, the mermaids just wore some regular white suits, with Curtis wearing black as their featured presenter. And for the "land routine," they all wore decorative white capes for a single-file march past the crowds:

> They entered from beneath a deck, which had been built out over an area of Lake Michigan that had been partitioned off into a swimming pool arena. Both the floating routines and rhythmic swimming routines were performed to a twelve-piece band. The audiences, seated on both sides of the pool area, were estimated at more than ten-thousand people for each performance. The Century of Progress Publicity Division's news release of August 24, 1934, [stated], "Performing ten complicated routines in perfect unison, thirty-five modern mermaids are revealing to patrons of the Lagoon Theater at the Chicago World's Fair, the highly modern art of synchronized swimming."[25]

This was the genesis of the phrase "synchronized swimming," which was first coined by the Modern Mermaids' charismatic announcer Norman Ross, and thereafter "applied to all kinds of water ballet."[26]

"The Modern Mermaids"—Publicity photo (1934).

Naturally, these performances displayed only a rudimentary form of the future Olympic sport, but the subsequent surge in public enthusiasm would prove essential for later developmental efforts, also led by Curtis.

> The swimmers were initially signed for one week of performances, the last week of June. This was extended another week, then two weeks, and finally, so popular was the show, the last contract was for the entire summer season. The publicity release stated, "They will be featured in the Lagoon Theater until ice forms in the Lagoon or the Fair closes on October 31 [1934]."[27]

Curtis later recalled that "the fur-coated audiences in late September were so cold they complained of the cruelty of forcing swimmers to perform." But the spectators were undoubtedly transfixed, and "the shows had proved so popular that, on their final day at the Century of Progress, it was announced that the Mermaids would present their picturesque swimming act each Friday night during the coming winter in the pool of the Medinah Athletic Club, [now the InterContinental Hotel], in Chicago."[28]

In March of 1935, the Modern Mermaids were commissioned for two 30-minute shows at the Illinois Athletic Club, whose chairman wrote to Curtis, requesting, "I wish you would arrange for the photographs that you now have, most of which you advise were taken at the Century of Progress, to be delivered at the Club as early as possible, so that we may use them for publicity purposes."[29] Curtis also began offering instructional programs to meet the rising public interest in synchronized swimming, and was soon writing a book from compiled notes and swimming routines to reach a more widespread audience across the nation.

While a more famous Katharine Whitney Curtis was actively gaining ground for her cause, and sleeplessly dreaming about every possibility for the future, her only nephew was born on February 22, 1935. George's wife, Marion, had been pregnant at the time of the world's fair, and the young couple was understandably preoccupied with laying the practical foundations of their family. They eventually received a letter from Lee Rankin Whitney, who wrote on his official stationary with these delayed congratulations:

Dear Marion and George,

[Pearle and I] certainly appreciated your good letter, George, and naturally, I am proud to have you name the boy Gaylord Lee Whitney. We like the name Gaylord, and if we had received a letter that Katharine sent from Chicago on Thursday eve in time to join her, we would have been in Chicago last Sunday to see the christening. Katharine sent it to our house and we did not get it until we arrived home, Saturday afternoon, and then it was too late to connect with her. She wanted us to drive back with her that day, as she was here on business. Darn sorry that we were not there.

[…] We often think of you and Marion, and know how much you appreciate the baby. As time goes along, you will notice so many changes that will tickle your ribs when they show up. You should make notes of the changes, with dates, for later on, as you will be glad you have them.

We went to see Katharine and her swimmers when she had them up here, and we enjoyed them very much. Did not have much time with Katharine as she had to dig back to Chicago. […] Both she and Vic [Vacha] looked fine.

All well here, and we hope that we will either be able to get to Chicago and see you both and the baby, or that you can get away so that you can bring the boy up to Milwaukee and pay us a visit. We would love to have you.

It was mighty fine of you and Marion to include me when naming the baby. I surely appreciate it, and am anxious to see him.

Curtis holding Gaylord Whitney on Washington Island (c. 1936).

Pearle joins me in sending heaps of love to you both and also to Gaylord. Write again when you have the time. Always glad to hear from you.

Affectionately,
Dad[30]

Curtis was making so much progress (and history) by this point. "In 1935, she bought a house on quaint Washington Island, off Door County, Wisconsin, where the view of Lake Michigan waters is engrossing and far-sweeping."[31] She also kept an apartment in Chicago for her continuing commitments at Wilbur Wright College, where, since 1934, she would make invaluable efforts toward establishing "synchronized swimming" as a codified sport.

The old "Henry Miner House" on Washington Island happened to be the first original homestead in Washington Township. And Curtis soon arranged for her recently retired mother to take up residence there, at what they eventually decided to rename "*Ferda Lokin*," Icelandic for "Journey's End." And although that poetic conclusion would not arrive for many years—for either of them—it was a beautiful prophecy that was bound to be both profoundly appropriate and self-fulfilling.

4

A Change of Plans

In his first memory of his Aunt Kate, a much younger Gaylord Lee Whitney was being led along the humid corridors of some indoor swimming facility. He was about three or four years old at the time, in the late 1930s, and his aunt had brought him to what was likely her regular swimming pool at the Chicago Teachers College. Gaylord was often delivered to other family members by George and Marion, who, as relatively new parents, always looked forward to the temporary time off and privacy. It was plain to see that this little blond-haired boy was wearing a swimsuit, although perhaps he didn't quite understand what that meant. He was just following the lead of his determined Aunt Kate, whose larger-than-life footsteps would have been quick and difficult to match.

Katharine was smiling (as always), and it's easy to imagine why in retrospect, for she certainly had another amusing plan in action. Perhaps the boy simply thought he was brought to observe the fancy diving boards as she rummaged through a supply closet. And perhaps he thought it strange when she wrapped a thick yellow rope under his arms and made it secure. The fibers were rough and itchy against his skin, but he only fixated on that for a moment before she picked him up. And then, much more to his surprise, he was unceremoniously tossed into the water with a helpful bit of advice, heard just above the muffling surface, to "swim!" Of course, he only knew how to splash and wave his arms, so she kept him afloat and moving at a gentle pace. This was the characteristic way in which Curtis decided to introduce her only nephew to her favorite element, with an implicit life lesson that anything can happen. "I remember her laughing," Gaylord later described, "[…] but I liked the water, so I don't remember being frightened. The only thing I didn't like was that damn rope, because it was itchy."[1]

The Promise

Soon after Curtis acquired her house on Washington Island, and certainly by the time her mother took up residence there, George and Marion concluded that it would be the perfect place to send Gaylord during the summer months, just after school let out in Chicago. The three of them vacationed up there together for several years until Gaylord was sufficiently accustomed to the 300-mile journey, and then, when he was eight years old, it was finally arranged for him to travel unaccompanied. There were some tricky commuter transfers in between, and no way to call his grandmother if something went wrong, but it would all end up going "according to plan"—or, at least, according to the official narrative. Many years later, Gaylord revealed the details in a short story about what actually transpired, and the following highlights provide a valuable window into the Whitney family during the early 1940s:

4. A Change of Plans

> When my father said goodbye that time, he didn't hug me. Since this was my first trip alone, I wondered if he just might, but he already had extended his hand for shaking. So, I took it and shook it. You see, my parents weren't huggers. Affection was transmitted with words in our home, and there was no lack of it either. He turned away, starting back down the aisle of the [train] car toward the exit steps at its end. Father stopped as a blue-uniformed porter approached him, heading in the opposite direction. He spoke to the porter, and handed him a five-dollar bill.
>
> […] Father turned to me a final time, waved and smiled, and told me to, "Say hello to Grandma for me." Then, he went down the steps and disappeared into the Union Station throng. I didn't see him again until I returned three months later. The porter, while stuffing dad's fiver into his vest pocket, continued past me to the far end of the aisle and disappeared into the next car.

George had asked the (Chicago) porter to give Gaylord some extra assistance at the right stop, however, this would prove to be too hopeful of an expectation. Gaylord was on his own from the very start.

Halfway through the journey, and just before his first transfer in Manitowoc, Wisconsin, Gaylord got up to retrieve his luggage.

> My old, black valise was wedged into a row of other suitcases on the second shelf of the luggage rack. By stretching from my tiptoes, I reached and tugged on the valise's single handle. It didn't budge. I stretched again and pulled harder, but the bag didn't move. I seemed to be the only person in my car planning to get off the train, so I was alone at the luggage rack. The train stopped, and the door slid open. I could feel the June midday heat whoosh into the air-conditioned car.
>
> I reached again for the valise's handle and pulled as hard as I could, and it inched toward me. I could hear the conductor yell from a distance, "All aboard!" Time had run out. I pulled on the old leather handle again, this time using one foot against the rack for leverage. My valise lurched free. It fell to the floor in front of me. I bent over and tried to lift it, and when I did so, the frayed handle broke away at one end and became useless. I couldn't lift the valise to carry it since it must have equaled my own weight. So, on my hands and knees I pushed it over to the steps. I shoved it over the brink and it toppled, end-over-end, to the pavement outside.

The train, which was behind schedule, departed only seconds after Gaylord escaped, and he soon found himself standing alone on a quiet platform. He knew that he had to catch a bus to the ferry landing at Gills Rock, still a hundred miles away, so he dragged his heavy and broken-handled suitcase over to the station house.

"The top of my head did not quite reach the level of the counter, so I used my tiptoes again to peer over the top." The man inside smiled and told him not to worry, because the bus also happened to be late. When it finally arrived, the (Wisconsin) driver was refreshingly courteous, helping the boy with his luggage, and they traveled for nearly three hours until Gaylord was the only passenger left. The final stop at Gills Rock was on a steep hill above the harbor.

> "C'mon," the driver said. He retrieved my valise and carried it in his arms down the hill with me right beside him. On the way, we walked past several wooden sheds painted red where commercial fishermen process their daily catch. Their workday was over, but I'd seen them before, gutting and cleaning whitefish and lake trout, and crating them in ice for their journey to market. One of the sheds was the "ice house," which held huge blocks of lake ice from the previous winter.
>
> Half-a-dozen sturdy fishing boats rocked quietly in the slip behind the breakwater. The permanent scent of fish left no doubt of where we were. It nearly overpowered the just-as-permanent scent of cedar there. The evening sun cast long shadows and illuminated the low limestone cliffs along the shore. The harbor water was calm and deep blue. It was beautiful there, and quiet, except for the cawing of some gulls.

When Gaylord reached the ticket office and its solitary employee, it was revealed that, unfortunately, they were too late. The last ferry had come and gone for the day, on schedule. "Suddenly, everything had changed. Now, instead of being a [thirty-minute] boat ride and a [short] drive from grandma's pleasant cottage, I was stranded."

Anne Townsend Whitney would soon realize that Gaylord was missing, but had no way to search for him until tomorrow. He was on his own, once again, and with no real backup plan. He had several dollars in his pocket, so he made a general offer to the bus driver for a ride back to Sister Bay, 15 miles south. They discovered some lodging at a local tavern, where the bartender was soon introduced to young "Mr. Whitney." In a very professional manner, Gaylord promptly offered to compensate these gentlemen, "[Who] must have thought me amusing, because they chuckled in my direction." They seemed to have little to no interest in this Chicago kid's money, and furthermore, the driver offered to bring Gaylord back to the ferry in time for its early-morning arrival. The bartender gave the boy some hot food, and found him a cot upstairs.

> I awoke in darkness suddenly to the sound of a church bell clanging nearby. It kept ringing. The light in the room came on. I could see all the cots had sleepers, and some of the men had already gone to the windows to look out. In a moment, [...] the bartender pounded loudly up the stairs. There was a fire, he announced excitedly. A barn south of town was burning. Would any of the men volunteer to help fight the fire?
> [...] That was an easy question to answer. But instead of speaking, I threw off the blanket and reached for my shoes. I tied their laces while the men began hurrying down the stairs. [...] In a moment, I was in the cab of a pickup truck, speeding south out of town. With several men in the open back of the truck, holding on tightly, we quickly followed a line of other trucks and cars. The church bell continued clanging.
> It seemed only a few minutes before we could see the glow in the night sky. We could hear a siren now, probably from a fire engine on the way. The line of trucks turned right, off the main road, onto a secondary road, and we sped along toward the flickering glow. [...] A farmhouse came into view first, and we drove past it toward the fire. Vehicles already there pointed their headlights onto the barn.
> "You should probably stay in the truck," I was told as we stopped, but I got out and watched as the men in the bed of the truck hopped out and ran to help. A bucket line was forming. Then, I climbed onto the truck bed and watched from there. I could feel the fire's heat, which came in waves. One end of the barn was burning wildly, while the other end hadn't yet ignited. The barn's doors had been swung open to allow animals to escape, and some men with buckets of water ran in. [...] The truck's pumping motor roared and fed water out through a longer hose toward the barn. Two firemen, bracing the hose between them, directed a long stream of water onto the barn's roof.
> [...] Burning barns have a strong smell, one you can't forget. Maybe that's true of any building on fire. I didn't like it, and I found myself hoping I wouldn't encounter it again. Some other people, mostly women and their children, were watching too. I wondered which of them lived in the house that we passed coming in. The loudest noises came from the fire-engine's pump motor, and from the raging fire. I could see men shouting, pointing and running, but their voices were muffled. This went on for what must have been more than an hour.

When the fire was extinguished, Gaylord rode back to the tavern with his weary roommates. He heard somebody say it was 3:30, and their few remaining hours of sleep disappeared in the blink of an eye.

The bartender woke Gaylord on time, carried down his suitcase to the road, and offered him some food inside. He told the boy not to worry about leaving the suitcase unattended, because, "No one around here will steal it. This isn't Chicago." After breakfast, Gaylord offered up his money again, but it was refused all the same. Instead, "[The bartender] asked me to tell my grandma that he had taken good care of me." Apparently, the gratitude and goodwill of Mrs. Whitney was worth much more than some minor pocket money, at least, around these parts. The boy gratefully shook hands with the bartender, and soon also with the bus driver, who would once again carry the heavy suitcase down the hill at Gills Rock.

4. A Change of Plans

The ferryboat arrived on time, and it turned out that Gaylord had just enough money for a round-trip ticket.

The deep-water passage to Washington Island was named "Death's Door" by French explorers, who once witnessed a deadly canoe skirmish between the Huron and Potawatomi tribes. Curtis had also conquered these formidable waters, with a marathon swim by September of 1926. Gaylord continued, "[The waves] broke in big, white explosions over the port bow, and sprayed the cars and anyone on deck. I got splashed and drenched several times on that leg of the journey. [...] I couldn't help shouting and laughing whenever we plowed into a big one." Finally, they arrived at the island's southern harbor, and most of the passengers moved down from the observation deck toward their cars. Gaylord stayed to look for his grandmother, and sure enough, she was there waiting for him.

[Anne Townsend Whitney] was standing beside [a driver], who must have brought her to the ferry dock in the island's only taxi. In seconds, I made my way down to the main deck and over to the ramp to get my valise. The same man who helped get it aboard came to my rescue again, and carried it off the ferry. When he set it down, I thanked him yet again, and then ran over to where my grandmother was waiting.

She took both of my hands in hers, stepped back a bit, and looked me over. She said I seemed just fine, and none the worse for wear. She said I certainly did have her worried when I wasn't on last night's boat. So far, she hadn't said she was glad to see me, and, of course, she hadn't hugged me. Suddenly, she pulled me to her and gave me a nice squeeze. I admit I was surprised, and felt a bit silly (and a little reluctant) as she clasped me to her bosom. Being hugged like that made me smile. I was delighted to be there with her again. We walked hand-in-hand to [the] taxi, while [the driver] lugged my valise in his big arms.

"You must tell me everything that happened. Where did you stay last night? Start from the beginning."

On the way to her cottage I did just that, not leaving out anything important.

[...] "My, my," she said, "you've had quite an adventure." Then, in a more serious voice, my grandma asked me another question: "Do your dad and mom know about this, that you were on your own last night, and I had no idea where you were?"

I told her no, they didn't know.

"You know what?" she asked, not smiling at all. "Maybe we should make all of that our little secret. Or maybe it's our big secret. So they don't think you were in any danger. So that they don't think I can't take care of you, or that it's dangerous coming here on your own. [...] So that you can come again next year. I wouldn't want them angry with me."

"Not tell them?" I asked, starting to laugh.

Gaylord Whitney playing on Washington Island (c. 1942).

"Yes, it will be just between us. I won't tell them if you won't." Smiling again, she extended her arms for another big hug. As I went to her, she made it a question: "Do you promise? I will if you will."

"Okay, grandma," I answered. "I promise not to tell them."

A promise made is a promise to keep. So we kept it forever.[2]

Gaylord would spend 12 memorable summers on the island, exploring every hidden pathway, forest grove, and pebble beach. His grandmother would always seem to be hosting a cavalcade of interesting people, from Chicago and beyond, who all came to likewise regard Ferda Lokin as a welcome distraction from life. And soon after Aunt Kate departed for the adventures of World War II, she'd receive many joint letters and modest gifts from "Master Gaylord" (and company) to remind her of home. Indeed, it was this notion of "Journey's End" that would keep her going throughout the many difficult years ahead, and—as often as she could allow—with a happy tear in her eye.

Writing the Rules

Back in January of 1938, Curtis was just returning home from another Mexico excursion, the art of which she had much improved ever since her first attempt (in 1932). She continued writing travel notes, with the following highlights:

> As we approached the mountains about sundown, I never saw such beautiful colorings in my life. All one could say was, "Oh." Deep purple, shading to light. It was simply beautiful, and if one saw a painting of it, you would not believe it possible. After reaching Monterrey and getting settled at the hotel, we went to the square to see the sights at the band concert.[3]

Curtis and her friends soon ventured into new territory, including the bustling streets of Mexico City, where "the buildings are so close to corners that, at every intersection, you have to honk your horn, and it's 'toot' all the time." She then joined the roaring crowds for an exhilarating bull fight at "the biggest bull ring in the world," with a seating capacity for up to 30,000 people, "and it was packed." Two days before Christmas (1937), however, their celebratory mood shifted in tandem with that city's fragile and top-heavy buildings.

> I woke up about 7:15, and saw the chandelier in my room swinging so hard that it nearly hit the ceiling, and the hotel was swinging from side to side. It was the funniest sensation, just as though you were on top of a big tree and the wind was swinging you back and forth, and every time it blew you over one way, you wondered if it was coming back. That was just how the hotel was swinging. It lasted for over three minutes—my first experience with an earthquake, and one is enough. They had four other small ones that same day, but did not bother you any. [I] understand they've had only three as bad, and the reports said that four [people] were killed in the outskirts of Mexico City. There was no excitement on the streets when we went out later in the morning.[4]

In fact, there were at least ten people who died from this earthquake around Mexico City, as reported in the *El Paso Herald* for that day. Curtis returned to Monterrey just after Christmas, and was soon back in Chicago for the new year.

The 1938 spring semester at Wright Junior College would be her last stint in a three-year tenure, before being transferred to Chicago Teachers College (previously Chicago Normal College) on September 6. Since starting at Wright during the world's fair, Curtis had finished her groundbreaking book, *A Source Book of Water Pageantry*. Its first edition (1936) was released "privately" by the College Press (Chicago), which "made it available at $1.75."[5] Later editions were released under a new title—*Rhythmic Swimming: A Source Book of Synchronized Swimming and Water Pageantry* (1942; 1948; 1953)—by Burgess Publishing (Minneapolis). Early royalty statements indicate sales of over 3,000 copies, many of which would end up in public libraries around the country.[6]

According to Frank Havlicek, Curtis's former student at Wright College, she had created "not only the first collegiate synchronized swimming club [at Wright], but also the first co-educational synchronized swimming club in the world [by 1937]."[7] Another of her early swimmers, Ellen Wales, wrote about this period:

> It was in September of 1937, at Wright Junior College [...] that the name Kay Curtis first became a reality, [but] I had [previously] seen it in print on a Chicago World's Fair (1934) Aquacade program. [My] original contact [with Curtis] was in a Senior Life Saving Class. What she saw [in me] was a strong, natural swimmer, [...and] capable to listen and learn; years later, Kay explained it as an "undiluted brain." At that time, she asked me to consider her Creative Swim Club, a large group of swimmers. Their forte was swimming in unison with each other, and with many float patterns, [using] the music as a backdrop.
>
> [...] In January, 1938, Kay showed films of Canadian and German figure swimmers, who executed strokes and stunts in tandem. It fired our imagination, to incorporate new figures with ones that were already in use and explained in her book. [...] What she wanted was a swimming routine in which stunts and strokes were synchronized with each swimmer and the music.
>
> [...] From April to September of 1938, Kay and I spoke, demonstrated, taught and coached anywhere [that] an aquatic event was held—indoors, outdoors, schools, athletic clubs, country clubs, public pools, and all the Red Cross clinics; [in front of] amateur swimmers and professional coaches, and always stressing synchronization with the music and with the swimmers.[8]

Havlicek also described that, when transferred to Chicago Teachers College, Curtis took "some of her Wright students with her, and so a second co-educational collegiate synchronized swimming club was formed, called the Tritons."[9]

By May of 1939, Bernice Lorber Hayes was chosen to coach the team at Wright Junior College, and she later explained, "I was a swimmer, but I knew nothing about synchronized swimming. I learned from the second-year students, who were still in the club, and from Kay's book."[10] Havlicek continued about what happened next.

> Kay Curtis and Bernice Lorber Hayes [...] encouraged and co-operated with the clubs' members. As a result, a first dual demonstration meet in synchronized swimming was held between the two schools on [May 27, 1939] as a part of the Chicago Teachers' Day Program. The meet was very successful and tempted David Clark Leach (Central AAU Swimming Chairman), who had acted as chief judge at the meet, to lead a group of Chicago swimmers and coaches in developing the idea of synchronized swimming as a competitive AAU sport.[11]

David Clark Leach, who had been tracking the development of synchronized swimming ever since the Tarpon Club (1923–1927), appointed Curtis as chairman of this experimental rules committee, which also included Bernice Lorber Hayes, Victoria Vacha, and "representatives of various clubs and schools in the Chicago area, all of whom had worked with Kay."[12]

Synchronized swimming's foremost historian, Dawn Pawson Bean, confirmed that this athletic meet (at the 1939 Chicago Teacher's Day Program) was indeed "the first competition in synchronized swimming." She also explained the wider national context for this period:

> In the wake of widespread exposure to the charisma of the Modern Mermaids shows of the Century of Progress World's Fair, clubs began to spring up throughout the nation with eager young girls wanting to try to emulate the Mermaid's synchronized swimming, as water ballet had come to be known. [...] Rhythmic or synchronized swimming was, of course, not entirely new, [...] but both of these lacked what the Curtis method supplied, music.[13]

To clarify, Curtis was not the originator of "experimental" swimming, "water ballet," or any other non-competitive precursor. And neither was she the first to swim with an ambient band or record player nearby. The basic elements of water and song have always coexisted within a neutral state of potential. However, a singular agent was ultimately required to complete this formula, with the natural advantages of good timing and personal determination. It was because of Curtis's historical efforts that the name of "synchronized swimming" came forth, and furthermore, that it would become associated with her unique combination of standardized strokes and swimming patterns within a musical framework. This (more evolved) hybrid would later prove to be perfectly adapted for the rigors of physical competition. And it's because of Curtis's early chairmanship that water ballet became an officially codified sport, while she also ensured that it would remain such an enchanting artform.

About two months before the historic May 1939 meet between Wright Junior College and Chicago Teacher's College, Curtis had sent both David Clark Leach and one of her swimming students, Edward B. Mueller, to "demonstrate synchronized stunts for a group of AAU [Amateur Athletic Union] officials who were involved in establishing criteria for competitive synchro." Mueller continued, "I rode with Clark Leach, AAU official, to the [NJCAA] Swimming Championship held in Ann Arbor, Michigan, in the spring of 1939, on the day the Nazis invaded [Czechoslovakia, on March 15]."[14] It was only six months later that Nazi Germany invaded Poland on September 1, and so began the Second World War.

Throughout the next year, the United States remained dormant in isolation as the Japanese Empire conducted its own full-scale invasion of China in the Pacific theater. Americans would stay cautiously aware of these growing conflicts overseas, if only from the opening newsreel highlights at the movies. Meanwhile, for movie-goers in downtown Chicago particularly, there would also be some media coverage of a nearby synchronized

Curtis and pupils at Chicago Teachers College (1942).

swimming event in Wilmette, Illinois.[15] This was "the First [AAU] Synchronized Swimming Championship ever held," which had commenced at the Shawnee Country Club on March 1 (1940). Frank Havlicek explained, "Although this was not a national event (it was Central AAU), it set the stage for additional meets and recognition."[16] Seven teams were entered, according to a 1941 article, and "competitions were held indoors and outdoors in the central section."[17] This meet was historically noteworthy because "the rules, as devised under Kay Curtis' chairmanship, were [first] accepted by the Central AAU Committee."[18]

The more significant landmark arrived by December (1940), when the AAU, "In its national convention in Denver, recognized Kate's type of swimming and adopted [her] standards, rules, and terminology. [...] This recognition, which Kate prizes so highly, came through the resolution introduced by Clark Leach, chairman of the Central AAU swimming committee." The aforementioned 1941 article continued describing the following excitement:

> After the Denver convention, Leach wired Kate from the Burlington Zephyr [train], on which he and other delegates were returning home, that the AAU had approved synchronized swimming, and asked her to arrange a demonstration in her school pool at Chicago Teachers College [CTC] the next day, preferably in the morning. His wire came about midnight and asked for a reply.
>
> Kate was in such a whirl she could not sleep, and she could not wire because she did not know what hour would be free at the pool. So she got up at 6:00, arrived at school by 7:00 (when the doors were opened), put notes into the lockers of all the students she was inviting to participate, and, shortly after 8:00, had all arrangements perfected. Then she wired Mr. Leach, who was still on the Zephyr. The train rolled into the Chicago station about 9:00, and, by 10:00, the delegation was at the pool.
>
> One of the visitors was Robert Kiphuth, swimming coach at Yale [and] a member of the national swimming committee. Another was Herbert Holm, chairman of the AAU diving committee.
>
> The CTC students put on a gorgeous exhibition, swimming to "Hark, the Herald Angels Sing," Bach's "Choral," and other unusual musical accompaniments (unusual, i.e. at swimming events). Whenever the men were puzzled at terms used in the announcements of events, they asked the students for

Curtis (*center*) coaching at Chicago Teachers College (1942).

explanations. Kate said it was immensely gratifying to her to watch their expressions, for they were so visibly carried away by what they saw. Afterward, Mr. Kiphuth told Kate she had "opened up a marvelous new form of aesthetics!" Mr. Holm paid the highest compliment of which he was capable: "This is every bit as fascinating as diving."

Now that the AAU has approved synchronized swimming, the next phase of its official recognition will come in the running off of sectional championships in 1941, and of the national meet in 1942. [...] Kate had made a short film of synchronized swimming demonstrations in 1938, and now the AAU has appropriated funds for producing a complete teaching film.[19]

This article was published in *The Wisconsin Alumnus* for February of 1941, and its author (Lucy R. Hawkins) opened by stating, "When I asked Kate if she would consent to be written up, [...] her face lighted up in that smile for which she is famous." Hawkins eventually concluded, "I have known Kate for many years, and, in the fullness of my friendship and admiration, I call her 'the Billy Rose of Chicago.' Maybe that is the best characterization any of her friends will find for her, to describe her prestige and her showmanship."

Indeed, Billy Rose was likewise renowned for arranging various large-scale aquacades since 1937, which were invariably inspired by the success of the (1934) Kay Curtis Modern Mermaids. Rose would also discover Esther Williams (in 1939), whose Hollywood career would continue to popularize synchronized swimming immeasurably. This vital integration with American popular culture was already being established by the second edition of Curtis's book (1942), in which she enthusiastically declared, "I feel that the surface of this new field has barely been scratched. We will see much progress in the use of various types of accompaniment and the actual interpretation of the music. [...] The future is teeming with exciting possibilities."[20]

But as Curtis was testing these new ideas in the waters around Chicago, a dark storm was gathering on the horizon. The United States had been neglecting the rising threat of Japanese military expansion, which, after devastating much of Asia, was looming toward Pearl Harbor. On "December 7, 1941—a date which will live in infamy—The United States of

Curtis about to leave Wisconsin (1942).

4. A Change of Plans

America was suddenly and deliberately attacked by naval and air forces of the Empire of Japan." President Roosevelt spoke these words to the U.S. Congress on December 8, and continued describing his nation's fateful turning point in history:

> The attack yesterday on the Hawaiian Islands has caused severe damage to American naval and military forces. I regret to tell you that very many American lives have been lost.
>
> [...] The facts of yesterday and today speak for themselves. The people of the United States have already formed their opinions and well understand the implications to the very life and safety of our nation. As commander-in-chief of the army and navy, I have directed that all measures be taken for our defense. But always will our whole nation remember the character of the onslaught against us.
>
> No matter how long it may take us to overcome this premeditated invasion, the American people in their righteous might will win through to absolute victory. I believe that I interpret the will of the Congress and of the people when I assert that we will not only defend ourselves to the uttermost, but will

Anne, Katharine and Gaylord, together at Washington Island (1942).

make it very certain that this form of treachery shall never again endanger us.

Hostilities exist. There is no blinking at the fact that our people, our territory, and our interests are in grave danger. With confidence in our armed forces—with the unbounding determination of our people—we will gain the inevitable triumph. So help us God.

I ask that the Congress declare that, since the unprovoked and dastardly attack by Japan on Sunday, December 7, 1941, a state of war has existed between the United States and the Japanese Empire.

Curtis would have been listening to this speech on the radio, like everyone else in the nation, with a fierce and mournful determination for justice. And although she was certainly planning for a different set of circumstances, the fate of the world was genuinely at stake, and mostly every other member of the Greatest Generation was scrambling to volunteer and "follow the action." Of course, most of them were too young to fully understand what that actually meant, and what horrors might be waiting for them overseas. But even Curtis, a 45-year-old woman (in 1942), wasn't going to be left behind to float around in some pool. She pulled her strings with her old contacts at the American Red Cross, which made her an assistant recreational director with orders to report for training in Washington, D.C., by October.

Curtis after joining the American Red Cross (1942).

Curtis's noble attitude would have been duly praised and encouraged by her father, Lee Rankin Whitney, who had unknowingly prepared her for this moment. And while her mother was somewhat envious of this grand opportunity for adventure, she'd remind Curtis to write home whenever possible, to let the men do all the "heavy lifting," and to have a smart career strategy for when all the excitement was over. But last of all, Curtis would say goodbye to little Gaylord, who had already been shown that one must choose to sink or swim in circumstances like these. And that, while the experience can certainly be shocking at first, the choice is always obvious.

The Second Diversion
Hope (1942–1946)

Kay, when I remember back to our talks at rest camp, I feel very grateful to you [...] for keeping alive in me that spark of human decency that could have been so easily lost. I can hold my head up, now, with pride and clear thoughts, instead of feeling like a low animal with a distorted mind. [...] You did for me what the folks back home could have never done. My mind was becoming quite bitter, and, by your help, I was able to snap out of it. [...] It's hard to explain, but I'll always be grateful to you for making me realize that other things existed in the future besides [German fighter planes] and endless hours of combat. You will always be welcome in our home.
—An American Pilot (1944)

5

She's Over There

On a rainy October Tuesday at the crowded Annapolis Hotel in Washington, D.C., a 45-year-old "Katy-did" (Curtis) was writing back to her old Chicago friend, Estelle Angier, who was eagerly trying to volunteer for overseas duty. The endless vehicles were splashing puddles in the road outside, and everyone was wearing some sort of military uniform as the United States mobilized for World War II. Curtis explained to Estelle, "I have seen [the administrator], who thought you wrote 'the cleverest letter,' and [I] have done the best I can, but she seems to feel that 'the committee' will say 'thumbs-down' because of your age." Of course, Curtis was writing from the center of America's bureaucratic chaos, where nothing was known for certain, so she simply recommended patience before describing her own situation:

> We have been told to hold ourselves "in constant readiness," which is like sitting on a keg of dynamite! We have no idea of where we'll be sent. So, America, Iceland, Australia, British Isles, New Caledonia—or what have you! My heavy winter overcoat's going to look awfully silly if I land in the tropics!
> […I] was driven out to Mount Vernon, Sunday, and was thoroughly thrilled by everything. It was a beautiful day, and the sun on the river and the colored leaves were beautiful. We didn't have half enough time, and it was dark when we got to the Lincoln Memorial, but I had "butterflies in my tummy" when I saw that gorgeous statue!
> Washington is, of course, a bedlam, and we have had very little time to get around, except to eat. And it takes a whole evening to get dinner, the service is so slow! Almost like Mexico. […] Tomorrow, we go to Camp Meade all day, so I must to bed. Cheerio [and] don't work too hard.[1]

Fort Meade was a military training facility during World War II, and, shortly after this first letter, Curtis sent Estelle another brief note: "[I] am now working on a club activities committee, in between meetings. [And we] just completed our third consecutive day of rain!"[2]

Curtis had arrived in DC a couple weeks before, on September 28, 1942, and would later turn 46 years old on January 4, 1943. She was sent to the Hotel St. George in New York City for her general orders by January 24, when she then revealed to Estelle, "[I'm] on my way, at last, right into the thick of it. And as director of a rest camp for aviators, hooray!"[3] She wrote to her mother on January 27 with a fuller description:

> Dearest Moth,
> [I] do wish you could see this hotel, a teeming ant-hill of uniforms—atmosphere choking with intrigue, at least the possibilities for it—and then, the place where we have been going for final instructions and equipment. My! How I wish I could tell you half of it, but it's a military secret, and that's that!
> Weren't you thrilled by President Roosevelt's latest trip [to Morocco with Winston Churchill]? [I] do so hope that your radio was working enough to catch that [January 24 (1943)] broadcast! We were listening to it in the ultra, ultra, Colony Club, and you'd have loved the old dowagers who sat there with us! If only I could have asked who they were, sitting there (under the portraits of past presidents) in

their feminine glory—especially the one faded old blonde, who had a chapeau [hat] covered with black ostrich plumes!

[Gaylord] sent me his entire weekly allowance of twenty-six cents, to "buy something from me." I am having a hole put thru the penny to wear with my dog-tags! You can imagine what I did when I opened that letter! Anyway …

[…We] had gas-mask drill in tear gas today—and typhus shots! Hold your thumbs that I don't get too seasick!

Heaps of love,
Katie[4]

Curtis revealed to her other friends and family that upon receiving Gaylord's modest gift of 26 cents, "Of course I wept."[5]

By February of 1943, the first of Curtis's many "carbons," or general newsletters, was written aboard a large military transport ship with the start of her wartime chronicles:

I am ashamed to think of how many times you have probably thought of me and sympathized with all the hardships that you thought I was undergoing these past days. I am ashamed because this trip has been one of the grandest experiences that I have ever had. Enough of our old group has been held together to give good companionship, and the rest of our fellow sufferers have been a varied group, to say the least. The spirit and high morale has been better than one could ever imagine. Each day has been a jewel all its own.

[…] There has been a gorgeous moon, all the trip, for [anyone] looking for romance—although we have 10:00 curfew each night. The chaplain has a very nice library on board, so we all have plenty to read, too. The canteen, run by the ship, carries all the necessities of this life, at cheap prices; so you see, I have really not been suffering at all.

We girls are in staterooms, four to a room, which is slightly crowded, but we manage very well. And I have had a salt-water shower every morning since I left. I will admit that I would've had a bad time with the soap not lathering if one of the engineering crew hadn't given me some of the soap that they are using. It really doesn't bubble, but makes sort of a creamy mess that kids one into thinking that your skin is cleaner. Haven't dared to tackle [the] laundry problem yet. We completed our typhus shots on board, and I slept the entire next day, but otherwise no effects.

[…] We have been brushing up on our French and German, but I find that I am very lazy and would rather be out on deck in the sunshine. So, once more, I guess I will be depending on sign-language and a smile.

I know that there must be much that you wish that I would write, but you will realize that we are limited [by censorship regulations], and I will try to do better as time goes on. At present, you will just have to accept the fact that I have never been better in all my life, and only wish that all of you could be right here beside me as I experience all these new things. I am writing this before we have landed or reached our final destination.

[…We don't know any] more details about our individual assignments than we have ever known, but I am afraid that I will have to learn to like salt-water bathing after all. We are told that the city to which we are to report is very beautiful and modern, with tropical verdure. We have been in slacks, T-shirts, and sweaters the entire trip, so you can imagine how comfortable I have been. I got myself a tan windbreaker [jacket], which I have worn constantly, and have wrapped my head up in my red turban, which I notice, today, is all spotted with salt water.

And so, until next time—Cheerio, *Bon soir, Auf wiedersehen*—and much, much love to you all![6]

Curtis then typed a separate letter to her mother during this mid–February voyage (1943), which was described with additional details:

A few days ago the prettiest flying fish flew up on the forward deck—be sure to tell [Gaylord] in your next letter—I forgot to mention it in my general letter. The back is a gorgeous iridescent blue and the underside is silver.

[…] We all heard President Roosevelt's speech this week, and it was really stirring to be where we were, hearing his words. They were taken down in shorthand by a couple of the ARC girls, and read to us on our daily news broadcast. You'd have loved the sight of us all huddled around the loud speakers in various locations drinking in every word.

[…] The men have been boxing on their aft deck, every morning, and aside from the few who were seasick, they all seem to be having as good a time as we are. Morale is certainly high! Of course, it is a scream to see me in the mornings trying to get [my] body under the salt-water spray as we roll around [on the waves]—and our clothes are beginning to get a bit sticky. But you know me well enough to know that a little dirt never bothered me much. I have gotten a good healthy color from the sun and wind, and really don't think that I have put on very much weight, as the clothes all seem to fit just the same. I certainly will be thinking of [Gaylord] on his birthday this year. Tell him that he will have to wait for his present, but that it will be coming in some form or other, as soon as I am in a position to do something about it. […] Be sure to tell him where to look on his globe for me now!

Isn't it a scream how I never thought of this area in all my planning? I sit out in the sun and wind with my knitting, and smile a broad grin, and feel still that if I pinched myself hard enough, I would wake up at home with all of this a dream. Then everybody says, "Just wait! The worst is yet to come!" Well, let it! I'll bet I have fun anywhere, and I'm getting to be the best buck-passer there ever was! There has been a grand spirit of camaraderie during this trip, and I'm sure that none of us will ever forget it. […] And so, I will now go out into the sunshine—heaps of love, Katie.[7]

Curtis was referring to President Roosevelt's speech of February 12, 1943, wherein he described his January conference with Winston Churchill in Morocco. By this point, Curtis's friends and family would have understood why she said it was "really stirring to be where we were, hearing his words." Roosevelt was speaking about the historic Casablanca Conference, and it was to this tropical, "beautiful and modern" city that Curtis was being sent to receive her first assignment.

So This Is Africa!

At 9:03 p.m. on February 24, 1943, an official telegram was transmitted from Washington, D.C., to a regional Milwaukee office, which telephoned Jane Whitney at 9:28. The message: "Glad to report safe arrival [of] Katharine Whitney Curtis—North Africa—Col. Will Cross."[8] That same day, the United States lost its first major engagement at Kasserine Pass (Tunisia), where German Field Marshal Erwin Rommel, or the "Desert Fox," had U.S. General Fredendall's inexperienced troops hopelessly outgunned and outmaneuvered. They first converged while Curtis was still en route to Casablanca, where Allied forces (including U.S. General George S. Patton) had already landed in November of 1942—about 1,200 miles west of Kasserine.

On March 2, Rommel's armored divisions were advancing south of Kasserine Pass toward the British Eighth Army (General Montgomery), and Curtis wrote about her own landing in North Africa:

The first day, when we were taken [from the boat] up into town in an open truck, you should have seen the unbelief that was written on the boys' faces when we shouted "hello" at them as we passed. And then, the cry of "Real American women, fellas!" followed us wherever we went. [Charles] Lindberg, in his triumphant procession, had nothing on us!

[…] We stayed in this town [three or four days], attending meetings to become acquainted with our new director. […And] during this time, we were sorted out and assigned to various places throughout North Africa. […While] in between meetings, we walked the streets, talking to every [soldier] we saw, and we were weary at night!

[…] This city is high on cliffs, overlooking the sea. The streets are narrow and crooked, many having steps leading from one level to the next. We were not allowed to drink the water, […and] the only good liquor here is what is brought over on the ships. And, of course, that is at a premium. [I] met some very interesting people, naturally, and managed a laugh or two. [The] ARC has one large club and two restaurants there, as eating is such a problem. The Germans cleaned out everything, and the populace is on strict rationing. [...] So, we all eat GI food in its simplest forms.

While Curtis was prohibited from naming any specific geographical locations, it's clear that she initially landed in Morocco's capital of Rabat, before heading south to Casablanca.

ARC cars met us, when we landed, and took us to our billeting spot. [...] The horses all had "sleigh bells" somewhere in this larger city, and there were thousands of bicycles. The street noises were a confusion of these bells and funny horn squawks from the French auto horns mixed with the clatter of army vehicles of all kinds.

On the sidewalks were the most varied collection of human beings one can imagine (and it's not at all like the [movie] picture of its name): white-robed, veiled woman and black men; men in heavy woolen robes with hoods, some white, some gaily striped, shuffling along in gay Moroccan slippers; all sorts of headdresses; [...] children calling [out to us], "bonbon" and "chewing gum."

[...] The clubs in this city had been staffed very recently by folks who had been in service in another country. [...] There is a very large club staffed with Negro personnel, with whom I was [trained] in Washington. They gave me a great "lift" by their genuine welcome. [...And] there is a warmth here that we did not find in the other large club staffed with white personnel [...who] have all the same facilities planned, but there isn't the sincerity that there is in the other place.

[...] Of course, everywhere we walked, we were mobbed by enlisted men, who followed us "just to look at us," or who stood around the edge of the conversational circle "just listening," or who had become so "Frenchy" that they grabbed our hands and kissed them or smacked us on both cheeks. "Where are you from?" was the usual greeting. I never knew there were so many people I'd never known before!

We ate at the officers mess at the Excelsior Hotel, and the younger [ARC] kids spent most of their time with the officers, but us "old bags" spread ourselves all over the enlisted men. One afternoon, [a friend] and I were on our way back to the club when a group of enlisted men surrounded us and insisted that we have a drink with them in a large beer hall where there was an American orchestra playing modern US music. [...] The oldest of their gang finally said, "Let's dance," and you know me!

This social encounter (continued below) is particularly significant because the older GI—later revealed as Private Bill John—would charmingly lock eyes with Curtis, who'd eventually trace their subsequent wartime romance back to this night.

There must have been several hundred boys in there, [...with] a smattering of French women, and us. There was hardly room to walk between the tables, let alone dance! But we pushed back the tables, pushed the chairs in, and the boys picked up their feet, and what a hit we made with our "solo." Everybody whooped, hollered and clapped, and finally [Bill John] said, "And I'm forty-two!" Says I, "Shh! I'm forty-six!" And what a laugh we had! I danced there with any Tom, Dick or Harry for over an hour. At one time, there was a circle of boys just passing me from one to the other!

[But] one of the many strange situations here is that it is almost impossible to ever reach any of the people over here after your paths have separated. APO's are changing so rapidly, and so many of these folks are casuals and replacements! Plans are made, broken and remade in the winking of an eye.

[...] Once again, I dragged all my luggage (foot locker, bed roll, suitcase, musette bag, gas mask, helmet, gun-belt with canteen), [and some friends] saw us off at the field. [...] Our air transportation here is marvelous! [...] We flew above 5,500 [feet] on the way down, through a high mountain pass with snow on the heights, and landed here at this beautiful little ocean resort hotel.

This was Curtis's first official assignment, an ARC rest camp for recuperating aviators in Agadir, which she'd consistently refer to as her "Paradise."

Never in your wildest dreams could you picture this place—such luxury in this fantastic dream. [...] A beautiful, large room on the fourth floor—twin beds. [...] Lovely, thick wool rugs on the floor—a huge bathroom with ultra-modern plumbing—a real toilet that flushes. [...And] we also have a lovely, large dining room with good food (GI mostly), and I'm afraid that I'm going to be fat as a pig after this war! I'm eating more food than I ever have!

5. She's Over There

Curtis (*right*) with American GIs in Casablanca, Morocco (June 1943).

When we arrived, yesterday [March 1 (1943)], we were met by the major […] in his seven-passenger Plymouth, […and] we drove around and around the hill to the walled city [and the resort building recently acquisitioned for a rest home] on its top—all shiny white. I guess it was built before the fifteenth century […and] outside the gates, there were a lot of natives pounding on tom-toms and shaking things like small cymbals on sticks and dancing. A very ragged, bare-legged French sailor, such a young boy, guided us around the little narrow path which ran along the inside of the top of the wall. […] The "fattened calf" had just been slain, and some of the men were busy cutting up the entrails. […] (Perhaps I should say at this point that one feels as though they are sitting on a powder keg as far as <u>real</u> friends are concerned in this area!) I felt as though I were walking through the pages of the *National Geographic* magazine all the time.

[…] And now, we are at "observation" status. It is not clear to anyone just where we are going to fit into this picture, […but] just know that never in civilian life could I have achieved such comfort and luxury. No matter how much responsibility comes, this is the life! If this wind ever lets up, I'll go for a swim. Whoopsie! Of course, I need a haircut, and would thoroughly enjoy a chat with my old friends, but *C'est la guerre!* ["That's the war!"]

[…] It's now Wednesday [March 3, 1943], and we have been kept busy with our guests, so that I have had a bad time trying to type this off. […] I went for a swim with a couple of the boys yesterday, and the water was like ice, but the beach was grand, and we took a long walk in our suits on the sand. This bunch [of aviators constitute] a couple of crews who have cracked up [psychologically] more than once, and are here to recuperate. They are <u>so</u> young, and are such swell kids. They are doing better work than you folks are ever told, too. Don't ever worry about their ability and spirit. I wish that I could write [to Gaylord about] some of the stories that I have heard the past couple of days. Some of them you will undoubtedly hear in your papers and on the radio, and maybe I can get some pictures to bring back with me, and tell you then.

[…] Will each of you be kind enough to send copies [of this newsletter] to the friends I have previously mentioned? […And] will someone please add Uncle Jim to their list? […] Among the things I forgot to tell you is that the local busses here are packed worse than the Mexican ones, and are charcoal-burning! […] When we were in the walled city today, I saw some black prisoners doing "street cleaning." They had their feet shackled together with a metal plate, about a foot long, which gave them the most peculiar gait you ever saw, the poor things. I'm getting so [experienced] that I can distinguish many of the planes [constantly flying overhead]. These ports have all the types you ever heard of—and then some! Again, I certainly wish that [Gaylord] could be here with me.[9]

A few days after Curtis finished this newsletter, the Germans reached General Montgomery's forces on March 6, 1943, at Medenine. British code-breaking intelligence gave Montgomery an early warning, and the assault was quickly repelled. Rommel was thereafter called back to Berlin "in bad health" (to save face) as his forces retreated.

Meanwhile, General Patton took over General Fredendall's command, and engaged the western German flank at El Guettar Valley by March 23. A day before that, Curtis wrote a private family letter with some rare commentary about her daily frustrations:

While I am on duty in the lounge this afternoon, it looks as though I might get a line or two off to you all, [...] and then the interruptions begin! First, it was some of the boys wanting to know where in the [hell] they could get something to drink, now that the canteen in the hotel has given out all their allowance, and since there wasn't any liquor anywhere today—[so] that took some little time. You see, the first thing they all want, as soon as they arrive here, is to "let down" by the liquor route, and it's a darn shame that they don't get some good American stuff over here so that these kids won't ruin their insides trying to get "drunk" on this red wine. They drink it like they would beer, and boy what a mess!

[...] I came back to my room facing the highway—across which, is the sea—to get the sewing kit, and stopped long enough to go out on my private sun-porch to see what was going on. [...] The boys play horse-shoes in a wide gravel path [that's] used by the camels and Arabs as a street. There the boys were (oblivious of their growing audience), pitching the shoes, while along the edge of the walk squatted at least fifty men and boys of various ages—almost every one of them in a different sort of clothing. A little farther back stood two brown-skinned beauties, all wrapped up in their "spook clothes," as the boys call them—one with a yellow face-veil, and the other with a white one.

[...] Words cannot do this place justice. I could spend all day just sitting on my balcony and watching this world pass by, but I never get a chance. [...] We've been having exquisite moonlight these days, and with the ocean rolling in at the front door, it has all been even more fairylike! [...] I've had a chance to walk down along the shore, and one of the boys asked me to walk with him at 6:00 a.m., which I did, even though I had sat up until 3:00 a.m. with six of the new arrivals, listening to their stories and watching them try to drink themselves to death in wine! When they [all] first arrive, it's always the same pattern, and we've already gotten used to it.

I sat in one of the rooms with the six of them, each [of my hands] being held by a different boy leaning against the knees of a third, [while I was] wearing the English brown suede "mosquito boots" of a fourth (a gift from him so that I could ride these Arab horses and god-awful saddles more comfortably); [I was also] smoking the cigarettes of the fifth [pilot], and wearing the ring of the sixth. Most of the evening was spent looking over snapshots of Palestine that one of them had taken, and listening to their tales of their travels. This particular unit has been in all the war areas, and has been in continuous service for the past fifteen months. Of course, they're anxious to get back to the States, even for a short time, and I for one don't blame them. It's difficult to take a gang like this and expect them to settle down here for quiet and sleep.

[...We] have made a valiant stab at trying to arrange some sort of social life with this community, but they (the powers above us) will persist in sending us both officers and enlisted men, and I'm discovering that you just cannot mix them socially. It sounds ridiculous from an American standpoint, but it's so. Then, too, the French are disapproving of dancing—sort of in mourning for the war situation—and all the dancing we try to manage has been done "sub-rosa." As a result of our efforts for the boys, we [ARC women] are being flooded with social engagements for ourselves. Tomorrow night, I take one officer and have dinner with a French-Moroccan family—the mother having cornered me in the hairdressing shop last week, and begged me (in fairly good English) that I come and bring "one nice officer."

[...] And another week is nearly at an end! But we got fifteen new "guests" in today, so the "circus" begins all over again! Nice war, eh what? Please pass this letter around because I'll not get another chance like this for some time, I'm sure. I'm stealing this time as it is! Am enclosing some snapshots that I bought—sorry I am not allowed to label them, but they are all sights that I see every day. Must get ready for dinner now. My love to all of you—I think of you often.[10]

Even more to her frustration, Curtis would soon get rebuked by the military censor, who would reject sending this message because "information in letter is detrimental to home morale. Also, all pictures enclosed show clearly geographical locations."[11]

One of Curtis's official duties as recreational director was to submit a comprehensive narrative report, which was begun on March 1, 1943, and described (without censorship) their activities since its opening earlier that year, "In the large, ultra-modern Grand Terminus Hotel—just across the highway from the ocean at Agadir, Morocco." This building was acquired by the U.S. Air Corps to accommodate various enlisted men (EM) and officers, who each stayed there for about ten days on average, up to a month.

> The boys all seemed to go through the same stages of recuperation during their rest period. The boys are all very young and very tired when they arrive, and their eyes have the "deadest" look one has ever seen. Most of them, I am sure, don't care too much about what the war means to anybody.
>
> To counteract all this, the ultra-modern hotel on the sea offers them all the conveniences of home (and more than that, to many of them). There are uniformed Arab boys to carry their luggage to large airy rooms with twin beds (with sheets), private baths with hot running water (twenty-four hours a day), and sun-porches facing the sea. […There's] electric light and a telephone, with an English-speaking person at the desk. After cleaning up, they come down to the lounge where there are flowers and candy on the tables; books, cards and games where they can reach them. Their laundry and cleaning problems are cared for right at the hotel (and what piles they had!). Usually, the Victrola [record player] is the first thing they use, and it runs continuously thereafter. Then come the letters home (and the Red Cross personnel offer to write and tell the folks how well each boy is looking).[12]

Curtis provided many other details about their abundance of food, drinks, and recreational activities, which included swimming, bicycle and horse-back riding, horseshoes, tournament softball games and sailing. Furthermore, "As far as the duties of the Red Cross workers are concerned, I feel that each [separate] Red Cross camp is a problem of its own. Here in North Africa, […] the personnel should be mature, well-balanced emotionally, independent individuals with an understanding of program needs and personal service."

As General Patton proved victorious at El Guettar, and the North African campaign advanced toward the last German-held territory (in northern Tunisia), Curtis continued to enjoy the temporary privileges of her Paradise, and typed a letter to her mother on March 31, 1943:

> Here I sit, in my swimming suit, on my private sun-porch, in a comfortable wicker chair, gazing out over the ocean, and writing you while I add to my sun-tan! It's a hard war I'm fighting! The boys are down on the beach, quite happy without me, and my co-worker is up in the big city [Casablanca] for a brief change of pasture, and I am bitten with the "lazy-bug." We have only a few of the most recent crowd left, and they are re-awaiting transportation (as usual).
>
> Your letter of March 1 reached me this week, but I have not seen the one written earlier. […] This is the first mail I have gotten, and it sure seems good. […] Censorship rules are still so strict that I am never sure that I can say any of the things I would like to say, but will do the best I can, and you will just have to be patient.
>
> We are still very happy here, and I am firmly convinced that this is the "softest" and safest assignment in North Africa. I had a chance to go up to one of the larger towns this week—[we] flew, as always here—and saw several of the other Red Cross workers. They are all working so much harder than we are, and are so "crabby" that I was only too glad to get back here to my happy family again.
>
> […] Thanks for all the bits of news. This, over here, seems so awfully unreal that I need those bits to keep my feet on the earth. I can't tell you how many times I have to pinch myself to see if this is really

[me]. I feel so sorry for all those kids you mentioned. They are just like all these "guests" we have. I about tear myself apart over each group, and all the visiting "brass-hats," including my CO [commanding officer], have told me that I'll never last the war out if I don't stop taking all this so personally.

But these kids are so young. Majors at twenty-six! Most of them under twenty [years old], and the grandest set of high-stepping "horses" you ever saw anywhere—doing a marvelously inspiring job—all anxious to get the thing over and get home to "nay" and settle down for the rest of their lives. Of course, many of them are already married, too. The French are so surprised to see at what an early age our people marry! So very many of the boys come to me to talk about their mothers and fathers. I offer to write to any of their relatives, and have so far quite a range—from "sweeties" and wives to fathers, mothers and sisters and brothers. That's another thing that keeps me from writing you all. I feel that my time really belongs to them first.

[…]I am trying to learn this darn French—we had three lessons so far—so can't do much. But our desk clerk, who is a refugee, is giving us lessons without a dictionary or books, so you can imagine what a job it is—for all of us! I must at this time stop letter-writing and study my lesson.[13]

Shortly after this letter, General Montgomery continued his northern advance toward Tunis on April 6 at the Battle of Wadi Akarit, where German forces withdrew along their supply routes to Sicily.

General Patton was soon called back to Morocco for the planning of a greater Allied invasion along that same pathway into Europe, while Curtis also received new orders, as she wrote to Jane on April 2:

I am here, in town [Casablanca], on business—"monkey business"—[and it] looks like my [Paradise] is about to be disrupted "in order to make use of my administrative ability." And the job is to be plenty big, [so] goodbye little pleasures of life. The area for this work is the same—use the same APO—the new "prospect" is in a large city, and I will no longer be associated with my beloved fliers, but C'est la guerre. And I have had a month of "heaven!"

[…] Now [April 4], and I have promoted [or acquired] a "jeep," which I have been driving all over town myself today (Sunday), having the time of my life! Of all wild things, never did I think I'd be flying, hurry-scurry, all over—in "my own" army jeep![14]

Curtis then wrote to her mother on April 11 with some additional updates and important details about the return to Casablanca.

While I am waiting to drive to a nearby town, where they are opening a new ARC club today, I have been reading the stack of mail that has been waiting for me to arrive here in this large city, where I am to act as "procurement officer" (note that the word is not "procuress"), for one of the largest clubs here. I hate the thought of the job, and was heartbroken at leaving my Paradise. […I'm] sure that the atmosphere of "hominess" that we have tried so hard to establish will be changed, […] but I guess that is just typical of the war.

[…] Really, I think that I will have a lot more personal life here [in Casablanca] than was possible at the "Paradise," but Lord, how I will miss the personal contact with those swell kids who brought "the front" right down into my lab. Here, when I was in town last weekend and "crying" about the change, the lieutenant gave me a jeep, and I had the time of my life driving it all day by myself. I have never seen another woman driving a jeep any place in North Africa, and I surely made the most of this opportunity.

I found [Bill John], the "private" from California, with whom I had such a good time dancing in the beer parlor when we first arrived here (remember?)—the one about my age—and he came into town the two evenings I was here. We found a nice little French restaurant that served late, and we certainly "clung" to each other. He would definitely fit into our old Chicago circle, and you can imagine what a life-saver he was. When I reached the hotel yesterday, there was a bouquet of bright geranium blossoms on my desk—in a tomato can, with a note from him. So I think that we will manage to have some nice moments, in spite of the war! So there is an occasional bright spot—in fact, I am still having the time of my life!

[…] The club is a huge "marble palace." […] I have [Gaylord's] large photo on top of the dresser, a map of the city covers most of the dirt spots, […] my pink geraniums in the tomato can, […so] the place is quite homey. My best boyfriend (the private) is having fits because I have no bath or toilet, but that's the least of my worries. […] The private and I are hoping we can sneak a plane ride back to Paradise this coming Sunday—don't know whether I can wrangle it or not, but it's worth a try—and am afraid [that having a boyfriend] will be quite a blow to the "rank" [younger enlisted men] that we'll meet!"[15]

This is the first (known) instance of Curtis openly revealing her romantic involvement with Private Bill John, who was providing logistical support for their military supply lines.

Leading up to Easter Sunday—April 25, 1943—Curtis was busy planting flowers and arranging for "the boys" to paint Easter eggs. On the last day of her vacation, she wrote to her sister, "I thumbed a plane ride back to Paradise for me and my private—and that took all day, was very pleasant, but tiring, since it ended with the Studebaker truck (ARC) breaking down. But it wasn't very far to walk!" Curtis was subsequently treated to a fancy dinner by her superior officers, and later sneaked away by an ARC friend "to have chow in the chow line, in the field mess of 'my private.' […] There, we put the two boys (in their fatigue clothes) into the car, […] and drove over to the seashore and watched the water 'til dark. I didn't go to church, but I managed to get pretty much at peace with myself!" The next day, she continued, "I enter 'society' via a dance at the major's villa, and I'm planning to wear my black-lace dress! Hope I can borrow an iron somewhere to press it! It's been so peaceful—I dread putting myself into this hectic social whirl. If only there were one-million American women here, it might help!"[16]

During this Easter period, Curtis was diligent as always to record her next carbon newsletter, in which she colorfully described her daily surroundings:

> I am now located back in the city where the traffic overtone is the tinkling bells of horse-drawn traffic; where one seldom sees a goat or a camel, but dodges millions of bicycles; […] where the light reflected from the white, white buildings is fascinating in the rain, sunshine or moonlight (we are of course, in blackout); where one rides in "*Voitures*," when one hasn't seen a car. These small, high-set carriages, with canopied tops, where the passengers sit facing each other riding sideways, have amazing drivers who always seem to execute the wrong traffic movement—and the seats are usually packed with sailors and soldiers of all Allied Nations.
>
> […] I have been transferred from my Paradise to act as assistant director to the largest club in this city, with the prospect of taking over the entire club when they see fit to move the man on.
>
> […] As I walk toward my club, I pass the bus station—a triangular corner where modern-looking "Greyhounds" (or a reasonable facsimile thereof) are panting at the curb, while passengers of every race, creed, color and costume loll in chairs at the sidewalk café, squat on the sidewalk beside their pile of worldly goods, [or] wrangle with small, shoe-shinning urchins. ("American polish, Miss?") Shouts of French and Arabic intermingle as they crowd into these busses like sardines. Even the tops are packed with bags, boxes, bundles, and squatting natives!
>
> Next door, on the corner where I turn, is a large old building now occupied by the American Military Police, and I smile and speak to our white-helmeted boys as I go past. […] On I go, past a souvenir shop, the windows of which are now filled with exquisite samples of North African handwork. […] Then our entrance, over which hangs a huge "American Red Cross Service Men's Club" sign. […] Up marble steps, one trots into a rotunda under a high-domed ceiling. In the center is a lovely large table with the register, over which the boys pore constantly (seeking to find someone they know who has signed before them). Today, the center of that table is occupied by a huge Easter egg (3.5 feet high), made entirely of red and pink geranium blossoms! (When I left the club at 11:00 last night, the [ARC] gang was still working on it.)
>
> […] To the right, is the entrance to the snack bar, where yesterday we did 14,800 francs of business, at two francs per item. […] At present, the snack bar is my greatest grief because it was all wrong when I came in (this club was opened in February), and it's so difficult to un-do and re-do! The steps from the lobby-rotunda lead directly to the food bar, which has caused a great deal of congestion, and I am

having a cafeteria-style railing put in (if and when we ever get through this Easter holiday so that these [local] "gentlemen farmers" can do a little work! Just don't talk to me about getting "help" in these parts to do a real day's work! Wow! You should just hear me when I get burned up!)

[…] We need at least seven reasonably intelligent people to keep that bar going. One, of course, is "off" each day. […] There have never been any Red Cross workers in the bar before I came, and I have one in there all the time now, trying to clean it up and "organize" it! In the kitchen, I'm still not sure how much help I have. I know I have a Parisian chef that is half crazy—as most of them are—and an Arab cook, with whom the chef won't work, and at least three or four other men of varying ages and abilities. There is a grand little Parisian woman […] who guards the supply room, and is the only member of my household with any brains.

[…] I have the sweetest walled patio you'd ever want to see. It used to be the tea-garden where folks talked business, sitting cross-legged, on bright rugs. […] There is a little tiled, blue-edged fountain in the center, and tropical trees, plants and flowers. It's a peaceful resort in this ant-hill of humanity, and I always sneak my favorite callers down there to visit! So far, it hasn't been used much by the [GI] boys, but we are moving table-games out there. And, as soon as I can think how to control the flies, I'll try serving free lemonade out there!

[…] Then, there is the Liberty Club, manned with Negro personnel (whom I knew in Washington), and catering to more whites than blacks. They have a beautiful building with much more warmth than we have been able to conjure up, to the present time, at least. They also have the best food, but don't serve the numbers that we have to serve.

[…] Josephine Baker—who, I am told, is the favorite of the [Thami El Glaoui] household in Marrakesh—was there last week, and I met her and talked with her.

[…] Much as I loved the luxury of Paradise, and the more personal contact with those grand young fliers, this job is much more of a challenge and certainly keeps me on my toes constantly. […] It's truly fantastic and unbelievable.[17]

Josephine Baker was a famous African-American entertainer who also served as a secret agent in the French Resistance movement. She first moved to France in the 1920s, and, after achieving cultural notoriety alongside Ernest Hemmingway and other avant-garde expatriates, she moved to French Morocco in 1941. Her public life was the perfect cover for passing along valuable intelligence about local Nazi collaborators. And, when she encountered some dire health problems, it was the local pasha of Marrakech (Thami El Glaoui) who supported her recovery. By 1943, Baker was entertaining Allied troops at venues like the Liberty Club in Casablanca, where Curtis was glad to make her acquaintance.

Meanwhile, General Patton's relief commander, Omar Bradley, was beginning the forward assault against German fortifications in Northern Tunisia. Bradley wrote in his autobiography, "By the third day, April 26 [1943], we had slugged forward about five miles, but then we got bogged down. The enemy had dug in atop a stark, rugged peak, Hill 609, so named for its height in meters on our French maps."[18] On the same day, Curtis, who was secluded in her own corner of North Africa, wrote to Jane with this light-hearted anecdote:

A couple of our boys were eating at a table with a couple of French sailors. Both tried to talk with each other, and one of the French boys was so proud of the fact that his mother used to rock him in his cradle and sing him an American lullaby (demonstrating the rocking of the cradle all this time). After much thought, finger-on-temple, he finally burst forth singing, "Hail! Hail! The gang's all here!" And he sang every single word without understanding a single syllable! You can imagine the laughter that caused, and what trouble our kids had to explain why they had laughed at the boy's lullaby! C'est la guerre! And I still can't speak French![19]

By May 1, 1943, General Bradley succeeded in penetrating the German defenses at Hill 609, and the Allies advanced toward their final destinations in North Africa.

Curtis wrote to her mother on April 30, wishing her a happy Mother's Day and concluding, "I'm well and happy myself, and know that you would love everything that I am doing—think of you at every decision—and the boys are now 'mom-ing' me!"[20] She then wrote to her sister about some local excitement on May 3, after returning from a beautiful villa where there "was a full colonel, a one-star [brigadier] general who had just arrived from the Pacific area, their two aides (a captain and a sergeant), my little snack-bar manager, and me! […] Most of the after-dinner, coffee-in-the-lounge conversation was political, and I found it very interesting! I can't tell you how fantastic this all seems to me." Curtis was obviously exhilarated by rubbing shoulders "with these men who are 'running' this war, talking 'trivia.'" She modestly concluded, " It just doesn't make sense, but I thought you all might enjoy hearing how I was fighting [this] war!"[21]

The final Allied assault in North Africa was launched on May 6, 1943, with the British entering Tunis from the south, and the Americans capturing Bizerte in the north. Curtis provided a contemporaneous account of this good news, writing to her mother, "The Tunisian collapse has been expected so long that it came as a relief to most of us, although there were parades and much display of the British, American and French flags."[22] And, on the same day that the ranking Axis general, Hans-Jürgen von Arnim, surrendered to British forces (May 12), Curtis wrote to her mother much more candidly about recent romantic developments:

> Do you remember the private who danced with me the first time I hit this town? Well, he and I are very much "that way" about each other, and it certainly helps a great deal under the circumstances. Please don't say anything to anybody else about this, as so many things may happen to change conditions, but I thought that you might be glad to know that, at long last, I had found an awfully nice person who is grand to me.
>
> Since he is a private, he has very few privileges, but we manage to find some little French restaurant where we can eat at least three times a week, and since I usually have a car, I have managed to get him back to his quarters in time for his "bed check" (and he is my age). It really has given us many a laugh. I haven't asked very much about his background, but I am sure he would fit smoothly into any circle we have ever been in. He knows his music, books, and art, and is an old Taos [art colony] person—travels in the art and theatrical groups, and I am sure at some time has had money. Not my luck that he should be rolling in wealth at this time.
>
> His "home" (an aunt a bit older than me, I believe) is in California, and the story at present writing is that we will live in [Mill] Valley, wherever that is. So you will have a warm place for your winters after all. It seems that he has been in the hotel business, and last connection was with the Mission Inn in Riverside. Don't you think that he will pass? He is taller than I am, skinny and quite homely, but we are two old "love birds." He is in the supply department, so may not get very far away from here. But, of course, one never knows. And we are very happy now. However, I am not forgetting to be very practical.
>
> […] I am sorry that I have not gotten around to writing to many of my friends, such as Vic, but I can write to you on the spur of a few stolen moments, and am sure that you will not mind whether they are coherent or not. […] I managed to run out to the major's villa on my lunch hour today, and had a ten-minute swim and washed my hair, so that I feel like a new woman. This is a "hard" war? Of course we will have a "million" at the dance tonight, so I will more than make up for the little respite I stole at noon. […] Much love to you all, and I hope that [Gaylord] will be with you soon [on the island].[23]

A month later, Curtis was made full director of her Casablanca club, with a full staff working for her by June 20, 1943, when she wrote to her mother, "I am most apologetic for not writing, but this period of transition has been a most difficult one and I am pretty tired most of the time, so spent most of my 'leisure' sleeping. My days are so full that night comes before I even get a start on the day's work. I have even given up my good habit of swimming every day, which was quite a jolt as the weather has warmed up considerably."[24] On June 24, Curtis wrote to Jane with a notable update about her aviator friends:

I'm finding a bit more time to "hob-nob" with more of the boys than I have had since leaving the [Agadir] rest camp, and I do enjoy that. This week, a group of half-a-dozen of the crew of one of the bombers has been here awaiting shipment to the States, now that they have completed their fifty "missions." These youngsters are all twenty to twenty-three [years old], and were at the rest camp when I was there, so we have had quite a fine reunion, and are already planning a hilarious time at the first Legion Convention after this thing is over! Most [in] this group are hoping to be able to take more training, to become pilots, etc. Imagine that, after fifty missions of high-altitude bombing! They sure are a great bunch of kids doing a swell job. This crew was especially lucky, in that they didn't lose a single man! And aren't they happy at the prospect of getting back home![25]

She also wrote about these bombers to her mother on July 1 (1943), recommending, "If you'll look […] in the April 26 edition of *Time*, read the article on the 513th Squadron of bombers. […] They were my best friends at the [Agadir] rest camp—grand fellows! One of them phoned George."[26] Indeed, the following highlights are worth reading:

In an average of forty-five missions per plane against Japs, Germans and Italians, the 513th's ten "Flying Fortresses" were riddled by ack-ack and enemy pursuit, but not one was shot down, and not one was cracked up.

Copilot Victor Bartholomei was the squadron's only casualty. He lost an eye to German shrapnel over Bizerte.

[…] Every airman in the squadron has flown 150,000 to 200,000 miles. […] They moved to Biskra [Algeria] after the Americans invaded North Africa. Because the mountains over the Kasserine Pass were high, they could get only twelve-thousand feet above heavy German ack-ack (they usually flew at 25,000 feet). When intelligence officers asked Bombardier Milton Stevens about the anti-aircraft strength, he replied: "Heavy to unbearable."[27]

Soon after Curtis hugged each of these young aviators goodbye in Casablanca, the invasion of Sicily commenced on July 10, 1943. Operation "Husky" was comprised of both American and British troops landing on the southern beaches; Patton from the west (at Gela), and Montgomery from the east (at Syracuse). Patton came ashore with a cigar in his mouth as he directed their impressive advance—naturally, in full view of the American newsreel cameras. The Germans pulled back slowly to Messina in the northeast, as Montgomery pursued them over difficult terrain. Meanwhile, as Patton was securing his southern beachhead on July 11, there was a disastrous friendly-fire mishap when an Allied bomber group arrived unexpectedly in the dark, and 23 C-47s were shot down by (Allied) anti-aircraft guns. Commanding General Eisenhower was understandably furious at Patton's oversight, and punitively relegated him to support the British flank.

Hungry for redemption, Patton pursued a more proactive opportunity on July 17, when he ordered a "reconnaissance-in-force" to capture Palermo in the northwest. And, with the Germans abandoning that region to increasingly demoralized Italian forces, Palermo was soon in Allied control by July 22. Benito Mussolini was deposed on July 25, and the new Italian leadership started negotiating peace with the Allies. All remaining German troops in Sicily were withdrawing across the Straits of Messina by August 5, when Curtis wrote to her old Chicago friend, Estelle, for the first time since Washington, D.C.

I surely was glad when told I could have a whole week at this aviators rest home in the mountains [of Agadir]. I have become a recluse here, shutting my door to all "eager beavers," and trying to catch up on my sleep, relaxation, peace, and letter-writing! My room is a huge airy one with French doors (second floor) opening out onto a vista of green meadow with a trout stream ambling through, and, in the distance, one of the sultan's many palaces.

[…] As for me running a hotel [with Bill John] when I'm through here, who knows? I'll not go back to teaching unless finances demand it. But, at present, one doesn't seem to be able to think about what

General Patton to the left of Curtis (*center*) at the ARC beach club in Mondello, Sicily (September 1943).

one will do when this mad thing is over. It just doesn't seem possible that it will ever be over, somehow! I hope that my next assignment will be one "in the field," and not another metropolitan club, but one never knows. All one can do is wait and wonder.

[…] Jane got [Gaylord] up to the island OK, so mother is holding her usual court quite happily. […I] am returning all the snapshots you sent me, except the one of you which I am carrying with me, if you don't mind. It wasn't fair for you to wear that coat in the picture if you've lost thirty-eight pounds—you look swell! I haven't lost any, I don't think, although I haven't seen a scale since I came up to the city.

[…] Nothing more in mind at present, and the gang is getting ready for tennis and a swim. Tennis balls are $85.00 a dozen on the "black market" here, if and when you can get them. I'm seriously considering writing [to my old colleague…] that, if the PE department would like to help the boys overseas, they can ship me a dozen (or any part thereof) tennis balls from the central stock. They surely would be a God-send! And, so, to fight the war—best of luck and love.[28]

The ARC club at Curtis's "Paradise" had been officially closed for about a month, and, with the conquest of Sicily concluding by August 17, 1943, she was preparing herself to "follow the action" beyond the shifting sands, exotic oases, and romantic Moroccan sunsets. On August 6, she continued describing her final days in Agadir with this fitting newsletter highlight, which reveals her inevitable reunion with another old Chicago "friend."

The pool is fed by the mountain stream, which flows in at the shallow end, and out at the deep, so the water is always cold. The pool is always full of adults and children (no guards of any kind) of all shades and colors—and you should see the snappy suits the French gals wear. […] Today, I finally got enthusiastic enough to get myself to the pool, and took the [Victrola record player] down with me. It was quite fun "spreading the gospel" of synchronized swimming again, only, I would have hated to have any of my team gals see the way the old lady was executing the figures![29]

6

Lifting Morale

There would always be one heirloom of a story guaranteed to fascinate the descendant family members of "Aunt Kate" ever since she first entrusted that precious memory, with a wink and a smile, to her only nephew. And it was Gaylord who gladly nurtured this flame until it took root in a more recent generation. It's been 75 years since the unforgettable day in question, and, from Curtis's original words—as per her family's honest tradition of remembering them—the type has now finally been set for the record, and to be cherished by all future generations.

It was said to have happened in Palermo, when Curtis was with General George S. Patton in 1943 after the city's capture. She was sufficiently prominent in the American Red Cross to become personally acquainted with the famous general, whose no-nonsense and formidable swagger inspired the common soldier and ARC staff alike. He'd already proven his mettle by taking this city (against orders) in a quite unnecessary race against his British allies, and Curtis was proving just as much of a masterful commander for the many impressionable young girls working for her. Patton often relied upon Director Curtis's administrative acumen to "get things done," and a prime example of this arrived when she was put in charge of arranging a big social event at one of their newly opened ARC facilities. She received a concise set of orders from Patton to that effect, and, sure enough, she "got it done" just in time for the general's inspection (or so the story goes).

Curtis was notified of Patton's approach by a vigilant staff member, who spotted the gleam of his formal dress-helmet speeding up toward their facility. He was also equipped with his iconic horse whip and ivory-handled revolver to maintain his carefully cultivated persona, which never failed to excite a crowd like the one now mobilizing in the foyer to receive him. Curtis fixed her hair and adjusted her uniform before stepping through the ranks to assume her position at the front. Patton's entourage of officers and military aides were keenly in pursuit as he arrived in his jeep. He stepped sprightly from his mount and looked up at the impressive building façade as those other vehicles halted in the gravel.

He advanced with seemingly indomitable steps (and a mischievous smile) along a straight line to the focal point of gathering GIs, some of whom were greatly bandage-wrapped and naturally in need of encouragement. Curtis gave a competent salute, and the general slowed his hurry. The Sicilian sunlight was breaking around the three stars on his helmet, the curious and intimidated soldiers were rising on their toes to get a better view, and Patton walked up within a nose-to-nose proximity of Director Curtis. She smiled suspiciously before he barked with a rhetorical question for everyone to hear:

"How the hell are ya, Kate?"

Patton grinned without reserve, and then reached around to grab (and hold on to) her anatomical posterior.

6. Lifting Morale

Katharine Whitney Curtis (*right*) reaching across General Patton while the newsreel cameras are clicking away.

"Well, you feel fine to me!"

That social bombshell reverberated in silence before an explosion of uncontrollable laughter. Everybody was practically out of breath by the time that Patton finally let go, and, in a rather generous spirit of entertainment, Curtis postponed the natural urge to slap him. The maverick pair just smiled at each other with a mutual understanding in the spotlight, after the glorious victory of yet another bold and spontaneous battle maneuver—obviously intended to "lift morale."

Shortly after this legendary moment, Curtis discreetly encouraged its rumor by sorely rubbing her "caboose" whenever onlooking spectators were gossiping nearby, as if there might be a secret bruise in the shape of General Patton's hand. Many years later, she proudly reminisced to her full-grown and discerning nephew, who'd never forget the impact of her retrospective candor. And, although the scandalous nature of this event would prevent any chance for direct historical confirmation, the truth in her voice and (almost guttural) laughter never left room for any doubt.[1]

So This Is Sicily!

While Curtis was still vacationing in the mountains around Agadir, Patton was getting into some preliminary trouble after having slapped two soldiers for perceived cowardice by August 10, 1943. Following the swell of public outrage back home, Patton apologized to them both by August 23, began apologizing in public to each of his separate divisions, and then wrote a deferential explanation to General Eisenhower on August 29:

> In World War One, I had a dear friend and former schoolmate who lost his nerve in an exactly analogous manner, and who, after years of mental anguish, committed suicide. Both my friend and the medical men with whom I discussed his case assured me that had he been roundly checked at the time of his first behavior, he would have been restored to a normal state.
>
> Naturally, this memory activated me when I very aptly tried to apply the remedies suggested. After each incident I stated to officers with me that I felt I had probably saved an immortal soul.[2]

Meanwhile, on August 18, 1943, Curtis was flying up through the recently captured cities of Tunis and Bizerte to her new assignment, just outside of Palermo.

The ARC was renovating a recently acquisitioned building, still known locally as the *Antico Stabilimento Balneare di Mondello*, and Curtis oversaw its (informal) opening to military personnel on August 28. They had a more official opening-day parade scheduled for shortly thereafter, and Curtis excitedly wrote her first letter from this new location to her mother on September 8:

> Just a line or two to let you know that I am OK, and love Sicily. [...I'm] in charge of a perfectly lovely beach club which used to be one of the most elaborate Mediterranean Spas. [...] Of course, it is in an area which has not escaped bombing, so many parts need repair. But, on the whole, I have been told repeatedly that this is the finest Red Cross setup of the war, as far as recreational facilities are concerned, and everybody is crazy about this beach club.
>
> It is located in a small village [Mondello] near a large city [Palermo], and the drive out here [is one of the loveliest you can imagine]. I am driving a little German car, which carries an Egyptian license plate, has four speeds, and a reverse [gear] where no descent reverse [gear] should be. And most of

"Peeling grapes for General Patton and Norman Davis [*right*] at opening of beach club."

the time, it is, or should be, in the repair shop. [...To get to the club], we pass through some gardens and tangerine orchards (pretty bad shape for want of water), and always with the grandest mountains on every side. The water is the most gorgeous blue, green and aquamarine, you can ever imagine, and there are sailboats all over the surface. [...] We have a big float out in the deep water with a springboard and a five-foot diving stand, all of which is most popular. The water is very salty, and no one could possibly sink in it. It is also tropical enough so that the temperature is almost tepid. [Gaylord] would love it here, too. And boy, how he could swim in this water!

[...] As you can probably see, I have been writing this in spurts—and now it is evening, almost bed time—of the night when rumor has again told us that the Italians have surrendered. And if it is true, I know that you will be wondering what I am doing.

[...The famous musician], Al Jolson, who has been at the beach club the past two mornings, sang several songs up on a table, and everybody sang with him. Yesterday, [actor] Douglas Fairbanks Jr. was out at the club, too. Just a rendezvous for artists, that's all!

[...] I found Bill John here when I arrived, but since he is not an officer, it is very difficult for us to get together often. We did a bit of sightseeing yesterday, since we both had the day off. There are many ancient things to see, and the scenery is never to be forgotten![3]

The "rumors" she mentioned regarding an unconditional Italian surrender were in fact reliable, and it was on this day, September 8, 1943, at 5:30 p.m. that the good news was officially announced by General Eisenhower. Meanwhile, U.S. troops under General Mark W. Clark were moving against the Germans around the Italian mainland port of Salerno, about 200 miles north of Curtis in Palermo.

By September 2, General Patton had flown over to Algiers for an in-person "verbal thrashing" from Eisenhower, regarding the slapping debacle. It was also exclaimed that Patton had "ruined [General Montgomery's] career by getting to Messina [via Palermo] first," and was to apologize to Monty, who was continuing to lead the Italian invasion effort alongside General Clark.[4] Additionally, Eisenhower would snub Patton's (all-too-transparent) ambitions for the upcoming Normandy invasion, the command of which would instead be tasked to their mutual friend, and Patton's former subordinate, General Omar N. Bradley.

A few weeks after all this administrative drama, Curtis woke up at 6:00 a.m. on her day off—Sunday, September 26—to write her first newsletter from Mondello:

So this is Sicily! And I love it!

[...Our Mondello] villa is about six blocks along the coast from the beach club, all of which is set [among the] lovely summer homes of the wealthy [families] from the large city [Palermo], about six miles away. [...] Many of the families are back here now, although there were none here prior to the submission of Italy. I understand that most of them were up in the mountains to escape the bombings of the city. The same situation prevailed in [Palermo]—when I arrived, there were very few civilians on the streets, which were filled with debris from the bombings. [...] But now, the place looks like Chicago, only, the civilians will walk in the streets, although there are narrow sidewalks on both sides where they could walk.

[...] As usual, every GI mess [hall] has a following of old and young civilians with tin cans to snatch the scraps and garbage at the end of the meal, and every GI solider seems to have "adopted" at least one emaciated child to fatten and clothe. It's amazing how these soldiers treat all the children, who really are little pests with their incessant begging for "*caramello*" [caramel candies]. As soon as our car stops, there are faces poked into every window, old and young alike, all speculating as to whether we are Americans or not.

The ARC women here are the only women they have ever seen driving a car, I think, and everyone seems to think that is a big joke. I have a beautiful eye-rolling acquaintance with all the handsome Italian traffic cops along the main drags of the city. And after the "eye," you should see the variety of "salutes" I get! And such smiles!

[...] I flew all the way here, so you can imagine what a grand trip it was. Stopped in Tunis and Bizerte on the way, but not for long—got into my first air raid en route. Was sleeping on the roof of a building without any glass in any of the windows, and you can believe that I didn't waste any time getting down from the roof to the first floor, where we watched the rest of the raid. I have some nice pieces of flak [shell casings] that I picked up around my cot in the morning. I wasn't the least bit afraid, but I was furious that there had to be so much waste of money with all the stuff shot up into the air without every shot bringing down a plane! Queer folks we are, aren't we? We had a raid here when I was still in the city, and there was a hit within two blocks of our apartment, which wasn't what you could call <u>fun</u>. But it's all so peaceful now that it's hard to believe that there is trouble anywhere.

[…] The war passes by me all day and night, over my head, across my horizon, and by our front door, but I still look forward to my delayed copy of *Time* [magazine] to find out what has been going on in this fracas which I have found myself. It is strange, but the closer one is to it all, the less one seems to know!

She continued this newsletter with what should be historically noted as her first interaction with General Patton, only a month after his public scandals and apologies.

You might be interested in the story of our formal opening day, which some of you have undoubtedly seen shots of in the newsreels recently. After all the ARC services in this area were completed, we had the big opening [parade] with all the "big shots." It really was a scream! There were ten cars of celebrities from the various army and navy circles, including the British, of course. There was a Red Cross "hostess" in each of the cars, and the "kingpin" was the commanding general, of course.

The course of the parade had been carefully timed according to the speed limits which he had so strictly set, and what did [the commanding general] do to the schedule but get into his car with all his flags-a-flying, and go hell-bent for heaven along the course in such a hurry that he was forty-five minutes ahead of schedule when he arrived at the final club where the speeches were to be (the band hadn't gotten there yet and the audience wasn't there either!). He is sort of like that! […] He got up and said, "After hearing all the good things that the Red Cross has said about me, I have about come to the conclusion that perhaps I am not the son-of-a-bitch that so many think that I am!"

To go back to the opening—the parade came to [our Mondello] beach club first, General [Patton] and all the ARC officials from Washington and Algiers, etc. We met them at the sidewalk, and there is a long approach to the club building. I thought I would die when I found that I had to walk all that distance <u>alone</u> with the general, whom I had just then been introduced to. But, with the newsreels grinding and cameras flashing, I managed to make it without stubbing my toe.

We had a hurdy-gurdy [musical instrument] at the front door, and one of the familiar, gaily painted Sicilian carts with a tiny, "mouse-like" donkey at the other side of the door (the cart was loaded with white grapes). I thought, all the time, of how much [Mother] would have loved that day with all of its effects! We ended our march of inspection on the upstairs balcony overlooking the sailboat and swimming races, and drank a glass of lemonade. The races were being run for and by GIs, although the boats were sailed by their Sicilian owners. Below us were "a million" GIs having such a good time that they never even knew that [General Patton] had passed through behind them.

[…The ARC] sort of "sneaked" into this [Mondello] villa (since this small town is supposed to be restricted to generals). And, the very first day that I had obtained the key and was inspecting the house, who should walk in but two of the general's staff to ask me if the ARC girls would accept an invitation to the general's villa for a buffet supper—which we did, and it was a very pleasant evening with good food and company. Frankly, it was quite a pleasure for me to have the opportunity of conversing with somebody my own age for a change.

[…] I have found many "old friends" here, and have made many new ones, and Sicily will always find a warm spot in my heart. It is so much more colorful and friendly here than it was in North Africa. […] The beach club is on a bay that is nestled down in the heart of the "sweetest" mountains one could ever want to see. And one of my favorite thrills is to swim out near the float, hang there in the buoyant salt water, and "inspect" the mountains on either side of "my" club and the palms behind it.[5]

Although Curtis's first meeting with Patton undoubtedly confirms their historical proximity, it's likely that her "legendary" (and considerably scandalous) moment occurred more toward the end of their three-month acquaintance, rather than here at its beginning with all the reporters and newsreel cameras probing for additional scandal.

6. *Lifting Morale* 71

Curtis performing her administrative duties around the Mondello beach club opening (September 1943).

Following this first Sicilian carbon newsletter, Curtis wrote to her father on September 29, "I am having the time of my life, and I really feel very selfish most of the time." She also mentioned an update for her dormant teaching career: "I understand that my assignment has been transferred from Chicago Teachers College [back] to Wright Junior College, but I just can't get interested. It all seems so darned remote, and, since there doesn't seem to be any immediate signs of a speedy return to the USA, I certainly am not concerning myself with Chicago Board of Education vagaries!"[6] And, when writing to Jane on the same day, she added, "I had quite a surprise the other day when [General] Paul Harkins, [General Patton's chief of staff] appeared at the beach club. [...] He certainly is a handsome devil, but just as nice as ever. Jack Benny, Al Jolson, Douglas Fairbanks Jr., [and Arthur Rubinstein] are some of the other celebrities who have been out to the club during their Sicilian visits. [...] Mother would love this assignment, as well as the house in which we live."[7]

On October 1, Allied troops captured Naples with a slow advance as the Germans traded ground for time to retreat. The Naples port was incapacitated by both Allied bombing and German sabotage upon their retreat. And, while those fortified lines of engagement were retracting from one boundary to another, Curtis wrote her mother on October 10 with some more details from Palermo:

> I have seen Bill John several times, and have been out to several insignificant social affairs—except for the Seventh Army Headquarters dance, which was quite an experience [...] since it was my first really big army dance. As usual, I was left cool and unimpressed—had a lot of chuckles, and several good

dancing partners. I went with an ordinance captain, who had been especially kind in giving me transportation for my civilian help [staff] ever since we opened. One of his men told me that he "was one of the few gentlemen left in the army," and he certainly has been a great relief to me from many others who haven't been such. They had a grand dance band for music though, and everybody enjoyed every bar [of music] they played. It still seems so strange to me, to go to social functions and to have so few women there. I just can't seem to get accustomed to it.[8]

Curtis continued describing the general atmosphere of her local surroundings to Estelle on October 12, 1943:

Our rains are here, but, when there is no wind (which becomes almost a twister in these mountains around the club and villa), they are quite refreshing. [...] I am the happiest I have ever been in this exquisite beach club assignment on the Tyrrhenian Sea. [...] It's so delightfully calm, peaceful and green (after tonight's rain) that it's difficult to think of the horrors of war that have made this all possible for me! [...] Over here, naturally, we are all wondering where our next move will be! [...] Love—always—Katy-did![9]

Curtis also wrote a brief note to her mother on October 29, stating, "I am still in the pink of condition and am having some grand dances with [a] nice second lieutenant. [...] So, while the good times last, I am making the most of them—and it is really great fun. I still manage to see Bill John as often as he has the time off."[10]

The rainy season fully arrived by November, and the Italian cold was starting to cause trouble up north for the Allied troops, who were getting stuck in heavy mud with some reported cases of trench-foot. The Mondello beach club served hot coffee (instead of lemonade) for "the boys [...] still coming over, although in much smaller numbers. [...] The hardy ones are still swimming, since the water is quite comfortable."[11] Curtis wrote her last letter from Sicily on November 11, commiserating with Jane about their failed attempts to get her mother to leave Washington Island for the winter. Furthermore, it was by December that Curtis started having serious doubts about her romantic future with Bill John, especially after she was "suddenly" transferred to her next assignment (another rest home for aviators) on a small but famous rock, just south of Naples.

The Isle of Capri

About a hundred miles away from the enemy entrenchments at the "Gustav Line," which ran across the width of Italy (between Naples and Rome), Curtis scribbled a brief introductory note to her mother on December 12:

I hope you're having a happy birthday, wherever you are, and boy! Do I wish you were here with me, you'd be in seventh heaven! It's like living in the midst of a musical comedy. This small community is an entity of its very own, and if the ARC will only give me a little help, we'll really have something here. If they don't send me help soon, I'll be completely "nuts!"

[...] I am "wound up" already in local politics, social feuds, community problems, etc.! [...] You'd split your sides laughing to see me and the "mayor" (Italian) and the "governor" (Allied Military Government representative) having our conferences over requisitioning space for the ARC. I have been labeled *"Comandante"* [...] by the local Italians! Details when I have more time, must rush off. [...] Lord help us![12]

These promised details were given (at length) in her next carbon newsletter, which was started during the week after Christmas, and laboriously finished while she was sick in bed on January 12, 1944. The following highlights provide a valuable and micro-level glimpse into her various responsibilities, and it should become abundantly clear just how many colorful stories she collected during this period:

> Dear folks,
>
> I hope that I can write this letter in such form that the censors will allow me to greet you and tell you somewhat of this, my new assignment. As you all know, the theater [of war] is a moving one, and Red Cross activities are keeping as close to the front as possible. Hence, I move on and on, never seeming to stay long enough in any one spot to become part of it. Yet, in each new assignment, in the short time we <u>do</u> spend there, I <u>must</u> become an integral part of the community in order to have our Red Cross installations function properly.
>
> [...] I am back in the rest camp field, in an administrative capacity. I have thirty US gals working with me, only one of whom has had any previous ARC field experience. So, as you can imagine, I have my moments when I wish that they were all back in the States! There is nothing that can take the place of "seasoning" by previous experience, and, while all these girls are grand and are working hard, it really was a job when they all arrived here just before Christmas to be tossed directly into an already functioning program!
>
> I had come into the community, a couple of weeks before, in order to survey the needs and possibilities, and to secure buildings, etc. The rest camps were already functioning from a housing standpoint, and my job was to determine what part the Red Cross could play in this unique setup. I am sorry that censorship forbids my giving details here, but suffice it to say that this is the only place in the world, so far, that an attempt has been made to function as we are functioning here. It has been an ideal situation for me since we are an isolated community, a comparatively small one, and I was the first and only ARC person to "open" the location. My supervisors came in with me the first day, and then left me to my own devices.
>
> This is one of the beauty-spots of the world—an artist's paradise—each of the residents an interesting international personality, and most of them are "interned" here, far from their properties and relatives in the active war-zone. Many of them speak English and French, in addition to their native Italian, and have traveled a great deal; although the "native" population speaks only Italian, they are rapidly learning American expressions. When we first arrived, [their] greeting was "Allo! Tchooing gum!" And, of course, all the little street urchins smoke cigarettes!
>
> The streets are all cobblestone paving, winding around, up and down the mountain sides—some of them so narrow I can touch both walls without stretching. [...] These marble (and tiled) floors and huge glass windows may be OK in warm weather, but they're much too cool for now! When the sun is out (like in Mexico), all is well—<u>but</u>, this is the rainy season! When I get back to the States, I am going to live in a "hot-house!" The streets are so narrow that only on the main ones can any vehicle move, so most of our supplies must be carried by man-power. A "jeep" can manage to go where no other vehicle has ever been before, but even that miracle can't cover half of this community! Our uniform leather oxfords (with heels) are getting an awful beating, and I am suggesting that the gals purchase the local rope-soled shoes for service purposes.
>
> The villas, perched up and down the mountainsides, are among the most famous in the world, and I spent my first day or two with the major in charge of this area, inspecting various villas. This was an education in architecture and interior decorating in itself! The scenery and views from these various locations cannot be beaten anyplace in the world. [...] I searched the community for space for an information center, from which tours to points of interest would originate. [I also searched] for an [EM] enlisted men's club, a snack bar, and for living accommodations for the ARC personnel, if and when they should arrive.
>
> This searching necessitates inspection and measurement of the space in the buildings to be requisitioned—and a report to the military, who then requisition the space. But this requisition must meet the approval of the local mayor and the local AMG governor, who is a captain in the US Army—and what a time I had! Every time I thought I had "just the right spot," the [local] proprietor would turn out to be a widow with children whose sole support was the shop I was requisitioning—or an old couple with ninety-nine relatives they were supporting, etc. I had my moments when I thought we were too lenient with our "co-belligerents." And, when the smoke of many battles cleared away, I found that I had the resultant installations [...] a little off the beaten path which had more space.
>
> [...] The EM lounge villa had been the home of a bachelor and was very comfortable and completely

furnished. [...] The girls have already made this most homelike, serving coffee late in the evenings, and making fudge when they can "mooch" the supplies from the mess officers. They did a grand job of Christmas decorating, and had a nice American Christmas tree. They have a radio and we are now looking for a piano. They do have an accordion, and each week some GI appears who can play it (and how he loves it!).

A little candle lantern sits outside the door on the rocky window ledge, blinking its welcome to the men so far away from their homes. The first night, some poor civilian apparently needed the candle more than we did, because it disappeared entirely, but the little tin lantern was left. Candles are at a premium here, as are most supplies for civilians. The poor things have been without so many of the so-called necessitates of life that you wonder how they have ever managed. Most of their supplies come through their black market, if and when they can get anything at all.

[...] The villa we have for the recreation center is an elaborate, large-roomed palace with a nice old garden filled with palm trees, dwarf irises, roses, and narcissus in bloom (at present). It was an old English-American hotel, and a wealthy Jewish woman—who is now in German-occupied territory, poor thing—had remodeled the place, and started on the furniture when the war stopped things.

[...] The week before Christmas, the powers-that-be dropped thirty gals into my lap as most-welcome Christmas gifts, and I dispersed them into the various rest homes to prepare for their first Christmas away from home—and how they worked! They were weary from the long trip over, and many of them had colds and a few gastro-intestinal disturbances, but they managed to spread the good old Christmas cheer like a group of old troupers, and I am awfully proud of them! The following week, [...] the Red Cross delegate in this theater came on an inspection tour, and I think [he was] quite happy to see everything [up and] running in so short a time (three weeks from the day of my arrival).

During this time, [...] I hired [Olga], the daughter of a Russian princess, [...] as my "social" secretary, and started out with her to make the necessary social contacts to secure the cooperation of the best women in the community to help us with dances and other social affairs.

After meeting several of them separately, I called them together at a meeting at the hotel, opened one of my boxes of Christmas candy, and explained my problems [before asking] for their help. You can't imagine the "conversation" that that instigated! After listening patiently to the rapid-fire Italian conversation for some little time, I asked Olga if they had reached a decision, whereupon she said that the officers' dances would be simple, but the EM affairs would be a little more complicated since the "nice" Italian girls were so closely chaperoned. However, the dowagers (the *marchesa*, the *contessa*, the baroness, etc.) would grace our first EM dance, bringing with them their own household personnel and shopkeeper friends. This was to be a Sunday afternoon tea dance. Thus, the stamp of social approval would be put on the affair, and the "nice" girls would be allowed to attend.

So, even before my US gals arrived, Olga and I had tried two officers' dances and two EM dances, which we thought were quite successful! At the EM dance, the boys couldn't tell the difference between the dowagers and the "hoi-polloi" [common folk], and would grab one of the former by the arm with a "How about a dance?" And—before the poor soul could gather together her little English to say "No!"—she'd be whirled off into the middle of the floor! One of the most charming of these lovely ladies came to me with tiny beads of perspiration on her forehead and gasped, "That's the first time I have danced in twenty-two years!" And a good time was had by all!

[...] I almost got myself all mixed up in local politics through [a communist agitator] because I had planned the community Christmas party for the children with his help, instead of the help of the mayor, who was very busy getting food for his community and almost never at home. However, after "sweating out" two days of conferences—when I thought the whole party would collapse—finally, the lamb and the lion laid down together, and the party was a huge success. There were over 450 children, [...and] the nuns gathered them all in the vaulted stone halls of the ancient school building on the afternoon before Christmas, and there they stood, two-by-two, for "hours" waiting for the rain to stop.

[...] You see, this "theatrical" ceremony had been planned by my man, "Friday" [the communist]. The children of the community were presenting huge Christmas cards (painted by one of the local artists, with two scenes topped with an American eagle)—one to the governor, and one to me. There were to be the usual speeches by the children [...] and then the large group was to be split up [at] each of the hotels to be fed, and [also to] receive their Christmas candy from the [soldiers].

The rain held up the affair for almost an hour, and, just as the children were entering the village square, one of our highest ranking generals (who was here on a very brief visit) came into the square from the other side! It couldn't have been more perfectly timed, and the governor and I stepped out of the picture and turned all the speechmaking over into the general's lap! The children were perfectly adorable, and the general, quite moved! [...] It was a howling success, I can assure you, particularly so to me because the mayor and the governor were in the general's party, and <u>had</u> to admit that my man, Friday's party was the best ever—after having criticized him the previous week![13]

Curtis would later reveal the identity of this high-ranking general for the *Milwaukee Journal* on September 26, 1944: "I'll never forget the mutual joy of General Ike Eisenhower and the two-hundred Italian kids at the Christmas party given for the children by the Red Cross. He wasn't expected, of course. But he has a way of popping up suddenly, in the midst of things. [...] When the door opened and they spied Ike, they thought his four stars were a part of the tree decorations, and all rushed him. He had a great time, too."[14] She continued describing that Christmas on Capri in her (January) newsletter:

We had expected a GI show to arrive Christmas Eve for special entertainment, and when, on top of pouring rain, it did <u>not</u> arrive, my morale reached its lowest ebb. However, each of the girls rose to the occasion in her [respectively] assigned club, and the boys (most of them) seemed quite satisfied. Some sat around the fireplace and sang carols for a while (one group asked the girls to stop after ten minutes, because they couldn't take it).

[...] As for <u>me</u>, I had decided that perhaps I could steal a few hours "just for me," so I tried to move some of my things from the big bustling hotel to a tiny two-room suite in a large villa, where a "young" countess lives with her seven dogs and a pet gazelle. It was pouring rain, but I thought of the corner fireplace in that tiny living room and persisted in my efforts to find somebody with a jeep who would move my bedroll and "accessories." After a struggle, I finally got my things and two GIs to move them into a jeep, <u>but</u> there was no room for me, so I set off on foot with <u>no</u> flashlight!

<u>Never</u> have I been in such blackness, and such a sheet of water! Even my raincoat pockets filled up! My flashlight had been stolen, and I haven't been able to "promote" another yet, so I stumbled along—first bumping the wall on one side, and then banging into the trees on the side toward the sea! To make a long story short, I fell up the 146 steps to the villa, and I fell <u>down</u> them. Where the walk divided, one leg went down the hill, and the other straight ahead, and I barked both shins on the cement dividing the curb! Never have I been so wet and so mad at myself for not having a light!

I finally reached my new home, and one of the boys tried to start the fire in the corner fireplace while I set up my little artificial Christmas tree [...] and piled my many Christmas packages up. The fireplace smoked like a smokehouse, so we opened the windows and doors, and, while the smoke was clearing, we opened my packages. First, I would unwrap one, and then Andy would unwrap [another] one (of mine), and such laughs we had when he would say, "What's this?" And it would turn out to be shoulder straps, a stocking mender, or some such un-gentlemanly giftie [*sic*]. It was great fun. And, finally, he retired to his room on an upper floor, and I got into dry clothes and my slacks, and settled down on the chaise lounge before the still-smoking fireplace to peacefully re-read *The Story of San Michele*.

Curtis was naturally interested in this bestselling memoir because the author, Axel Munthe, was a famous resident of Capri until 1942, and the title refers to that island's medieval chapel, which still overlooks the town in full view of Mount Vesuvius.

After a couple hours of this peace and quiet (with many memories of previous pleasant Christmas'), Andy came down to say that the Christmas Eve party was in full swing, up in the living quarters of Countess Maria. So up we went—slacks and all—to a very gay party of local men and women and American officers!

[...] The Christmas Eve party was a nice social event, and I finally broke away in the small hours of the morning. However, I was up in time for a short walk before church, Christmas Day, having been too wet to go to the 11:30 p.m. service the night before. Services are held by an Episcopalian chaplain (a grand person) in a tiny German church with German phrases on the ceiling (over the alter) and on all the beautiful stained-glass windows!

I ate a turkey dinner at one of the hotels, and then [went] to the children's (two-hundred of them)

Christmas party in one of our instillations, a short distance from the center of things. [...] These children [were] even poorer (suffering more from malnutrition) than those of the day before. They really were pathetic, and the way our boys took care of them, carrying a glass of cocoa to each child, was touching.

In the evening, my own morale needed a lift, so I decked myself out in my dinner clothes—brilliant ear buttons and all—to attend Christmas dinner at Countess Maria's. Somewhere, someway, Andy had managed a "whole" turkey and all the fixings, and there were twelve for dinner at a beautifully appointed table with a white-gloved servant. And at least twelve more guests dropped in after dinner, when we talked and danced to the radio and Victrola music. The Countess is a charming hostess, has travelled all over the States, and speaks English beautifully.

That brings you all just about up to date—except that, today, I have stolen the entire day, spending it here in my little hideaway (snuggly in bed), and trying to cure a nasty cold (which I think I caught from the children). You'd all split your sides [laughing] to have seen me today, sitting here in bed (in-state) with a beautiful silver tray and coffee service on my lap, and two servants busy in the other room trying to get the fireplace started.

[...Just to] describe some of the interesting folks I have met in the short time I've been here: there's the baroness, who was the companion for years of one of this community's world-renowned authors. [...Then] there is the Italian writer and editorialist, who dresses so theatrically [and] has a strange villa, which looks like an airship perched on a huge, bare rock jutting out into the sea. They say his floors are of glass, through which you can see deep into the sea.

And [there's also] the tall Italian prince, who is worried for fear that when the Germans move north they will take with them his wife, who is an Italian Red Cross nurse. (I have much to be grateful for, because, although I am separated from you all, I at least know that you are safe). [And finally, there's] the sweet little old Russian princess (who reminds me so much of [Mother]), whose husband was one of the Russian officers stabbed to death in the last revolution.

[...And] at the last party here, one of the American lads was dancing with me and said, "Do you know who all the fellows say you remind them of? [Actress] Marie Dressler!" So, now I guess I am a character myself! And, personally, I am flattered![15]

In addition to entertaining Curtis's immediate audience, this chronicle was eventually paraphrased by *The Chicago Tribune* for anyone else who wanted to read about Capri's population of interesting characters.[16]

As the Allies struggled to overcome the Gustav Line throughout early 1944, Curtis stayed busy with her ARC operations on Capri. She then took a "pleasure jaunt" to visit Bill John in Sicily for their one-year anniversary, with this cluster of letters (starting on March 1):

Dearest Moth,

[...] I have completed my first year over here (I'm celebrating "our anniversary of meeting" with Bill John), and sometimes it seems as though I'd never been anyplace else. Other times, as though I'd just gotten over here! Having no real personal obligations and responsibilities is a very different feeling, I can tell you. It gives me a queer, detached feeling, but it does relieve one of a lot of personal strain—living very comfortably, never having any bills to pay, and walking into a new situation requisitioning everything.[17]

Dearest Jane,

[...] I'm over here [for a brief furlough in Sicily] to celebrate our first year anniversary of meeting Bill John in Casablanca—that was February 26 [1944]—but I couldn't get here on the exact date. [...] Since they've taken half of my ARC personnel, the rest of us have had to develop rabbit characteristics—hopping frantically from one job to another! This week, it's renovating a civilian movie [theater]; next month, it will be opening up bathing facilities! And so it goes![18]

Dear Estelle,

[...] I am here on a brief visit, celebrating one year since meeting Bill John (who is assigned here), [...] and I will soon return "home" [to Capri], where there is plenty to be done since they took half my staff for more urgent assignments! [...I] can't understand why you've never heard that the tennis balls arrived OK. [...] Why don't you drop Dad a line, and ask him to put you on his list for my [newsletter] "serial?" I'm sure he'll be glad to do so. My time is so terribly limited and "confused" that there is almost no time for personal letters of any kind anymore.[19]

Curtis wrote to her mother again on March 28, 1944, revealing, "My former supervisor from Morocco is going to arrive any day to take over my job here, as (I guess) I'm on the move again. [...] Maybe I can get caught up on my sleep, letter writing, and reading."[20]

Curtis was more transparent about her subsequent emotions in a letter to Jane on April 2:

I'm going through another period of reassignment, the details of which will have to go unwritten. [...] I am so mad over the whole affair that I am refusing a reassignment at this moment. I'm taking some "leave time" to cool off, and then may demand (I'm not asking at this point) a transfer from [the ARC branch of] club personnel to Clubmobile. If such happens, I may get a cut in salary.

[...] It's nothing vital, just a regular army runaround [...and] another example of "it's whom you know, not what you know!" And you know how mad that makes me! Anyway! It's been the most interesting assignment I've had so far, and if I don't change over to Clubmobile, perhaps I can scrape another beach club for the summer months. The next month will tell the tale.

I'm sorry I haven't written often, but when they took away half of my personnel, I had to reorganize the whole setup, and that just about filled my time and sapped my energy. I've had a cold for the past month, which is unusual for me, and I think a little rest and relaxation will get rid of that too.

[...] I really haven't been doing anything unusual lately. I come into the city, most every weekend, for a dance with Lieutenant [Al] Davis, my old Palermo dancing partner. He and his colonel [...] have a nice apartment where we've been cooking our own dinners lately (when the gas power is strong enough), which has been fun for a change. [...So] I'm calmly sitting here in a comfortable apartment listening to Fred Allen's show. [...] The colonel is sitting near me, looking at a copy of *Life* (showing typhus in Naples), and Al is writing a letter to his wife. [...] How's that for a family picture?

Some time ago, I had a chance to drive to where there were some very interesting ruins—not so cluttered with guides as Pompeii was—but it's still difficult for me to believe that all this is real, and that I'm where I am! While on this trip, we took along our sandwiches, and made our coffee on a little field stove in a lovely Greek temple.

[...] There just isn't another darn thing I can write about. So, until next time. [And] never worry about silence on my part; bad news always travels fast![21]

Indeed, when the news spread around Capri regarding Curtis's inevitable (1944) departure, her remaining ARC personnel composed some fitting and lighthearted words to the form of a popular 1934 song, "Isle of Capri."

To Kay Curtis:

'Twas on the Isle of Capri that we met you,
Just before the Christmas season of joy.
We gathered 'round in the old Quisi [Hotel] lobby
For a brandy and soda—oh boy!
We dined, we danced, and we ran Red Cross villas
We roamed the streets with the boys on Capri,
We opened library, snack bar and lounges,
With Kay Curtis directing the spree.
We've had a lot of misadventures,
Getting fuel and H_2O.
For six long weeks we saw no Air Corps,
And one by one, we watched the old gang go.
And now our leader, Kay Curtis, is leaving,
And even old Mother Nature complains,
We see Vesuvius smoking and grieving—
Saying, "Capri just won't be the same!"[22]

The Second Diversion

On May 18, 1944, the Allied forces finally broke through the Gustav Line at the (fourth) Battle of Monte Cassino, which was critical for their subsequent advance toward Rome. So after the "smoke of many battles cleared away," it was with a heavy heart that Curtis left behind another precious and makeshift ARC community. This was one of the few chapters of her life in which she made no specific mention of synchronized swimming, perhaps, because of that uniquely captivating wartime period, with its fleeting opportunities for adventure.

One of Capri's other local "characters" saw fit to paint a modest portrait of Curtis, who'd appropriately remember that island as a genuine "artist's paradise," and this painting still shows her modeling the same conspicuous red turban (with saltwater spots) that she wore on her initial voyage across the Atlantic. It may also be significant to mention that, on the opposite side of this recycled canvas, there's an unexplained tableau of another woman (sprawling nude on a chaise lounge) with long, black hair. Curtis would later donate this interesting portrait to the International Swimming Hall of Fame, when the time came for deciding how she would like to be remembered. And so, it's with a simple backdrop of reedy palms along the beach that her Mona Lisa smile still offers the world a tantalizing mystery, about whether one could ever fully know her secrets, and all the stories she could tell.

Katharine Whitney Curtis portrait, Capri (December 1943).

7

Victory Lap

By the start of the Normandy Invasion, and the "beginning of the end" for World War II, there was one American pilot (back home) who had already done his share. His friends called him "Whitey" because of his lucky, platinum-blonde hair. And, in combination with his charismatic and indulgent personality, he was perhaps too good-looking for his own good. Upon his return, he began an unhelpful relationship with alcohol (and no shortage of women), but he was young and shell-shocked with such extreme wartime experiences that it was easy enough to empathize with his emotional troubles and distractions of folly. On June 12, 1944, he wrote a charming and confiding letter to someone that he could always rely upon for hope and understanding:

Dear Kay,

You write a wonderful letter, and I raved about it to everyone who would listen. It gave me a touch of homesickness, mainly because "home" is where I hang my hat. [...] All my best memories are of that place [in Agadir] and the people there. Only, I hate to think of it now, because it can never be the same.

If I wouldn't have been grounded so long, I would be back with you already. They nailed me with "operational fatigue" and I thought I would never fly again, so I tried to drink myself to death. I was doing pretty well until I met the right flight surgeon, who straightened me out, and I've been making a comeback ever since.

I've been flying since April 4 [1944], and have just now attained the old skillful level I used to live on. About one more month, and I'll be ready for overseas duty again. Where I will be sent, I have no idea—wherever I'm needed most, I guess. The normal thing would be to send me back to Italy, because I know every landmark so well. However, that's not the army way, you know so well.

There are many of us [working] here as instructors, and most are married, so they have little desire to stick their necks out again. Every once in a while, though, a few get disgusted with regulations and ask for overseas duty. It's so easy to get, that most of us expect it sooner or later anyhow. All I'm waiting on is some more gunnery training. I've never had any [actual] "aerial gunnery," except that in actual combat. I proved it's no use to fight without being a good shot.

As far as getting married goes, I still haven't met the girl. I have no steady woman, and I'm beginning to think I travel in the wrong circles to meet one "sweet one." The creatures I meet should be sent overseas.

The fellas that get back almost all fall into the same groove: a big celebration for three months, during which they buy a car; then flying duty, where they get restless. So they either get married or go back over in disgust. Many plan to cease all but very little flying after the war. As for myself, I'm an unusual character because I never do anything the normal way.

They sent me to the east coast after a P-39 [fighter plane] and I left it in a cow pasture (forced landing), not too far from home. Then they gave me a P-40, which I took to Phoenix, Arizona, in twice the time a trip like that should take. Then I took a P-38 [fighter interceptor] to Texas, and it caught fire and blew up. Fine! Makes life interesting.

Now they won't let me leave the base. I've been instructing in P-38's ever since. The fools! If an accident is going to happen, it will happen here, as well as anywhere else. Strangely though, I've had no trouble since then. Naturally, I didn't get a scratch. I just rub my lucky white head for luck.

You asked me for a smiling picture, and, I'm sorry. But the only one I have is [this] one, taken while I was "plastered" and doing my best to put my arms around seven women at once. When I sobered up, it was a small consolation to notice at least the one [girl] that I ended up with wasn't as bad as the rest were. What a bunch of mummies! So, you will have to accept the sourpuss [picture of me] enclosed. If you wish, I shall have a lovely one made especially for you. It's a rare event when anyone wants a picture of me, so I hasten to oblige, "Toot sweet!"

So, life is sweet, as long as I fly my head off. And, right now, I'm happy. Hope your new assignment works out OK, and, if I can get sent up your way, you'll hear from me, definitely. My best regards to everyone who still remembers "F/O [Flight Officer] Whitey." As for you—mmmm—you have my wholehearted respect, and, I can say, a little more than. Affectionately, Whitey.[1]

After Capri, Curtis was sent to one of the Fifteenth Air Force rest camps along the eastern coast of Italy. Throughout July and August of 1944, she toured other encampments across the Italian peninsula, including Lecce, Bari, Foggia, Naples, Anzio and Rome. This tour included that of a transient camp for refugees, where they had "over one-thousand Yugoslav war orphans (three to twelve years old), most of whom [had] seen their families slaughtered."[2] Curtis continued about the Yugoslav people to Estelle on August 2, declaring, "I think they're a grand group of human beings, with principle and the backbone to fight for it!"[3]

Curtis requested a 21-day furlough from ARC headquarters, and she was back in America by late September (1944). She headed straight for Chicago and Milwaukee, where she was received with much celebration, and *The Milwaukee Journal* published some of her favorite war stories:

Katharine Curtis, after nineteen months overseas, brought back to Milwaukee, the other day, brief but very human and revealing word-pictures:

[…] "I had General George Patton for a neighbor [in Mondello, Sicily]. 'Blood and Guts' is a peculiar man, a wonderful poet, and a ruthless fighter. It makes an odd combination. Where he is, there is bound to be strong feeling. You either like him very much, or you don't very much—no half measures. His men swear by him. I like him. He entertained the Red Cross personnel not long ago, and, after dinner, each member of his staff had to do something to amuse guests. At the end, General Patton himself volunteered. Leaning against the grand piano, he recited one of his own war poems. As he gave it, in his dramatic, deep voice, it made your scalp creep. This picture I will carry with me forever."

Curtis "on rotation" in Chicago (September 1944).

7. Victory Lap

[...] One of the most amusing things that Kay experienced was a feast with a Berber chief, in celebration of the arrival of cotton goods [to North Africa] from the United States. When the guests arrived, they were seated on low cushions, scattered upon large oriental rugs, and spread outdoors along the mountainside. The main course consisted of hunks of roast lamb, smothered in dark-brown gravy and roasted almonds. It was put before the guests on large silver platters, two guests to a platter, and no silverware! The idea was to use the thumb and first two fingers of the left hand to forage in the steaming heap!

"My [native] dinner partner dug deep and came out with a fat, overgrown kidney (the *piece-de-resistance* of each platter). She promptly plumped it down on my plate as a friendly offering, [whereby] to be fed at their feasts is a signal honor. I looked across at one of the fellows, who was dejectedly emptying his plate for the 'nth time, only to see it heaped again by a well-meaning caïd [Arab official]. His mild protests were misunderstood [because nodding gestures are interpreted differently], and more was added each time he shook his head.

"Then I started in on the kidney. The proceedings were all very solemn until it began to rain. With no shelter, we were soon sitting in puddles. The servants' attempts to shield us by holding rugs over our heads only made the damp situation worse. Every time they shifted weight, we were showered with a direct downpour. I didn't think I could keep a straight face much longer, so I looked over at one of the caïds to see how he was taking it. When our glances met, we both burst into helpless laughter. Mirth is a universal language. And the villagers dancing in their new, white ghost-gowns (imported from America) were really something to see."

[...] Kay has been kept busy ever since she got to America, calling the girls she promised hundreds of servicemen she would call.

"Those boys are all grand persons," Kay says. "They wanted to talk and talk to an American woman, and I listened as long as they could talk. I always wanted to be with them when they were taking off for a mission. They didn't want to awaken me, but the propellers warming up served as excellent alarm clocks, and I was always on the field to see them—counting them as they took off, and sweating them in as they came back."[4]

On September 27, Curtis's aviator friend, Whitey, who was now trying to settle down with a girl in California, wrote another noteworthy letter:

Hi Darling,

Your oh-so-sweet letter arrived today, so I'll answer, real quick-like, while I have some time (as if I'm too busy, ever!).

[...] As for those seven women I told you about—if you would have been there, I dare say, people would talk, because we would spend so much time together. I've never met anyone, except you and Opal, who really knew the fullest feelings involved in fighting a war. That's why I said "the creatures I meet should be sent overseas." If they could see what was going on, there would be a little more appreciation for the smaller things in life [that] they all take for granted. I wasn't there when it was "rough," but, even so, when I turn a spicket [*sic*] and cold water or hot water flows out, it's damn nice to be back. A glass [cup] is a beautiful substitute for a canteen cup. Little things.

Oh gee, Kay, I wish there was some way I could get to see you [in Chicago]. We never knew each other very long, but we were so close for a short while that I hope we'll never lose that feeling. Let's keep in touch with each other and perhaps, someday, I'll be able to see you (because I'll know where to look for you). I'd hate to miss you ever [if you're passing through town]. So many people miss each other because they didn't know. Let us know!

As far as going overseas, right now, I am very valuable here because of my earnest efforts to become a good instructor, in order for me to marry my woman. Of course, I may go, regardless. But, chances are—if anything—I'll just get shifted around the States, instructing. My day at fighting this war is over, and I feel very guilty to be enjoying so much happiness with a wonderful woman while my buddies are dying on their second tour.

The way I feel is that this love is so big that it can't be wrong, even though I've never done anything to deserve such a return of love. It's rare and good. A wonderful, clean, well-raised American girl—my ideal. It took a long time to find her. The beauty of it all is that she feels the same way. You know how a fella feels, he figures that, when he does meet "the" one, he won't be good enough. And yet, she wants to spend at least fifty years with me. It's awful hard to believe. Makes my head spin. She's the first girl I've ever bought a ring for, and she wears it proudly. I'm proud, too, 'cause I never expected to be so happy—a wonderful girl.

Kay, when I remember back to our talks at rest camp, I feel very grateful to you and the others—you especially—for keeping alive in me that spark of human decency that could have been so easily lost. I can hold my head up, now, with pride and clear thoughts, instead of feeling like a low animal with a distorted mind (like others I know).

You see, I was almost ready to come home when I met you. And then, later, was able to spend two weeks again at rest camp. So I had a whole month, very fortunately.

You did for me what the folks back home could have never done. My mind was becoming quite bitter, and, by your help, I was able to snap out of it (with very little help from the people back home). It's hard to explain, but I'll always be grateful to you for making me realize that other things existed in the future besides [German fighter planes] ME-109s and endless hours of combat. You will always be welcome in our home, and that comes from Anna Lee's heart too. She appreciates your efforts, and looks forward to someday meeting you.

So keep up the good work, and, when this mess is over, we hope we'll be seeing you—or sooner. Keep in touch! Luck, love, and kisses—Whitey.[5]

While Curtis was reading about Whitey's new and optimistic romance in September 1944, her own (long-distance) relationship with Private Bill John was lingering toward its inevitable end. Many other "grand" gentlemen, especially officers, were starting to catch her eye. And there was one particular lieutenant colonel, later referred to as "The Colonel"

Flight officer "Whitey" and Anna Lee (1944).

(John A. Brock), with whom Curtis would fall hopelessly in love. They most likely met when he was working for the inspector general's department in Bari, Italy, and this hopeful connection was undoubtedly the primary reason why she was so eager to leave home and return to war.

Once More

By late August 1944, General Patton had already arrived in Europe, and his famous "race across France" was being slowed only by a shortage of gasoline. Curtis was saying hello and goodbye (just as quickly) to her friends and family, and wrote to Estelle on October 21 from "on the high sea."

> Just a line or two to let you know that I'm really "en route." I spent two days in Washington [DC], talking my head off, [...and] we had almost a week in a camp somewhere on the east coast before sailing. I'm really resting and reading because there is an unusually large group of women on board. The whole "home trip" was so hectic that I'm really welcoming what little relaxation I can get now. We are packed in like sardines, as usual—twelve in our compartment, six of whom are a United Service Organizations [Entertainment] Troupe of glamour gals, with all their wardrobe, luggage and makeup! I get plenty of entertainment, as well as exercise!
>
> We have B-Deck with the officers for exercise, and A-Deck for sunning. First day of sun, today! Two very good meals a day, and a transport commander with a sense of humor! Our bunks are three-decks high, and not far enough apart to allow us to sit up on them. [...There's] very congested toilet facilities, the worst yet for me, but we're all managing to live through it with gusto. [...I] can't write any more tonight; my fanny [posterior] is paralyzed from sitting on a suitcase, and I'm almost blind, writing with this poor light. More another time.[6]

She then wrote a newsletter from her "new Italian assignment" on December 13, 1944, including one of her first public mentions Colonel Brock:

> As some of you know, I am not at all sure just when I wrote any of you last. I am now acting director of the EM's service club, to which I was sent when I first arrived. The director was reassigned about three weeks after I arrived, and this is no small club. It is located at the place where The Colonel had been transferred to, but he has since been sent to France—so that is that. I feel that, at last, I am rightly placed.
>
> The club is an old stone hotel, without any heating facilities, so the first thing I did was to put in several fireplaces, and board up all the holes through which the summer breezes have been whistling. You can imagine the size of the operation when I say that I have a civilian staff of ninety Italians to keep the place functioning.
>
> [...] I've hoped to get over to Capri, but haven't dared take any time off until I had all the help [staff] reorganized. It won't be too long, now. I had a chance at a bigger job, farther north, but refused it in hope of being allowed to finish this job before being moved again. [...] As far as my demotion is concerned, I have not finished with that yet. But I am still getting $50 less a month, and working harder than I have ever done—except in Casablanca, perhaps.
>
> [...] Our club's Christmas plans are driving us mad, with the usual too many details. [...] In the midst of all this, I am still trying to get the building finished. [...] Between us all, we have two jeeps and a one-ton truck, and I wish you could follow me around my domain, just one day, to hear the details that arise during the day. They are numbered by the millions, I can assure you. Just now, I have to wrestle with the hauling of coal some distance, with no place to lock it up after I get it. [...] So maybe you can understand why this letter is as it is. [...] I hope the holiday season has been a good one, and that all are as good as I am.[7]

Curtis's "demotion" was likely just the result of her request to be transferred closer to Colonel Brock. Her ARC club was in the AFHQ (Allied Force Headquarters) city of Caserta, just 25 miles north of Naples. And it was out of the Caserta Royal Palace that General Harold Alexander would serve as supreme commander (Mediterranean Theater) until the end of the war.

Germany's last military offensive campaign, the Battle of the Bulge, began on December 16, 1944, with a surprise attack that endeavored to force a peace treaty in Germany's favor. However, once they trapped an Allied army in the Belgian city of Bastogne, General Patton came to the rescue, in his finest hour, by crossing 100 miles and ending the siege on the day after Christmas. Both Generals Patton and Montgomery turned the offensive by January 1, 1945, and this is also when Curtis wrote a full description of her operations in Caserta:

> Little did I think—last Christmas on Capri—that I would be spending another holiday season in Italy! But, here I have been, and it hasn't been much warmer than last, either. Although, we haven't had quite so much rain, up to the present time.
>
> [...] We arrived at the same port [of Naples] I came into Italy through before, so it seemed almost as good as coming into New York harbor, with all the familiar landmarks! And, believe it or not, I really was glad to get back! [...] My assignment was that of assistant club director in a club for enlisted men in [Caserta], very near to this large city [Naples]. As you can see from the APO, I am at Allied Force Headquarters [AFHQ]. That means "rank," of course, but there are also many replacement men in the vicinity, and we naturally get many of them at the club. Some are the new boys, just arriving, and some are the fellows who are returning to their units after a session at a hospital somewhere.
>
> The town itself, I feel, has little character—although, it has a huge palace, and beautiful ancient gardens with a picturesque cascade up on the mountainside. We are surrounded by low mountains, the town being on a sort of plateau in the center. The streets are the usual winding, narrow, [and] dirty alleys. And the houses are the customary blockhouse-type of stone house, with high-ceilinged rooms with fancy pictures all over the ceilings.
>
> [...] The club was an old Italian hotel built around three sides of a patio, and consists of endless little rooms. A bomb in the neighborhood didn't help the exterior of the place any. [...My projects seem] very endless and impossible at times, but it is a real challenge, as compared with the Air Corps rest camps of my past. I think that I am correctly placed at last, and hope that ARC will keep me in this assignment.
>
> The first thing I tried to do when I arrived was to chink up the holes in the building, and get some sort of heat in the place. That meant having fireplaces put into all the rooms that I could. [...] Now, I have the army engineers from AFHQ in the building, and they are going through the place like a whirlwind—rebuilding the fireplaces, plastering and repainting the whole place. [...] So you can imagine the state I am in. Today is the first day I have taken off in about six weeks, and I hope the place doesn't fall apart! [...] All in all, it is quite a large installation, and when the engineers get through with the face-lifting process, I will be very proud of it.
>
> [...] I suppose you all are interested in what went on during all the holidays. [...] The week before Christmas [1944], we were a beehive of activities, [...preparing] for the children's party. We asked the [GIs] in this vicinity to bring in anything in the line of candy, cakes, etc., that they did not need, and we got much too much. The [GIs] themselves wrapped all these things before the party. Then we had a huge tree in the stairwell, and all the trimmings had to be made. [...] Then, the ordnance group near here gave us a lot of metal shavings, and the tree looked real nice. We had other small [Christmas trees] at other spots in the club, and if I do say so, the old "barn" looked real festive!
>
> I had a huge fireplace built in one wall of the patio, and that was where we had the children's party. The youngsters ranged from five to ten [years old]. We expected a hundred, and got [nearly two-hundred]! They were from an orphanage, [in addition to] the children of the [local Italian] employees. The former were very well-disciplined and accompanied by such sweet [Catholic nuns], but the latter were "brats," and we almost had a riot! We offered them a magician [...] and an Italian dog act, which they adored. Then, they sang songs in turn, and recited with fascinating gestures. They had some of the youngsters dressed up like angels, and I never saw cuter things anywhere. The patio was jammed with the soldiers watching, and they were crazy about the youngsters; many of them even asking if they could adopt one of the children.

> [...] New Year's Eve, we closed the club at the regular time, but had an "Owl Show" at the movie [theater...] and then we served free coffee and cookies from the stage. Personally, I thought it was rather sad, because it was only natural that the people at the show would be the men who had no other place to go (while most of the [intact] army units in the vicinity were having parties of their own). It went off OK, though. And, when midnight struck, we were singing "Auld Lang Syne," both in the audience and on the stage—led by a big limey [British man] without a tooth in his head, but with a rather nice voice, and a good feeling of leadership.
>
> [...] For those of you interested in my "romance," when I arrived in port, there was no colonel, and no word from him! I wrangled an assignment in the place where I had last heard from him, and, in about ten days, he returned from an assignment "in the north" with news that he was being transferred at once to France! So, here I am, and he is in France! We had about ten days together before he left, and I guess that is a lot to be thankful for these days! Maybe we can get together [afterwards] in some army of occupation. At any rate, there is nothing we can do now![8]

The complexity of Curtis's wartime romantic life can be further observed (among other details) in this letter to her mother, written on February 21, 1945.

> The greatest, and most pleasant, surprise was a visit here to see me by the colonel who "did the talking" in France to the WAC [Women's Army Corp]. He is not the [Colonel] Brock, in whom I am so interested, but the "major" in the air transport services, whom I liked so much (a year ago) when I was on Capri. Remember? [...] He is one of the finest (if not the finest) men I have met while overseas, and, although we correspond, I had not seen him in about a year. He had his choice of two business trips—to Italy or to England—and chose Italy in order to see me. And, believe me, I was flattered!
>
> But, you should have seen my face when I realized that it was he and not John [Brock] who had "done the talking." I laughed until I cried, but I have not heard from John since I wrote him about what you and Miriam had written me. I'm terribly anxious to see what he has to say now! Such a tempest in a teapot!
>
> [...] Did I tell you that Colonel John [Brock] had turned down an appointment to a higher command in Paris to accept an appointment in southern France—in order to be nearer me—in hope that we might get together, or perhaps make the "next move" together if we were closer when the time comes? At any rate, he will have more chances to get over here from southern France, than from Paris, and maybe we can see Paris together when the time comes.
>
> [...] So tomorrow is [Gaylord's] birthday! I wish that the family would let him write to me, once in a while, but I suppose that is asking for too much!
>
> You'd have laughed to see me struggling to get a picture of George Washington, surrounded with garlands, hung up on the tree that occupies the center of our patio. Of course, nobody at the club has such goofy ideas, except for me. I think that my ideas are swell ones, and I push them through![9]

Less than a week after writing this letter, Curtis tried to visit the elusive Colonel Brock on a couple of days' leave, "Only, John was missing!" She was writing in a postcard to her mother from a luxurious hotel, and concluded that she was "enjoying every minute, even though I am too lazy to go sight-seeing."[10] And it was on March 25, 1945, that she wrote to her old synchronized swimming pupil, Margery Turner, about "toying with the idea of trying some water pageantry here [in Caserta], this summer, if I can find the swimmers! [...Also, I] am now landscaping a garden so we can serve our Easter guests (including ten generals) outdoors! I hope [John Brock] will be here, too."[11] Notably, this is one of Curtis's earliest mentions of what would become the Caserta Aquacade.

Back in Germany, General Patton crossed the Rhine River on March 24, 1945, and recorded in his diary that he "went across on the pontoon bridge, stopping in the middle to [urinate] in the Rhine, and then pick up some dirt on the far side as a *Seizin* [symbol of land possession] in emulation of William the Conqueror."[12] Soon after, Curtis wrote her next newsletter on April 2.

I have just lived through my second Easter season in Italy, and that is really something to brag about. [...] You all know, of course, that I have been struggling all winter to make a real club out of what was handed to me in December. [...] So I set to work with about eighty civilian employees, and the help of the army, [...] to do "the impossible." We now have a very attractive club (if I do say so myself) with a great deal of atmosphere, and everybody who comes to see us is saying the same thing. We finally set Easter Day as the deadline for the major projects, and most of them were completed by that time.

[...] We had a lovely fashion parade with twenty-five "real American girls" modeling civilian and military styles. We held the affair in our roofed-over patio, [...and] the orchestra [that we hired] was to have been the best string quartet in this vicinity, [...] but nothing is perfect, [and] somebody did not send the transportation for them. After a full half-hour delay, a handsome blonde GI—who had been playing at the club, one night a week, all winter—stepped into the breach and carried off the entire program in grand style. Leave it to the average GI to be able to take care of any emergency! [He] had theatrical experience, but, when he saw all the "Brass" in our "Reserved Section," got so embarrassed that he did not do himself justice. [He] opened the show by presenting me with a beautiful bouquet from the staff. [...] One of our ARC gals modeled the [standard issue] raincoat, under which she wore a modern bathing suit, and she was the hit of the day! [Virginia Schakel] is one of my new girls, [...] a former water ballet girl. [...] She and I are scheduled to try to stage some sort of water show, when the local pool is opened—heaven help us!

After all the beauty, we had an "Easter Bonnet Contest," with six [bonnets] designed and modeled by GIs. The hats were representative of the units offering them, and the first prize was a dance for the winning group. It was won by the local postal delivery service, with a large hat—its crown made of letters. [...] The brim was draped with a veil, spotted with postal stamps, and some ribbons (down the back) were attached to two small packages. The other [hats] were just as clever as the winner, and we were all very pleased with so many entries. The boys were a scream when they modeled. Two came dressed as women, much to everyone's amusement, [...and] we had the biggest crowd we ever had in the club for any single function, and everybody seemed to be having a good time.

In the celebrities [section], we had some two-star generals and the CO of this area [General Alexander], so I was satisfied. They were astounded when asked to come out into the garden for refreshments, because, when they were last in that spot, it had been a mudhole. When they stepped out—lo and behold—we had transformed the place into a blossoming flower garden with a lovely cement terrace, the whole length, and a huge barbeque fireplace in the center with many little cozy corner-seats between garden plots. [...] It was my dream-come-true, and the ARC authorities were just as surprised as the military. Of course, it had all taken persistence and faith in the impossible, but it had materialized.

[...] The Saturday night before Easter, we had a group of forty of the sweetest tiny girls from one of the parochial schools come over to sing, dance and recite. I wish that we could have had a picture of the tiny things in the patio with all the [GI] boys looking on [emotionally]. It always sort of tears me to pieces to watch them, but I try to get some sort of children's affair [arranged] every holiday season. I think it does the boys good.

[...] There is quite a little social life here—for them as likes it—and I have managed my share of it; although, I wouldn't say that I was the most popular gal here, by any manner of means. I have been up to the "General's Club" on "Snob Knob," a few times. And, upon one occasion, I sat at dinner with six generals, including one who is now a four-star! He sat right across the table from me. This AFHQ area is thick as pea soup with "rank," and one soon gets used to it! I can still have a better time with a bunch of GIs anytime.

[...] As for my "Heart Interest," my one and only (Colonel) is still in France. I was sure that he would get over here for Easter, but he didn't, and that was that. One is never sure over here.

[...] Must get to bed. There is a big beautiful moon, and it must be the same one which is looking down on all of you. I hope that it carries to each and every one of you the many loving thoughts I think of you all, even though I don't write as often as I should.[13]

As Curtis was shutting her eyes at the end of that colorful day in early April, the light of her "big beautiful" moon (drifting over Italy) was the very same leading American troops toward a tragic sight at Ohrdruf, Germany. With sure knowledge of their defeat, the Nazi SS had already moved their remaining victims on a death march to Buchenwald

(April 1), bringing the total number of perished for the Ohrdruf Concentration Camp to approximately 7,000 souls. By April 4, evidence of this nightmarish operation was discovered by American forces for the first time. And, on April 12, Generals Eisenhower, Patton and Bradley visited Camp Ohrdruf for themselves, where they were solemnly overcome with another fierce and mournful determination for justice.

In Poland, on the eastern front, the Soviets had also discovered the horror of Nazi concentration camps throughout their wide march toward Berlin. The German capital was soon the target of their revenge with a relentless artillery barrage, which shook the dust from spreading fissures in Hitler's underground bunker. As was consistent with Nazism's reductionist "survival-of-the-fittest" worldview, the increasingly neurotic dictator sought to punish his own people for failing to realize his ideals for a thousand-year Reich. Hitler eventually subsided, gave leave to his officers, and married his (equally neurotic) mistress in a twisted ceremony of last rights. His evil hallucination of a "perfect" world was burning all around them as they killed themselves on April 30. Germany's unconditional surrender arrived on May 8.

It was on April 24, during these final days of war in Europe, that Curtis wrote to her mother about some more pleasant concerns:

Dearest Moth,

I found your letter [back in Caserta…] when I arrived from a few days "up north," in the city where I had the "black marble bath tub" on my last leave-period. This time, I had the best time I've had in many moons.

[…] I have never tried to eat and drink so much good food and drink in such a short time in my life—and me, with a shrunken stomach and the delusion that I ought to try to reduce if I am going to do any swimming myself in this aquacade!

[…] In the evening, we had one of the loveliest lobsters (with real mayonnaise) that I have seen since I was at Santa Cesarea [in southern Italy], and then went night-clubbing. […] We giggled and laughed until our sides ached, […and] I only wish that I could keep on feeling like I do now, but I am afraid of this darned old aquacade. Perhaps I can get enough real help that it won't be too bad. I will tell you of plans in the next letter.[14]

Aside from enjoying some minor comforts, Curtis was even more determined to actualize her biggest "goofy" idea yet—to teach synchronized swimming to hundreds of male and female Allied military personnel—for the enjoyment of thousands. Now was the time for celebration, and there was nobody better suited to make it happen.

The Caserta Aquacade

After Germany's surrender on May 8, 1945, referred to as "VE" (Victory in Europe) Day, millions of people around the world had the perfect excuse to kiss, drink and dance in the streets, and even Princess Elizabeth "snuck out" of Buckingham Palace for the night. Curtis's local ARC club in Caserta would have hosted a joyous pandemonium of British and American troops. And it was only 16 days later that their AFHQ Aquacade was announced in the *Stars and Stripes* military newspaper, which initially stated that "the premiere […] has been set for June 2 and 3, at the palace swimming pool in Caserta."[15] Soon after, another local advertisement was posted with the following pitch for volunteers:

The response to last week's request for swimmers who wish to participate in the upcoming Aquacade has been excellent. However—according to Kay Curtis, director—still more participants are wanted.

The spectacle, which is to officially open the Palace swimming pool, [...] is expected to be one of the largest and most unusual entertainment ventures to be undertaken locally.

Well over fifty potential Johnny Weissmuller's and Eleanor Holms' have, so far, volunteered their services. However, the entire cast will number over one-hundred people, when completely filled. Both British and American men and women are invited to take part. So far, the British have responded in greater number than the Americans. It is hoped to have fifty percent from each army. Therefore, this second call is for more American "water babies" to come to the force.

It is planned to make this local aquacade one which will compare favorably with those seen at the world's fairs.[16]

Their expanding preparations were reported in *The Chronicle* on May 27, 1945, with these highlights:

The AFHQ Aquacade—the first production of its kind in Italy [...] which utilizes the talents of 250 swimmers, actors, and musicians—combines the water stage and the land stage with music used as the central theme. [...] The program will open with background music by two chapel organs, [...and the narrator] will give the story of the aquacade. [...] To the background music of [the Army Ground Forces] Band, [...] the grand finale will feature the entire cast, with swimmers stretching red, white and blue streamers to all corners of the Aquacade pool. [...] There will be seats for approximately one-thousand persons.[17]

Due to both the growing demands of their production and "unsuitable rehearsal weather," the original performance dates were delayed by a week, to June 9 and 10. There was soon also an update in *The Chronicle* for June 3, that "tickets are necessary for admission to the water show, and will be available to all American and British personnel—enlisted men and officers—[starting] June 8 at 0830 hours at the palace information booth. There is no admission charge. However, no one will be admitted to the aquacade area without a ticket."[18]

Curtis provided the first account of her aquacade on the morning of its second performance, June 10, after they "sold out" of every ticket.

Dearest Moth,

The Aquacade yesterday was a huge success. Of course, I knew it would be. But it certainly has been fun to see the absolute wonder and unbelief on other people's faces when this "spectacle" really was produced. Folks at home will see snatches of it in the newsreels, I'm sure, as well as in the papers. We were lousy with photographers—movies, color photos, big cameras and little ones—and today, "The Mighty" are to see the show: [US Deputy Supreme Allied Commander] General McNarney, [Supreme Allied Commander] General Alexander, [...] and all the other generals in this area!

I was told, yesterday, that we could not tour with it—(now 11:30 a.m.)—but I have just been told to repeat it next weekend. So that's that! I will try to get a long (carbon) letter out this week on the aquacade, its preparation, etc.

Colonel Brock came over last weekend (but we had to postpone the show because of weather), and spent four days with me. Of course, I was up to my ears in aquacade, but we managed quite a bit of time together, in spite of that.

Since you ask, [John Brock] has been married (he is getting a divorce), [although they've] not lived together for [the] past ten years. He is forty-five years old, a graduate of Temple University, and he thought, at one time, that he was going to be a protestant minister (I've forgotten what religious group). He plays piano, as well as football, baseball, and rides [horseback]. His only son (a handsome lad) was killed in the Normandy invasion last fall [1944].

[John] seems to have plenty of money. I really haven't pried into his past too much. It's the present and future that concern me. I definitely want companionship from now on, and I think that John and I could work out a very comfortable future. He seems to think that he will stay in the army for some time yet—over here, as long as he can—and my plans are his plans from now on. We talked about "the ring" on his last trip (which he says he has ordered), and will marry [me] as soon as his other situation is cleared.

> I have asked to be transferred closer to him, and to go into the army of occupation, when and if the ARC in this area knows anything about what the next moves will be. I will stay here until such time, [...while] all of this is speculative. At present, we are all "marking time," and trying to keep the [GI] boys occupied and happy until they get their trip "home."
> [...] I've had so many interruptions—this note is a mess—but I wanted you to know that the show was a whopping success. Heaps of love, Katie.[19]

With the aquacade's final performance dates being extended into the "next weekend," June 16 and 17, Curtis hurriedly finished her June 10 letter before scurrying off to prepare for that day's second showing, which was promoted by this update in *The Chronicle*:

> The colorful and spectacular AFHQ Aquacade, which was first presented before a crowd of fifteen-hundred spectators, yesterday afternoon [June 9], will again be seen this afternoon at 1600 hours. The water and land show was enthusiastically received at its first performance, and was acclaimed as one of the finest and most novel productions ever staged overseas. The aquacade features a cast of over 259 swimmers, actors and musicians, in several intricate numbers—all of which are beautifully and unusually staged.[20]

Curtis then wrote to Estelle on June 16, the day of the third performance, with some additional mentions of John Brock:

> I'm expecting and hoping to find time for a "carbon letter" on the aquacade soon. I have been working on that for two months now (in addition to the club), and am pretty far behind in club work now, so must put the screws on here now. No time for the wicked!
> [...] I expect to be here four to six months yet [in Caserta], and then hope I can get nearer Marseilles, where "my" colonel is. And that, maybe by that time, we can have made arrangements to marry. He expects to stay over for the army of occupation, and his plans are mine, nowadays. This being "so near and yet so far" isn't too happy. He can get down here only every two months, and I can't get up to him at all, yet. I hope that [this] "ban" will be lifted soon, because it's only three hours (flying time) to Marseille, where he is inspector general of the Sixth Port.
> [...] Life can be beautiful, you know. I've come to the conclusion that we Americans miss a great deal of "life" by trying to cram too damn much into it!
> More, when I have more time. It's not because I don't think of you that I don't write, but there's just never the time and energy at the same moment. We've changed the whole emphasis of our [ARC] program work since "V-E Day," and that, in itself, has been difficult. [...] P.S. Ain't got no "ring!"[21]

Three days later, at the height of her aquacade's resounding success, Curtis wrote to her mother about more pressing matters:

> It looks as though I would soon be able to get over to France to visit Colonel Brock, and that is what I want most to do. At present, it looks as though we ARC folks would be allowed to go to the army rest area on the Riviera. How do you like that? And then I can get to the colonel in Marseilles from there, without too much trouble. Or, better yet, I may be able to coax him to come down there, although he is swamped right now with all the evaluation being done at his port, poor guy. They have to work at least eighteen hours a day, and it's not easy work, all this inspecting![22]

On June 24, she finished typing her laborious and long-awaited carbon newsletter, which, while also mentioning Colonel Brock, recounts the extent of her involvement behind the Caserta Aquacade:

> Most of you know that I am expecting to stay right here [in Caserta], where I landed when I came back from the States, for at least four to six months more. Then, I hope to move into one of the armies of occupation in Germany or Austria. There are no definite plans, at present, so we all just "sit tight and wait" for the next move. I am quite content and comfortable right here, and have no desire to move—except to get closer to "the one and only man," who is at present the inspector general for the Marseilles port. He is a lieutenant colonel, whom I have known since I first came over, and we hope to marry sometime in the not-too-distant future (if Fate is good to us). He is an old army man, so I sup-

pose the rest of my life will be tied up in the army. At any rate, we both hope to land in the same army of occupation.

[…Then] there has been the Aquacade! That all started when the ARC sent me Virginia ["Ginny"] Schakel, from Indianapolis, where she had been doing competitive and ballet swimming. When the "powers that be" discovered the pair of us, they asked us to stage an aquacade for the Allied Forces Headquarters Command in the beautiful cascade pool, behind the palace here in Caserta. They gave us one month to prepare for the thing, and there was no water in the pool when we started. We ran a "story" in our local paper, and had our first dry-land meeting of about fifty men and women (British and American). […] Not one of them present had ever seen an aquacade, or tried to swim to music. Ginny and I "briefed them" as best we could, and then we all tried dry-land swimming to a terrible old portable Victrola, and some worn-out records. There was nothing promising about that first effort! However, we believed it could be done, so we went ahead and ordered water put into the little officer's pool, near the tennis courts, and tested our aspirants' swimming ability in the icy mountain water.

After a week of catching folks during their meal hours for tryouts and training, I insisted that we move to the big pool, where we had "hit or miss" practices until, two weeks before, we put on the show. It was originally scheduled for the first weekend in June [1945], but the week before was so cold and rainy that all [members of] the gang were catching cold, so I postponed the show for one week. By that time, we had [everyone] in pretty good shape, and were having "scheduled" rehearsals, to which the members were supposed to come. Getting folks out of their jobs was the worst job, but we came out pretty well in the end, and didn't have to give up any of our original numbers.

A week before I started on the show, a GI who had done a lot of decorating of local clubs—a former decorator from San Francisco, Owen Bayne Jones—came in to ask if there was something he could do in the club. So I asked the authorities to "loan" him to me, to do the "land work" of the aquacade. Wonder of wonders, they gave him to me, and he was the one who really "staged the show." We worked so unusually well together, and he knew so many people in the show that he was a Godsend to me.

Two British boys […] did the costumes—both the designing and making [of them]—with the help of some local sewing women. If you could only imagine how scarce all the necessities for making costumes are, you could then appreciate the fact that all the audience spoke about the colorful costumes. […] We did manage to find a lot of sequins and "jewels," which made the costumes much more elaborate, but it was the fact that the fundamental styles were so good that made the show the hit it was.

[…] The setting was the "Fountain of the Dolphins," at the head of one section of the cascade pool of the Caserta palace, which was built in the eighteenth century. Using the fountain as the background for the wooden stage we built (with staircases leading down from both sides), we cut off about one-hundred feet by placing bleachers across the width of the pool, and bleachers along the sides. We had dressing tents, up on top, and some "cave" dressing rooms on the water level. The "sides" and the steps were covered with silver barrage-balloon material, and palms. […Then] there was a center throne for Neptune and Aphrodite, and minor side-thrones for Miss America, [Miss Britannia, and all of their followers].

[…] There was a set of center steps, leading right down into the water. And, on either side, we had a sort of water-screen made by puncturing holes into a pipe and having the fire-engine give us the pressure necessary. Along both sides of the pool, we built runways, on which were the thrones of the twenty "Rivers of the World." As these [characters] made their appearance, at the head of one staircase or the other, the sixty-five-piece band played music characteristics of the country represented. They came down the steps, paid homage to Neptune and Aphrodite, crossed over and sat upon their throne throughout the performance, making a lovely stage setting.

[…] They wore swimming suits for foundations [to their costumes], and all [the river characters] were boys, some British and some American. […] I really found the former very easy to work with, and most eager to try this new project. I soon developed leaders in each unit, and they did all the detail routine drilling of the group, just like a school project, so I felt right at home! And how those kids worked!

[…] The first number in the water was military maneuvers with a breast stroke. Twenty-four boys marched down the steps (twelve on each side), lined up behind the water-screen (in lines of four across), and dove in through the spray.

[…] The second number also came down the stairs—girls wearing pink and white-flowered cotton material, made into [Greek mythological] suits copied from a picture in *Life* [magazine], and they wore a hood of the same material with a white water lily on top.

[…] The center float, around which they worked, was covered with silver cloth, a huge bunch of real flowers, and three "mermaids" combing their golden hair! On their entrance, they marched down the center steps, right into the water. The number was very pretty, and they did it very well!

[…] The exit for the floating number was the old one, where the boys spring out first, and then "lift" the girls out. […] It was great fun to watch the formal British boys break down and learn to play the American way. The entire swimming group became the nicest friendly unit!

The Rhumba [routine] was my old one, out of the [*Rhythmic Swimming*] book, but adapted to the space we had. Have I told you that the water was only five-feet deep all over? In a way, it was a blessing, because I didn't have to struggle with any diving features, but it did make the number quite simple, too. The Rhumba was all men, and they wore red-and-white striped (cotton material) trunks, with a double cock's comb of Celloglas [rainbow-colored reflective material] down the center.

The "musical interlude" was the good old, comedic life-saving stunt, with wild costumes. We almost didn't have any comedy, because the man I had first tried to work out something with—an Austrian refugee, who had spent more than three years in concentration camps, […] and who was the swimming champ of Austria—didn't work out so well. And I just went along, waiting for Fate to drop something in my lap. And, sure enough, she did! Three boys in striped suits began showing off in the part of the pool, just beyond where we were rehearsing, and there was our comedy! Of course, they had to [travel] from Naples for rehearsing, but we managed to, somehow. Although, I felt like a regular kindergarten teacher before I was through.

The Tango [routine] was done with a duet in the center of the pool, working around the float, and two sets of ballet swimmers (on either side of the float), working the length of the pool. The ballets had three couples each.

[…] The finale was swell, even if I do say so myself! The Tango swimmers finished at the float, the duet pair stood in the center of the float with three of the mermaids, [while] each of these six people held the end of a red, white or blue streamer, which had been pulled out to the float by a swimmer with a "harness" during the end of The Tango. And, when all the audience stood while we sang the [national] anthems, it was something worth remembering, I can tell you.

[…] Did I tell you that the bleachers seated fifteen-hundred to two-thousand [spectators] each time?

Aside from being well satisfied with the production, "behind the scenes" was just like a circus. We had four dressing-room tents, and one costume tent, where four Italian sewing women and two sewing machines (of undetermined age) were busy all the time for the week before the show, and for the two weeks [throughout] the shows. In order to protect our property, four of the [GI] "boys" slept up in the tents all this time. I used to call them my "boy scouts," and got many a giggle out of them. They were the boys who had done so much with the costumes and staging.

[…] Although the cast was awfully green for the first show, they were good troupers by the last one.

[…After the last performance of] the first Sunday night [June 10], we had a party for the cast in the Allied woman's club garden. It was as nice as could be, and we sang, danced, and had something to eat and drink. The British thanked us, and all was well. And such a mixture as we had there: American soldiers and officers; air corps and infantry; British officers and soldiers; infantry, air corps, and navy; men and women. There has been some talk of trying to take the show (with different local personnel) up to Rome for the finals of the Allied Swimming Championships in August [1945], but the ARC says that my place is in the club, and not running around the country with swimming shows. So, I am going to try to send my henchmen, if the request ever comes through. Anyway, it is flattering to know that they want it![23]

Curtis included many other details in this long newsletter, including those of an intimate dinner party of ten people at the beach house of General McNarney, who was in charge of all remaining U.S. military in the Mediterranean. And, while it's not currently known whether the AFHQ Aquacade was ever repeated in Rome at the August 1945 swimming championships, it's clear that Curtis's many efforts were aptly rewarded with the esteem of her administrative superiors. The July edition of the ARC's *Newsbrief* concluded, "Cer-

Aquacade in Caserta performing "Waltz of the Coral Nymphs" (June 1945).

tainly, this was one of the most difficult, large-scale overseas performances—one of the most lavish and colorful—and Kay Curtis deserves a big hand."[24]

Among Curtis's various commendations was one written by Helga D. Swensen on June 25, 1945, which was sent to the ARC national headquarters in Washington, D.C.

> On June 9, I had the privilege of being able to see the AFHQ Aquacade at Caserta. There was no time at which I was more proud of the ARC than at that time, for the whole performance was—(right here, I pause to think of some word or words which will do justice and yet sound sincere)—"out of this world." Having seen Billy Rose's Aquacade in San Francisco, I wondered just what to expect, and dared not to dream up anything like that. However, let me hasten to say that the whole natural setting had the [Billy Rose] professional shows beat to start with—some of the scenes left you breathless. All in all, the whole performance entertained all who came, and accomplished its purpose in this war-weary world.
>
> Having done work of this sort (entertaining and trying to get others to help entertain), I appreciate the effort put in getting all these people to cooperate. I feel the director, Miss Kay Curtis (ARC), deserves special recognition for the complete success of it all. She was so busy taking pictures and directing the "oh, so many details" which follow shows, that I did not have the opportunity to con-

Opposite top: Allied Forces Headquarters Aquacade in Caserta (June 1945) with Katharine Whitney Curtis's swimmers performing in front of the royal fountains, and a 65-piece band (on the balcony). *Opposite bottom:* Some of the 8,000 Allied servicemen who attended the performances of the Aquacade in Caserta (June 1945).

Allied military personnel who just learned synchronized swimming for the Aquacade in Caserta (June 1945).

gratulate her—or of meeting her—so I thought I would tell you. And I know that you would be proud too.[25]

Furthermore, on June 20, a similar report was written by Colonel C. W. Christenberry, the AFHQ adjunct general, to the "Commandant of Headquarters Command, Allied Force." Christenberry helpfully summarized the scope of the aquacade's attendance, whereby "the long hours spent in its planning and staging [produced] worthwhile entertainment for some eight-thousand people of the Allied Forces."[26]

Finally, it's worth looking at a brief note sent by a man named Peter Hausner, who was implicitly mentioned in Curtis's long June 24 newsletter. Hausner wrote the following farewell:

> I thank you very much for all, and I am only sorry that I could not see you before leaving Caserta, but I hope to come one day to Caserta and see you. Believe me, in the short time I was together with you, I found a lot of simpaties [sic] for you, and I hope sincerely to meet you again in USA. I will ever remember our nice Aquacade and our work together, and I remain with the best wishes for you. A sincere friend, your Peter.[27]

Just below this note, Curtis wrote an explanation to her mother, clarifying, "This man is an Austrian Jew refugee, [who] used to be one of the richest chocolate and biscuit manufacturers in Austria, [and was] imprisoned three times by the French. He was in the aquacade, having at one time been [the] Austrian [Swimming] Champ."

Peter Hausner was the "Austrian refugee" whom Curtis originally choose for the comedic role in their "musical interlude," although that "didn't work so well," and he was eventually replaced by those three GIs "showing off" in the pool. Hausner was given a more suitable part to play in "The Tango," and he certainly did so admirably, considering the extremity of his wartime experiences. Overall, he was just one of many tragically exhausted individuals in desperate need of distraction. And while it's appropriate enough to praise the Caserta Aquacade for all of its unexpected, elegant, and "goofy" pleasures, it was ultimately just a genuine and hard-fought attempt to help remind everyone of what they were fighting for: "To make life what it ought to be."

8

Loved and Lost

When the scientists in Nazi Germany first discovered nuclear fission in 1938, scientists in America (including Albert Einstein) sent a letter of dire concern to President Roosevelt. A provisional "Advisory Committee on Uranium" was formed in 1939, and, after Japan attacked Pearl Harbor in 1941, the "Manhattan Project" was expedited as a full-scale military operation. Leo Szilard and Enrico Fermi created the first nuclear reactor in 1942 at the University of Chicago, where their testing site was set up inside an abandoned squash court, just below the bleachers around Stagg Field. This scientific history was made only half a mile away from the swimming pool in Ida Noyes Hall, where Curtis started her more serious efforts in synchronized swimming with the Tarpon Club in 1923.

The Manhattan Project grew into a literal city of classified personnel at Oak Ridge, Tennessee, and approximately 10 percent of all electricity in the USA was diverted toward the project's completion. Even after the conclusive defeat of Nazi Germany, the Empire of Japan continued waging its campaign of ruthless warfare in the Pacific theater. And, as Curtis was still working on her summer aquacade in Caserta, U.S. scientists in Los Alamos were preparing for mankind to enter the Atomic Age. This landmark was achieved in secret, early in the morning of July 16, 1945, when the uncertainty of mere "theories" ignited with an atomic flash that warmed its creators' awestruck faces, 20 miles away. The sand below its birth was melted into glass as a shockwave emanated in all directions, producing the first of many horrifically distinctive mushroom clouds.

Just over a week later, on July 24, Lee Rankin Whitney was responding to a simple note from his 10-year-old grandson:

My dear [Gaylord],

So glad to get your good letter, and to know that you were with Gram on the Island having a grand time.

Uncle Bob [Robert Whitney] dropped in on me, last Saturday (about 1:30 p.m.), and left again for Fort Sheridan. [...] He looks fine, and is quite weather-beaten (tanned). [...] I asked him what badges he could wear, and he said, "Good Conduct," "A Citation," "First World War," [and a] ribbon with at least six stars (one for each battle he was in), etc.

[...] That is mighty nice that you have been given a rod and reel. Now, when you go fishing, you will have to put some salt on the tail of the fish [bait] so that they will bite your hook. Don't you think that would be a good idea?

I remember when Aunt Kate used to go swimming on the Island. She said that the water was pretty cold.

Tell Gram to put a ring in your nose, with a chain attached to it, and lead you around if you run away and try to get into pig pens [again].

Always glad to hear from you, Gay.

With heaps of love,
Affectionately,
Grandpa Whitney[1]

8. Loved and Lost

While most soldiers, including Uncle Bob, were returning home from Europe, Curtis was resuming her ARC club work in Caserta, just after the aquacade. And, on July 3, 1945, she wrote to her mother about an exciting opportunity to visit Colonel Brock in France:

Dearest Moth,

[…] My <u>great</u> piece of news (received late this afternoon) is that, at long last, I can go to the French Riviera; to Cannes (to be exact), I think. And, from there, of course, I can get to <u>The Colonel</u> in Marseilles. I expect to go on or about July 20 [1945], and will be there for about seven or ten days. Isn't that heavenly? I haven't any of the details yet. My supervisor phoned me this afternoon to let me know that, as of today, we could apply for leave there; and to give me first chance for the trip. […] Hooray! Hooray! I have been looking forward to this for so long that I am fairly incoherent over it, now that it is here!

[…] I sort of hope that you can get Gay to write me a note or two while he is with you. He never writes from Chicago [with George and Marion], and I so often wonder about him and what he is growing up to be, nowadays. I am packing a box to ship to him, and will ship it to you.

[…] Tomorrow [is July 4], and we are planning to have a truck take anybody who wants to go swimming. […] And—if I can find the things in Naples, tomorrow morning—[we'll have] some fireworks, but not the boom-boom type […because] the boys who have been under heavy artillery fire cannot stand loud noises. So, we are looking for some things like sparklers, roman candles, and the like.

[…] I was so glad to hear the news about everybody, […and] wouldn't it be swell if Bob would get back in time to enjoy the island for a while?

I have fallen asleep over this twice already, so will sign off for this time.

Heaps of love,
Katie[2]

It's apparent, by now, that Curtis might have learned this particular sign-off, "Heaps of love," from her father, who wrote the same in his letter to Gaylord.

On the next day, July 4—American Independence Day—she wrote again to her mother about their local celebrations in Caserta:

We had a <u>grand</u> Fourth. We worked like fools, but it turned out to be another one of our [more significant] red-letter days, and I thought you would like to hear about it before I got too rushed to write you about it. So, here it goes.

Everything started out wrong, early in the morning. […] We stopped the staff meeting and rushed around like a bunch of fools. […] By noon, we had just about reached the stage that we were usually at by 10:00. <u>But</u>, from then on, things went just as nicely as we could have wished!

The club had quite a gala atmosphere, [with all the ARC girls] in patriotic flowers. […] At 2:00, [we] took a load of the [GIs] up to the cascade pool for a swim. We even provided them with trunks, and, by the time they got back from their hour swim, we had a glorious orchestra playing in the patio. It was the "Grotto Ensemble," the best Italians in this area, […] and they play a very well-balanced program of classical and semi-classical music. It was a great relief to me from all the "jitterbug" stuff that we usually have. They are coming to play for us twice a week, now, thank heaven.

[Then] the crowd moved out into the garden, where we had Vienna sausages roasting on the barbeque, and we ate "hot dogs." […] We must have fed between four-hundred and five-hundred [GIs], and everybody was having the finest kind of a good time. It really did my heart good to see them all there. And the grandest part of it, to me, was that I didn't see a single drunk during the whole time!

At 8:00 p.m., we moved into the patio, where we had a very nice dance with about twenty to twenty-five girls. […] We closed that (with regret) at 9:30 to go back to the garden, where we had our "fireworks," all Italian handmade. You would have died to see the [GIs] with the sparklers, midget pinwheels, and roman candles (made for Italian children), but the [GIs] had the time of their lives burning these themselves. […] I'm sure there wasn't a soul there who didn't have a good time.

[…] Tomorrow, we start building another feature in the form of a "Hit the Baby" booth. For hitting the prize-winning number of "babies," the thrower will get free ice-cream, and we expect the game to be most popular. There are times when I certainly wish that I did not have such an active mind.

> It would be a relief to settle down into a rut and let the club stagnate while I "enjoyed" myself. It's a temptation, sometimes, but I'm just not built that way, I guess.³

Her "active mind" would have been helpful in distracting her from the absence of Colonel Brock. However, she wrote with increasingly transparent signs of impatience in another letter to her mother on July 8.

> Word from Colonel John [Brock] said that he was "being moved," and would <u>try</u> to stay in Marseilles until July 20, when I am supposed to be having leave [time] for Cannes. So, I am trying to get my "leave" advanced so that I can get to him as fast as I possibly can. And, if you don't hear from me for two or three weeks, don't worry. I'll be chasing <u>him</u>, again. If we can make connections <u>this</u> time, I feel that our plans for the future will be pretty well set. I've no way of knowing whether he is being sent out of Europe, or just to another ETO [European theater of operations] location, from what he writes. I'll just have to wait until I can reach him.
>
> I'm listening to the regular Sunday night radio programs while I write this in my apartment. [...] I took a GI to Pompeii, this morning (third time for me), and walked my legs off. So, I came home from the club early tonight. I'm jeeping into Naples in the morning to see what I can "force" on my leave. I've never asked for anything "personal" before, and I'm going to get to Marseilles, now, legally or <u>illegally</u>!
>
> Bill John is still phoning me plaintively from Naples, but makes no impressions on me! When I told him jubilantly that I'd gotten permission to go to Cannes, he said, "I don't know if I approve of that!"
>
> I sure wish that they'd get him started home! I'm beginning to think that he's a bit "Tetched in the Head!" [or somewhat mentally imbalanced].⁴

The next letter she wrote, on July 11, revealed a sudden jump in geography to Marseilles, France.

> Dearest Moth,
>
> I <u>got</u> here, and <u>before</u> I had planned, by telling ARC authorities that John [Brock] <u>thought</u> he <u>was</u> being moved. [...] So, everybody turned themselves inside-out to help "Dan Cupid," and I flew from Naples directly to Marseilles. [...] And, thank heaven, John was just as thrilled as <u>I</u> was!
>
> The inspector general's department has a chateau of their own, high on a hill, overlooking the city and the port. [...] So, I've just moved in with them, and I <u>should</u> have a glorious vacation. My papers read to the rest area in Cannes and Nice. But, you know <u>me</u>—<u>places</u> mean nothing—it's <u>people</u> that count. So, here I am with John, and he's working like a trooper.
>
> Today, I am down at the office with him, and will follow him through his day (he's at his early-morning "gripe session" now). [...] I've called [the] ARC regional supervisor, here, and [...] I'm hoping that he can be instrumental in getting me [transferred to] this Marseilles area eventually. John seems to think he will be here until next March [1946], at the longest.
>
> I got here, night before last [July 9], and spent yesterday out at the chateau, just loafing. The customary "*ménage*" [group] is there: a young French (Corsican) "housekeeper," and three Italian POWs, who cook and care for the house; three American officers (besides John), including one other lieutenant colonel, a major, and a captain. "Home" was never like this, if you know what I mean! (Sometime, you and I will have to have a long talk about all the things which can't be written in letters. In the meantime, read between the lines!)
>
> [...] I'm hoping that John can get some time off and go to the Riviera with me. It would be a crime if I didn't at least drive out there. Maybe we can make it this weekend! The weather, thank heaven, is cooler than usual. So, I'm not melting, yet!
>
> I have been allowed "seven days in France," and then "additional travel time." I wonder what would happen if I didn't go back <u>at all</u>! I can well see why some of the young kids go AWOL! Business meeting is over. I'd better fold this up!⁵

A particularly revealing letter to her mother was written on July 22, after Curtis had arrived back in Italy.

> While I'm listening to [this] radio that The Colonel left for me, and [while I'm] sitting in a comfortable armchair (with a board across the arms for a desk) in front of wide-open windows—opening out onto

the dusty Caserta street, where the children are crying, and the adults shouting their conversation—I'll go through some of your old letters, before destroying them. I keep them because, as I've told you before, they're my chief morale-builder, these days. And so many of my friends have enjoyed them too. Folks, whom I see only infrequently, always ask for your last letter. They enjoy them as much as I do!

[…] By the time you get this, Bob may be on his way home, I guess, from the tone of his last letter to me and to Dad. It would be nice if he'd come up [to Washington Island] with you for a while, but I suppose he'll want to try to get a job of some sort. […] I suppose you got that letter from Bob. […] I sent it to Colonel John because it was so characteristic of the confused, "after-the-war" attitude. It's too difficult for me to believe that all the atrocity stories about a people [the Germans] who make such excellent prisoners! Of course, I belong to a group who feels that, even in defeat, they are "outsmarting" us. They are far too clever for us (diabolically so).

[…] Did I write you that, the night I came home [to Caserta] from Marseilles, I had all this nice mail—including yours and [Gaylord's]—which I have saved 'til last, and had a grand weep over? I have my moments when I get awfully god-damned fed up with these people over here, and get disgustingly homesick for our nice, clean Ferda Lokin! I have my moments when I'm not too sure that I'm doing a very "essential" job, and have thoughts of "quitting." Then, I think of that horrible Chicago school system, and how awfully much I love John Brock (and he apparently loves me), and I think I can somehow manage to stick it out as long as he can. His job is worse than mine, for sure!

[…] After the whole week with John, I'm still afraid that I don't know what his plans are. But, whatever they are, mine are the same (until Fate decrees otherwise). The "change" that he expected was that he was being asked to become the executive officer of the port, which would mean that he would become a full colonel. But, he doesn't think he'll fit into a "desk job," and he hates the thought of more "rank." […] So, when I left, he was still undecided. […] Anyway, I asked the [ARC] supervisor there about a transfer, and he said, "When Italy becomes part of ETO," which may be any time between November and the first of [1946]. So, that's that!

I can just hope that John can get over here to visit, next month. We really are awfully "comfortable" together, Moth, and I know you'd like him. He's so kind, considerate, and true (sounds "gushy," doesn't it?), and I'm in this with my eyes wide open to get as much happiness as I can, while it lasts. I'm hoping that it will be permanent! That's as much as one can expect, these days![6]

A couple weeks after this letter—one of Curtis's most unequivocal professions of love for John Brock—the entire world learned about America's new cosmic power when it was unleashed upon the Japanese city of Hiroshima on August 6. "Little Boy" was released from the *Enola Gay* B-29 bomber, and triggered barometrically at around 1,900 feet for maximum collateral damage. Over 80,000 people were killed instantaneously as an iridescent plume of radioactive particles floated high above the largely wooden city, ruined by firestorm. Those apocalyptic embers were soon suffocated by an abrupt downpour of blackened rain that poisoned the region, and mysterious symptoms of radiation sickness continued the devastation. This scene was repeated on August 9 at Nagasaki, with the total number of casualties for both bombings being estimated at around 130,000 men, women, and children.

The next day, August 10, Curtis took some time to reflect upon this important turning point in history:

Dearest Moth,

I won't have much time to write coherently, tonight. I'm waiting to be picked up to go dance at the generals club, "The Cascades." I'm going with a major from AFHQ command, if he isn't already so drunk that he'll forget to call for me! He's a good dancer, when he's sober, but I couldn't go tonight 'til 10:00 p.m. Heaven knows, he may even forget me entirely. It's 10:20 already! So it goes!

We are all wondering if this "V-J" [Victory over Japan] Day rumor is really the end of hostilities. Wouldn't that be marvelous? Somehow, we have [all] become doubting Thomas,' and just go right [along] in our regular routine, simply hoping for the best.

It seems horrible that we were forced to use the atomic bombs. But, if it prevents further bloodshed by US forces, it has served its purpose! What a revolutionary force that atomic-bomb substance will be![7]

Less than a month after she resumed her regular ARC routine in Caserta, Japan's unconditional surrender was announced on August 15, 1945, and many long-suffering Americans rejoiced by kissing perfect strangers in the streets.

Curtis wrote her first post-war letter to her mother on the evening of August 26, squinting through far-sighted eyes to see the page:

> Excuse the writing, but (at last) someone managed to steal my handbag. And, in it (among other such things) [...] were my glasses. So, I'm not at all sure what I'm writing, but I wanted to enclose a note with this chronicle:
> [...] You'd have laughed yourself sick, yesterday morning, if you could have heard John and me yelling at each other over the long-distance phone: "Yes! I love you! Sure, I do!" Just think, Moth, all I did was to pick up the phone in my office, call my operator for "Freedom Exchange"; she called Leghorn [Livorno], Italy; they called Lyon, France, [where they] gave me Marseilles; and I had John on the wire in less than ten minutes! Sometimes, the most surprising things are possible here! His mail had not been reaching me, hence the call.
> I noted your remark about "leading a horse." Don't worry. I, too, have learned a lot! And, I'm not fooling, this is the real thing, even if we never work it out. We both still believe it will work out, though![8]

On August 31, Curtis wrote again to her mother, revealing, "I am scheduled to leave Caserta for the ETO [European theater of operations], September 9 or 23, and I'm sure it will be the latter. [...] I'm told that I will be sent to Paris and reassigned from there, but I've written to friends in the administrative field, asking for Marseilles, and we'll see what I get—probably Germany, which will be very interesting, but a heck of a way from John! I'm expecting him to fly in here, tomorrow, to talk things over. And I'll feel better if I can see him before taking off for Paris, of all places. It had to be Paris, where I said I never wanted to land!"[9]

On September 11, she wrote her final letter from Caserta with some last-minute thoughts about her overall time there:

> Dearest Moth,
> [...] I've gotten my new GI glasses, thank heaven, so I can scribble a line or two. [...] My "replacement" is here, a swell gal (slightly younger than I), [...so it] looks as though this club might run 'til February [1946]! Personally, I'm darn glad I don't have to [live in] that darned, old barn another year! [...] This area is "closing out" much of its personnel, [and] we are losing our [local club personnel] each day. The two GIs we have are going to leave soon, and that's not too good. [...] I'm pretty sure that I can be routed to Paris via Marseilles, and am shipping [my items] ahead of me to John. [...] It's awful to try to work in a new place when all your luggage is left behind to "follow" you! Phoned John last night, and he's as excited over the move as I am. Boy! Will I be glad to get out of Italy!
> [...] P.S. Dad has the [Capri] portrait, I think. So, ask him for it, for at least part of the year, if you want it![10]

After Curtis's departure, a friendly letter of encouragement and farewell, dated September 23—was sent ahead to Marseilles by LAC (leading aircraftman) Allan Potts, who was one of the "two British boys" in charge of costuming for the aquacade, and still stationed in Caserta.

> Dear Kay,
> I do hope by now that life is treating you more kindly, and that the affairs of the heart are a slight more satisfactory than when I last saw you. You do deserve so much more. God, I'm cheering for you.
> I do know so well, in my own way, what separation and having affection at a distance can do to one.

It sends you crazier than no love at all and being completely without that certain person. Kay, he's just got to do things, and quickly. You are too darling a person to see going around, being helpful, thoughtful, and always cheerful—when, underneath, you are so desperately alone. Give me but half-an-hour with the said "heartthrob," and I'd either kill or cure the whole setup.

[…] I feel nostalgic. So little time has passed, in reality, since you went away. Though, in the mental sphere, it seems an age. I haven't been 'round to the club, as I just can't get used to someone else in your place. This phase will pass a little, and, I promise you (for all the wonderful friendship you have shown me), I will go on and do what I can in any way I can. But, I fear, that though the mind and body will be there, my heart can't be in it as before. How I longed to pour out my heart at great length and detail to you, while you were here. But, somehow, it didn't seem fair to make you listen when there were so many other and really important things for you to do, think about, or listen to. Plus your own problems.

Can I say, thank you, Kay, for being so wonderful? [For] helping me when I got temperamental, and [also for] oiling the troubled or turbulent waters that I stirred up from time to time over the aquacade. I know that I did, and I've always felt I owe you and others an apology for being such an awkward, gangling, overgrown, school boy. Kay, I send you my kindest thoughts. My prayers go with them, and He must see you happy. If only there were more Kay's in the world, how lovely to live in this world would be.[11]

So This Is France!

For anyone seeking the whereabouts of Katharine Whitney Curtis in late 1945, there was at least one leaflet, typed on official ARC stationary, that offered the following reliable advice:

<u>Directions for Finding Kay Curtis and Col. John Brock</u> (at "Chateau Beauvallon")
Take *Nationale* [Boulevard] under the railroad bridge (tunnel). Turn right on *Belle de Mai* [Road], where the red sign says, "Chateau Beauvallon." Follow the street-car tracks and these arrows toward Ste. Barthelme, leaving the street-car tracks to pass under two railroad arches. Turn right on the hill immediately after the second arch. Go to end of the street, turn left, and into "Chateau Beauvallon" gate.[12]

Before her official transfer, Curtis wrote her first carbon newsletter from this new location on October 6:

So this is France! And I am to spend the next six months here, or approximately here!
I have, at long last, left Italy behind me. And I'm to begin all over again with making new ARC and army contacts, or so I thought when I left Capodichino Airport on September 20 to fly to Paris with a stop-over in Marseilles, […] because, you see, "my colonel" is the port inspector general there.
[…] The flight over was smooth and uneventful. We were over water most of the time, and all the islands were like jewels as we flew over them. I was met at the plane by two GIs and a jeep, and then information that the colonel was up in Paris on business, but would be back in a few days, and that I was to go right out to the chateau where the inspector general's department lived. I did so, and had a grand rest until Sunday, when John returned.
The old house is three-stories high, with many high-ceilinged rooms, each with its own fireplace. There <u>is</u> a central heating plant, but no fuel (again) this winter! The place is in good condition and there is plenty of furniture, although it has been in use by the army for so long that it's all showing signs of heavy usage. There are six officers living here, and I am moving in as a sort of "house mother," which suits me to a "T," as you can imagine.
[…] The city of Marseilles was quite badly treated, around the port area. But, of course, it is hardly noticeable by now, and most of the harbor facilities have been returned to the French. There are many old German gun emplacements, which make one think that they expected to be here much longer than they were. […] I visited this region in July [1945] on a pass for Nice and Cannes, so had a chance to drive through that part of the country too. It is quite fascinating, although quite GI [populated]

at present, with all the soldiers "resting" down there. The protective anti-invasion defenses along the sea-walls there were especially fascinating to me.[13]

The next day, October 7, she continued writing about John Brock to her mother, with some hopeful speculations about life after Europe:

It's heavenly being here at the chateau with John, and the rest of the gang are swell fellows, so we're really one big happy family, with John [being] the one who seems to be shouldering most of the responsibilities (we two are so much alike!). [...] He says, now, that we will come back to the States when Marseilles is finished (anywhere from March to June [1946]). But we'll see, as time goes on, whether or not this is true! Don't count on it, but it is a possibility! I haven't talked the matter over with him at all, but, should that work out, I think I'll come up to [Washington] Island until I see what he is able to do about his "affairs." Anyway, I'm crossing bridges one-at-a-time, these days, and it looks as though the next few months would be very happy ones.[14]

She continued this discussion on October 28, 1945, while starting with some noteworthy commentary on her brother's post-war mindset:

I don't imagine Bob will find "fitting in" any easier this time than last [after WWI]. It's just not "in his soul." Thank God that I was built from the start (I guess) on a pattern which now enables me to feel that, given nothing at all, I could manage quite an interesting existence. Maybe I'm crazy not to be worrying about my future (if I wasn't perfectly healthy, I might feel differently), but I have such complete confidence—ego, perhaps—in my ability to adjust to any circumstances, now, that I'll just take each day as it comes.

If I have to end my life as somebody's char-woman [cleaning fireplaces], OK! That's it, and I'll have fun while I'm doing it. While I can have "the whole loaf" over here, I'm taking it and loving it (and everyone else who knows us thinks it's a perfect combination, and they love John). If it's no loaf at all, when I get back, I'll worry about that then.

I've had the ARC men (supervisors) out here for lunch, a couple of times. And, this week, John and I made our official "debut" into the ARC "inner circle" at a cocktail party. [...] We both like hard work, and that's what we've been doing. It's nice to know that, at long last, somebody in ARC may use me in an administrative capacity. At this point, I'll welcome some evenings for myself.

The Calas [pronounced "Ca-le"] staging-area job [in Marseilles] is really a huge project, and the ARC is getting very little cooperation from the army. The staging and re-deployment areas, as well as the replacement depots of this war, are certainly the forgotten souls, when they should be first priority. I have, in the past (little more than) two weeks, tried to make order out of chaos, and that's about all.

[...] There's so much that should be done that's not even being thought of, so far as I can see! I can see, too, that if anybody ever did have an idea, it would be strangled at birth with the indifference of the army to the needs there! It's certainly been a challenge!

[...] I have to "sweat out" transportation of all my personnel, to and from the port, and the road is a mostly dangerous, winding, narrow road. [...] So, I am most anxious to move all the gals [from a hotel in the neighboring town] into the port (I don't think that's going to improve my popularity any), as soon as I can. Once they're moved, I'm sure they'll all like it better, and at least ARC won't be forcing them to take that dangerous ride.

A week ago, two of the girls were being driven home by two GIs in a command car, and were forced off the road. The car turned over, and both girls will be in the hospital. [...] One has a broken pelvis, a gashed thigh, and a broken arm; the other, a head injury, broken jaw, and all teeth loosened! The vehicle was not an ARC passenger-carrier, so I don't feel responsible. But, each club has some jeeps that "a friend" has donated, and I'm so afraid that somebody will take one of these off the port and get hurt, that I'm really most unhappy!

[...] This is my first "day off" in two weeks. [...] John came out and picked me up to come into the chateau for dinner [last night], after which, the rest of the house went out "night-clubbing." I took a hot bath in the tub and read my collected mail, while John went home to the port to inspect a ship. He came back at about 9:30, and we spent an "exciting" evening, sorting his linen, marking it all, sewing on his service bars and ribbons, and listening to the radio.

This morning (Sunday), [John] has a "complaint court," and I'm seizing this long gossip with you while sitting in the French "salon," in front of a fireplace with a fire going (a kitten in my lap). I'm wearing my Capri-tailored, wool slack suit, and writing on the ping-pong table! The [German] POW who started the fire for me stayed a little while to talk "*Weihnachten*" [Christmas Eve] to me: "Did we celebrate it in America? Was it [similar to how] they celebrate it in Germany?"

What a state we are all in, aren't we? And, fundamentally, the good in everybody is the same, no matter what nationality—and the evil, also the same! It's a relief to hear these people speak a language I can understand, but my vocabulary is so limited that, most of my time, I hesitate to answer them in German. If it weren't for being with John, I'd be much happier in Germany (I think). I'm pretty well fed up with such as Italians and French!

[…] John said, the other day, that he was scheduled about November 1 [1945] to be made a full colonel […and] the executive officer of the Sixth Port. In which case, we will probably be here in Marseilles until the end of next April [1946]. With things breaking with me and the ARC as they are, I can probably manage to stay here as long as he does. Nice, huh?

[…] Here comes John, back from his "court." Pardon the break!

[…] Now after dinner, and it's raining a cold, fall rain. Sycamore leaves are all over the ground in front of the house! In your last letter, you said to tell John not to let me bother him when he's working. So, he's sitting [peacefully] across the ping-pong table from me, going over his reports!

[…] I'm sorry that Jane has to go back to teaching. I know just how she feels, and I hope she can get out of physical education if she wants to. […] I hate to be "smug," but—honestly, Moth—I seem to be the happiest one in the lot, don't I? Maybe it's because I just don't have the sense to worry!

[…] I must stop this chatter with you, […] but I did want this chance to show you what an improvement in ARC relationships this move has made for me. And I know you'd be happy, too. It really looks as though the rest of the time here should be most agreeable, and that I'm fast becoming almost "smug."[15]

On November 14, 1945, a couple weeks later, Anne Townsend Whitney received a more candid disclosure of her daughter's growing discontent:

I sure get "homesick" these days! I'm pretty fed up on drafty houses with no rugs, no drapes, fireplaces for heat, jeeps for transportation (they're so blowy and cold), and always the language difficulty—to say nothing of fighting, fighting, fighting to get the things which the ARC should have for the asking! So much for that!

I was very much interested in your UNRRA [United Nations Relief and Rehabilitation Administration] reactions. They're the same over here, and were the same in Italy. I guess more of this "big money" stuff is what it's supposed to be. The waste and stupidity in these closing operations is beyond your wildest imaginations. Whoever planned this method of demobilization must have been a terrific knot-head.

[…] I wonder when you will go into the hospital. I hope it doesn't pain much.[16]

Anne Townsend Whitney was preparing for gall-bladder surgery, which was later mentioned (among other family updates) in this rare letter by Curtis's younger brother, George, on November 20:

Dear Kate,

[…] We expect to see Jane any day now, as the deadline for her release from the WAVES was up a couple days ago. Mother's last letter says that she expects to go down to [stay with some friends on] December 1 to stay for a month, and then into the hospital in January [1946].

You should have seen Gay's eyes bug when the German rifle arrived. He wouldn't even let me help him open the box, and he immediately tore through the neighborhood, showing it to all his friends. He thought it was awfully heavy, at first, but gradually got used to it. On Saturday mornings, we wake up to find him staggering around under the rifle and helmet, with that old "sweet potato" for a hand grenade, and all his old toy revolvers and belts on.

[…] Hope you get your Christmas package. Two days after I mailed it, Mother sent us your new address.

Love,
George, Marion & Gay[17]

With the start of the holiday season on December 1, Curtis wrote to Estelle with a colorful summary of recent events:

> I am now in the position of assistant area club supervisor of the clubs in the Marseilles-Lyons area, with the prospect of becoming the director in the very near future. Then, I imagine I will be one of the very last ARC workers to leave this area, which may be kept open until next spring. Although, we are gradually closing up everything except the Sixth Port, where Colonel Brock ("my" colonel) is the inspector general. As long as they are redeploying troops through here, we will have need for a lot of ARC work, and have a large setup in the Calas staging area, about twelve-miles [north] of Marseilles. I was out there for about a month, putting things right, before coming to the headquarters right in the city.
>
> [...] I, personally, am looking forward to this season (to be one of the happiest ones I have spent so far), because John and I will be together. I am living at the inspector general's chateau with six officers, and we entertain quite a lot. [...] The ARC workers at headquarters are the nicest I have [connected with] so far—just one happy family—and we have [had] some delightful evenings together at dinner, popping corn afterwards.
>
> All the rooms in the chateau have fireplaces, [...and] we had fourteen [guests] to Thanksgiving dinner, and had turkey will all the fixings. Both John and I like to cook, so we were up almost all night before fixing the salad and the "dressing," but it was so much fun! The following Saturday night, we [hosted] the same number for a farewell to one of the coastguards who was leaving. And, this week, we had twenty [guests] in for a buffet dinner for the ARC regional supervisor [...whom I am to eventually replace when he goes] back to the States. Now we are all so darn tired that we can't think! [...] Personally, I am very glad to have a "desk" job for a while, so that I can again live sort of like a human being. Old age must be creeping up on me, eh?
>
> The weather has been mild, thank heaven, and so much better than the two preceding winters in Italy. [...] The gardens are lovely, [...] and we will have our own holly growing on our own tree. There are some soft-evergreens from which we can make a wreath or two, I am sure. ARC is sending trucks up into Germany to cut our own Christmas trees, so we ought to have some nice ones. And I opened Mother's Christmas package, which came yesterday, and it was full of homemade Christmas tree trimmings, which thrilled me to no end.
>
> [...] I am typing this at the office before all the staff get here, but they are beginning to drop in, so, here this must end. [...] Mother writes that she is going into the hospital in Chicago this month for a gall bladder operation; Jane is getting out of the WAVES in November, I believe; Brother George is waiting to lose his job, and I haven't heard from Dad for some time now, but all was well when last heard from.[18]

Meanwhile, as Christmas trees were being cut down in Germany, and just a week after Curtis wrote this letter to Estelle, General Patton's larger-than-life story was coming to a tragic end. He received orders on December 7 to return to Paris, but fatefully chose to go pheasant hunting on December 9, when his Cadillac was struck headlong by a U.S. Army truck. Patton was rushed 20 miles to a hospital in Heidelberg, where he died on December 21.

Like all other Americans, Curtis would have been shocked and confused at such an anticlimactic fate for her seemingly immortal commanding officer, who would so convincingly recite poetry about his past lives within equally heroic timelines. However, while she would privately mourn the loss of a much-loved and respected friend, Patton's death would soon be transcended by the enduring life of his overpowering (and well-cultivated) cultural mythos—the only reincarnation, perhaps, that he ever truly expected.

Sink or Swim

On January 12, 1946, Curtis wrote a particularly happy and self-confident letter from a new location in France, "Sitting on the floor, in front of my fireplace":

8. Loved and Lost

Dearest Moth,

Two more good letters arrived from you today [...and] both John and I laughed and laughed over them tonight! [...] As for thinking that I'm "grown up," I'm here to tell you that I have my days when I'd like to scream, "Hey! I'm forty-nine! Just let me ease up a bit, will ya?!"

But, folks keep saying, "You don't look more than your late-thirties," so I keep struggling along.

I think that John looks at me questioningly [about my age], every once in a while, and now that two people have told him that he doesn't look over thirty-five, he just feels like a spring chicken. But, we manage to have awfully nice times together, Moth, I don't think I've ever been so happy and contented. [...A friend] wrote, after seeing John's picture, that he and I look enough alike to be identical twins—and he was a twin! (a sister who died). John and I do think and act much alike, and seem perfectly happy, so long as we're together.

[...] We went on a spree, quite a while ago, which I meant to write [about to] you, but haven't gotten around to it. There is a charming little French restaurant down on the waterfront, called "The Caravel," [supplied by the] black market, of course. [...] John and I had been window-shopping when he suggested that we go to The Caravel for lunch, so down we went—had a nice martini, a handful of very bitter local olives, three anchovies apiece, some French brown bread, a fish course (three small, baked "sardines"), and a "New England Boiled Dinner." John [also] had coffee, and we had a bottle of white wine. When we paid the bill, I almost died. 1,250 francs—equal, at that time, to twenty-five dollars [in 1946, or over $300 in 2020]. How do you like that?! [...] How these French people live, I'll never know (and I'll never care much either!). When I "rebuked" John, his answer was, "That is none of your God-damn business!" And I suppose it isn't!

[...Some of our mutual friends] have separated, after she found him having an affair with a younger woman. [...] I do feel sorry for her, just as I'll feel sorry for me, if John and I ever separate. But, I'm egotistical enough to think that I'll still find life very interesting, with plenty to do.

[...] I'm glad that Phil [a cousin from Milwaukee] got home. Have you had a chance to talk with him about my Caserta club? Do make an effort, because he should be able to give you quite a sample, and he is a nice chap! However he got sidetracked into religion, I'll never know. But maybe it will balance our crazy end of the family. Certainly, we didn't get the "religion gene," did we?

[...] I still wish that George and Marion would make Gay write [me] once in a while, but I guess I might as well give up. And, now, [at eleven years old], if he's at the "smarty-pants" stage, heaven help you all![19]

Curtis's recent New Year transition was more fully chronicled by her carbon newsletter, two weeks later, on January 27:

Dear Folks,

We have left Chateau Beauvallon for an even more comfortable "billet!" For the first time in three years, I am (at last) in a building which has some central heating! And maybe you don't think that is a luxury! At long last, I can begin to unlax [sic] a bit! This new home is, again, a huge chateau with formal gardens, and this time, we have very well-trained servants (POWs) and an excellent Russian "house manager," a DP (displaced person). We still have the two dogs and two cats, but they have a nicer area to roam. [...] "We" are still the inspector general's section, and Colonel Brock and I are still the "Papa and Mama."

The rooms are all large, [...] the furniture is all beautiful antique, and all the "bric-a-brac" [miscellaneous clutter] is authentic and in excellent taste. There are small fireplaces in most of the rooms, but we do not need them for warmth. The dining room is a beautifully paneled room with a large fireplace at one end, and we eat dinner every night to the light of a pair of beautiful silver candelabras on the table. [We] are able to have gay flowers, now that the new ones are coming in.

We usually have ten to sixteen [guests] at dinner, so that the long table is quite festive. After dinner, we go into the large salon, where the fireplace is crackling with more candles on the mantelpiece, and listen to the big radio, or dance to a large electric Victrola. [...] We have a tiny "bar" set up in the hall, way outside the "salon," for our cocktail and after-dinner drinks. And, of course, my greatest blessing is that the servants are all so very well trained already! At any rate, life has suddenly become much sweeter! Now, Heaven only knows how long we will be permitted to be here!

As you have undoubtedly recognized [from the newsreels at home], we are closing out this area, and there is no end to the confusion in the process. Contradictory orders come in almost [via] the same telephone message—one, telling us to close out an installation—and the other, to keep it open. Thus, we live only from day to day. The Calas staging area, which has been my greatest burden, has started to close, and we have closed an average of one club per day, all this past week. In addition to trying to get all these materials under-cover in the warehouse, I have to interview all the personnel and get them on their way—either "home," on leave, or to another assignment. I have been running in circles! At the same time, I have been trying to open up some small installations in two outlying areas, and try to anticipate the needs in the very near future while the rest of this area folds up completely. It's quite an interesting game. Maybe we will last here through April [1946]. But, at times, I have my doubts about even that length of time!

[…] We (the colonel and I) still play with the idea of taking a few days off, maybe to take the Swiss tour that all the others seem to be able to get in. But, up to the present, we have had to be satisfied with a weekend in Cannes, where we visited a spectacular spot called the "Gorge de Loupes," and we ate some delicious food at a little pre-war restaurant, called "La Reserve." […] This week, if anything goes by schedule, we are hoping to drive to Biarritz [in southwest France], where the ARC has a small club for the GI university there. We thought the university might last through May, but by this week's orders, it looks as though it will fold in March, so I must get up there pronto.

[…] As usual, we have guests coming for lunch, so I must get at other things, but this will bring you up with the "latest moves" in the Curtis-Brock "*ménage*." I have not as yet made the final decision as to whether I will move directly to Bremerhaven [Germany] when the colonel thinks he will, or whether I will try to get another [furlough] home first. Don't count on my coming home, though![20]

Her comfortable upgrade most likely arrived in tandem with John Brock's promotion to a full colonel, enhancing their already charismatic social status.

Another two weeks later, she wrote again from this "regal splendor," on March 15, with some particularly optimistic plans for the future:

Dear Estelle,

Thanks-a-million for that cute Valentine card. Both of us [Curtis and Colonel Brock] got such a kick out of it!

Now! Hold on to your hat! I'm coming home (much as I dread all the un-pleasantries that will ensue). John has said that he will come with me to see if he can straighten out his family affairs, so that we can marry. Please, this is for your information only! I hope that, before September [1946], I'll know what (if any) our plans can be. And if I have to go back to teaching, OK. Or if I don't think I can take it, perhaps I can find another overseas job. This all came about quite suddenly, since I had been told that I could move up to Wiesbaden to act as a club supervisor, "somewhere." But then John was transferred to Bremen [in Germany] (he left last night), and said that, if I'd go home, he'd go too. I thought that was the best thing I'd heard in three years. And since ARC is cutting activities over here fifty to seventy-five percent (due to cut in budget), I "got to go home!"

Things are folding with a bang here. We will have no ARC club activities left here by the end of next week. I'll have [the club in] Nice, and a small Negro club in Miramas, and a small white club […that] will last until April 1 [1946]. Then, I'll go up to Paris to clear [out with the ARC], expecting to reach Bremen about April 15, when John says he will have cleared himself, too, so that we can come home together. I have to clear again in New York, and he thinks he may have to go to Washington [DC]. But we're hanging on to each other as long as possible, hoping that we can come out west together; perhaps, even as far as Washington Island! It will be grand if it works out that way, but I've learned not to count on anything. However, no matter what happens to John, I will be coming home just the same! Enough's enough! And, as we say over here, "I've had it!" Just tell "folks" that I'm tired, I'm on my way, and have no future plans, except to get to the island as fast as I can!

[…] You'd die if you could see my "regal" splendor. I'm sitting in front of my lovely marble fireplace, with a small fire under the broad mantelpiece, upon which are five pots of hyacinths (the colonel's parting gift), reflected in the huge mirror. […] I'm writing [while] sitting on a velvet chaise lounge, with the radio playing softly across the room. And it's such a beautiful room, overlooking a nice formal garden, which the POWs have been busily cleaning up and planting. And I'm giving up all this luxury just to see what the future holds! Sometimes I know I'm nuts! But, Estelle, he's such a grand person,

8. Loved and Lost

and we get along <u>so</u> well together. It just seems "<u>the</u> right thing!" So, here goes for "all the eggs in one basket," or "shooting the works," so to speak.

I had a brief business trip up to Paris, last week, but was in such a hurry to get back to the colonel that I didn't stop for any sightseeing. I'm not a good tourist, anyway, and John and I had such a heavenly time on our Swiss tour that nothing can even touch that. We both loved Switzerland and the Swiss people. We took the southern tour—Basel, Montreux, Zermatt, Bern, Biel—then back to Mulhouse (France), where we'd left our open jeep. And then drove off in a blizzard, almost getting lost. It was all great fun, and even we "two old bozos" will never forget it all.[21]

After another couple weeks, Curtis wrote to her mother from the city of Nice on March 27, 1946, building up the suspense of her expected departure:

I'm down here at the Westminster Hotel on business, [...] trying to get the ARC out of <u>this</u> area, too. Naturally, <u>nobody</u> wants to leave! March 31 is the closing date here, too!

[...] I'm having new troubles about clearing. "Rumor" has it that I can't clear in Paris between April 8 and 15, because offices are being moved from Paris to Wiesbaden. If that's so, I may have to get out of Marseilles earlier than I had planned, because John still phones (from Bremen) that he will be free to sail from there any time after April 15! There's never a dull moment <u>these</u> days!

[...] Looks like Colonel John may even come up to [Washington] Island to rest with us, as soon as we reach the Midwest. It would be <u>great</u>, if he only will![22]

On April 9, she wrote her last known letter from this climactic period in France, while she was waiting for Colonel Brock to arrive from Germany:

Dearest Moth,

So far, so good. I'm now completely cleared with the ARC in ETO, and I'm "on leave" for a week to wait for John to catch up with me here in Paris, because they gave him a job to do which couldn't be finished last weekend. Fortunately, I have some leave time, so here I sit, "alone" in "Paris in the spring." It <u>is</u> beautiful here, now, [...with its street carts filled] with tulips, violets, lilies-of-the-valley, and forget-me-not's, [...] to say nothing of huge hydrangeas, lilacs (white and lavender), and carnations.

I "bought you" (in my imagination only) a little straw sailor hat today. Only, it cost twenty-five dollars [just like the extravagant lunch with Colonel Brock], and I just couldn't spare that much at this time! It's just too bad that I had to hit Europe at the time when all prices are so high! No gifts for anyone, I guess!

[...] On Sunday morning [April 7 (1946)], I was at the flea market with a couple of ARC gals, and saw lots of lovely things that many of my friends would love to have—but purchased nothing! It was quite an experience, though. And, in the afternoon, I went to the Louvre with some other ARC gals, and then walked through the Tuileries Garden, and along the Seine to Notre Dame. Believe me, I slept <u>that</u> night!

Tonight, four of us "old bats" [...] are going "out to eat," to the tune of about five dollars [or over sixty dollars in 2020] per person! Tomorrow night, [we have] tickets for us to go to the opera and ballet. So, I won't miss too much of Paris. You know what a lousy sightseer I am when I'm by myself. Of course, if John gets here Sunday morning [April 14], we'll still have three days in Paris <u>together</u>! Lord only knows how long we'll have to wait in [Port] Le Havre for a boat.

Both of your Milwaukee letters were here waiting for me, and I was glad to get them. Mail surely helps a lot, over here, and not a single one of John's letters has gotten through to me from Bremen in four weeks! It took <u>three</u> weeks for mine to reach him! I couldn't say any more about our (John's and mine) plans than I could before, since I haven't <u>seen</u> him, and all our conversations by phone have to be "business" (no <u>personal</u> calls allowed?!). But, <u>if he really makes the boat with me</u>, I wouldn't be a bit surprised if we tried to pick up a car of <u>some</u> kind and just plunked our luggage in it, and headed for Washington Island.

[...] From the tone of your first note, I thought you sounded kind of "low." <u>I</u> certainly can appreciate <u>that</u>, but we'll make up for it, if and when I get to where you are. Don't let Jane get under your skin too much. I, too, feel sorry that she can't grab more happiness as she slides through life.

As for <u>my</u> troubles and adjustments, don't worry for a second. I'd rather be with John Brock than anything [or anyone] in my life. But, if it doesn't work out that way, OK. I'll just go back to Wright

College and live as economically as possible, so that I can travel or <u>really</u> live during vacation times. My period of worst adjustment is behind me now. It was making up my mind to come home, now [rather than later], and <u>make</u> (?) John come, too, to see what he really will do about our future. I'm <u>sure</u> you'll like him, Moth, he looks enough like Grandpa Townsend that I'm sure you'll see the resemblance, too. And he's a very kind person! We three can have a swell time on [Washington] Island, if I can get him up there!

[…] I was [transferred] back to Wright from [Chicago] Teachers College since I've been overseas. So, in the fall, that's where I'll report (unless God is good!).

[…] John phoned that, instead of arriving this past Sunday (as we had planned), he wouldn't get here for another week, [so] wouldn't I try to get up to Bremen and we'd come back to Paris together; that was Friday night [April 5]. I tried on Saturday morning, but couldn't get travel orders until Wednesday (and then I'd have to pretend I was going on leave to Denmark, to get orders into Germany!). If I did that, I'd reach Bremen just as he was leaving. So, I said, "Nope! I'll sit right here in Paris and not tempt Providence anymore!"

That's what I'm now doing, and hope to heaven he'll get here when he says he will. I sure wish you were here to prowl around with me. I'll try to see the spots you'd like.

Heaps of love,
Katie[23]

As she signed off in April, hoping that John Brock would soon join her on the docks of Paris to return home and start the rest of their lives together, the only indication of what happened next is implied by a month-long, deafening silence. Something profound had happened; some life-changing event, epiphany or disagreement so rocked the foundations of their previously certain engagement, that the timeline of their romance ends here.

Beyond this period, she would not hear (or mention) anything about Colonel John Brock's whereabouts until 1949, and only rumors at that. Her correspondence resumed with a sudden change of plans, announced from Milwaukee on June 10, 1946:

Lt. Col. John A. Brock in Bari, Italy (1944).

Dear Estelle,

The "die" is cast!

I am going up to Hayward, Wisconsin, as soon as my trunks catch up with me [from Europe], to help Amy Holm with their summer resort on Spider Lake. They need help desperately, and have offered me a fair salary, so off I go. It's a good hideaway, and will "keep me out of trouble." Until I send you another address, Dad's will always reach me.

As soon as my trunks catch up with me, I'll head for [Washington] Island with them, and then up to Hayward with what few clothes I'll need there.

Sorry if I'm disappointing you, but I feel that they have <u>no</u> chance of getting the needed help up there [otherwise]. See you in the fall, but let's hear from you in the meantime. Thanks again for your hospitality, take things easy, and watch your step.

Love,
Katie[24]

Her seemingly heartbroken attempt to "hide away" at Spider Lake undoubtedly confirms that her engagement with John Brock had ended by this point. And, unless they discussed this in person (or even over the phone), it's possible that Curtis was left waiting for his arrival at Port Le Havre until the very last minute.

Although Curtis always knew that Colonel Brock was still married, the legitimacy of his marital "separation" remains uncertain, as so many of his so-called "affairs" were always shrouded in mystery. Perhaps there was never another woman in the equation, and perhaps there was always one waiting for him back home. His emotional life was unquestionably complicated by the death of his only son at Normandy. And, conversely, it would also make sense if Curtis, like her mother before her, proved to be simply too overbearing or "independent" for the relationship to work. Regardless, this narrative of her romance with John Brock must be carefully recognized as only one side of the story, with the open possibility for any other unseen variables or explanations.

As Curtis retreated from the world—perhaps in bitter contemplation (or even repression) of these difficult considerations—she was struck again by despair when her father, Lee Rankin Whitney, had a serious heart attack in Milwaukee. She had to drive over 300 miles south from Spider Lake to see Lee before he died on August 13, 1946. Whereas Curtis was seemingly at her happiest point only four months earlier, this subsequent period of her life was now indisputably one of her lowest.

It was only three days later, on August 16—that her young bomber friend wrote a characteristically troubled (but still charming) letter of sympathy:

Dear "Aunty" Kay,

Now doesn't that sound all formal-like? Tsk-tsk. Your encouraging letter was waiting for me when I got home, a few hours ago, and lots has happened since then.

You see, I got so [...] eager to get out of California that I called the chump who is peddling my car for me, and ran smack dab into a <u>rare</u> deal. Now all I have to do is make his heart bleed some more for me, and I'll own a 1941 Ford station wagon. [...] Aren't I terrible? [...] I've got all fingers and feet crossed. It means free transportation for me to Ohio, where I can sell it anytime for more than the investment.

[...] If finances permit, I go through Texas to visit friends, then to Milwaukee. But fast, [... because] it takes me two days to go to Cleveland from here, so expect me around Monday or Tuesday, any week. Depends on how grown up that little girl got in San Antonio (other secondary reasons also). Sort of a rebound, I guess, from my wife divorcing me, two weeks ago.

[Anna Lee] told me she was going to [divorce me], two months ago, but I didn't believe it for a second until the judge wrote me a nice letter, telling me I was a single married man. Yes, he granted the divorce on "Mental (Extreme) Cruelty" (am I really capable?). And now, under California law, one year must elapse. The case is studied, and

Lee Rankin Whitney, Curtis's "anchor to the wind."

granted or disapproved then. So, I'm not contesting. If it will make her happy, I'm all for her happiness.

She didn't leave me, I left her. Yes, we were living with her in-laws. And, one day, I moved out. I sort of got tired of being the hired man and living with the mother's daughter, not my wife. I asked her if she was tired of working for them, and how about working for us—let's pull together—and she said "nope." So she stayed. If I wouldn't have left, we would still be together. So my fault.

It's a mess. We are divorced. We see each other, maybe once a week, and then I can't kiss her hello or hold her hand—unless we're alone, and then just barely. So, I love her and make sarcastic remarks, like, "Oh, I'm sorry, I forgot we can't kiss goodbye in public." We're still man and wife, [but] now I don't see her unless it's unavoidable. It makes me feel bad—and her, feel worse. She won't let go of my heart, and I am—as the song goes—a prisoner of love. Isn't that sad? [...] Nuts!

You know, I traveled the world looking for that girl for a long time, and I wouldn't trade her for a dozen, even now.

Katharine Whitney Curtis sitting in silence (undated).

So, you have your troubles, too. I was sorry to hear about the funeral of your dad. I only hope I can be as fortunate as you in arriving in time [to say goodbye]. That means so much.

Now, don't sit on pins and needles waiting for me. I'll be there, just as soon as I can get my nose in the wind that's blowing. Be prepared for a shock, 'cause I only weigh 125 [lbs.] now, and, last time you saw me, I was 162. So, I'll need a shave and a bath, and I'll feel just like I did when I first met you.

Put a candle in the window, Aunty Kay, I'm coming home.

Yes, chin up, together.
Whitey[25]

Curtis would certainly have received this letter gratefully, having always had a soft spot in her heart for the young pilots that she befriended at her "Paradise" in Agadir. And, while she knew that it would be mutually therapeutic to see Whitey again, there were still many taxing and mundane details to put behind her.

On August 23, she wrote to a distant (Rankin) family cousin from Milwaukee, revealing her recent mindset among the funeral affairs:

Your red [flowers] were such a lovely bright spot in Dad's beautiful [arrangement]. I know they would have pleased you. And I so appreciated your note of sympathy. It was fortunate that we [siblings] were all in States at this time. It is difficult enough for me to lose him, even if I am here! I will miss him more than most folks will ever realize, since he was my one "anchor to the wind."

8. Loved and Lost

I am finding it a bit difficult to adjust, these days, but I'm returning to my old teaching job at Wright Junior College. [...] Please remember me to those [other cousins] I met when Dad and I were in Flint. My love to you—hastily, Katharine (Curtis)[26]

Curtis then wrote to Estelle from Chicago on August 31 with some important and supplementary details:

Things have been moving so fast for me, recently, that I haven't been able to keep you informed of all the changes in my plans.

First, Dad died quite suddenly and unexpectedly on August 13. I got down on Tuesday morning, and he was gone by noon (hardening of the arteries). As you can imagine, that was quite a blow to me, and I'll miss him terribly. Then, in the settlement of the estate, I lost the car to my brother [Bob] on a cut of the cards.

I am grateful to you for your kind offer to take me in, but I feel very strongly that I want to live alone. And, after much cogitation, I'm moving, this Saturday, into a two-room suite. [...] I will have a sort of "light housekeeping" arrangement / "share the bath" plan. The building is only now being rebuilt, so doesn't look like much, but it will be nice eventually.

[...] I haven't had time to get in touch with anybody, as yet, but will do so soon. I've been [staying] with Zella and Vic [Vacha]. They'll always know where I am. [...] No time for more [writing] tonight, but I'll be seeing you soon.[27]

Curtis's plans continued to change both quickly and substantially. She soon chose to return to Europe, rather than resume her teaching job at Wright Junior College in Chicago. The Nuremberg War Crimes Trials had already begun within occupied Germany, where she always wanted to be assigned, and so it seems that she was simply "following the action" by her letter of October 21:

Dear Estelle,

Just a line to say, "So good, so far!"

Everything has been fine, even the weather. I spent the time I planned in Cleveland, and (with one exception) saw the folks I hoped to. Even my little Agadir bomber ["Whitey"], whom I hadn't [seen] in over three years. He showed up to repeat [the usual charming overtures], just as though it had been the day before yesterday when we last met: "If only you were a little younger, or I were a little older!" But, since there was nothing I could do about that matter of age, I came on to New York City as planned.

I had to wait four hours to get into a room, in spite of an advance registration, but did get into one. I've been pleasantly busy (with plenty of time for bathing, resting, etc.) ever since. I've seen the people I wanted most to see, [...including] the latest [1946] Gary Cooper picture, *Cloak and Dagger*. I've eaten too much good food, and drunk too much good liquor, for my own good. And now it has come to an end.

I catch a 6:30 a.m. train to Washington, tomorrow, to start "clearing" at 10:00. Hope I'll know by tomorrow night about when I'll sail, and will let you know. [...] There has been a rumor that we might go on October 25 [1946]! More, when I know more. Best to all. My love to you. I think of you often, and wonder how things are working out.[28]

Both Curtis and Flight Officer "Whitey" would have reminisced extensively, no doubt, with a very admirable sense of buoyancy as they joked about what it would take for them to "get together" themselves.

Ever since the beginning of World War II, the essential life lesson that Curtis once imparted to Gaylord, to "sink or swim," would have seemed all the more appropriate by this (equally decisive) turning point. And, also in retrospect, it would have been encouraging to think that the worst was truly behind her. There was still a profound need for self-contemplation, private grief, and healing; not only for herself, but especially the devastated nations of Europe. And it was perhaps because of this noble mission to help people rebuild their lives that Curtis would not return to live in the United States for nearly two decades. On November 6, 1946, she got right back on the choppy surf without looking back—the autumn wind beckoning sweetly across her face—as she embarked with a courageous hope that life had more to offer.

The Third Diversion
Harmony (1946–1980)

I'm not a big enough thinker to know how Russian [communist] thought can be overcome, but, as long as they keep that "iron curtain" preventing their masses from knowing how the rest of the world lives and thinks, I don't think the rest of the world has a chance. And, when I think of the similar masses in China, I could give up myself! But, since I continue to live and exist, I shut out as much thinking as I can, and I concentrate on my silly little tours—hoping that, perhaps through them, I can give a few Americans a better understanding of a tolerance for the wide, wide world, and humanity as it really is! Amen!
—Katharine Whitney Curtis (1949)

9

Rebuilding

During what are now often called the "dark years" of German history, one woman (among a respectable percentage) who never joined the Nazi Party was Renate Renk, a physiotherapist from Nuremberg. After being displaced by the end of World War II, she was finally able to return home from along the eastern front. Fortunately, her brother-in-law was a highly skilled engineer with a specialty in aeronautics that put their entire family on a shortlist for relocation by the U.S. Army. They were moved along to the western sector with strategic haste, because the "Iron Curtain" of Soviet Russia was descending across those ruined cities with a long shadow. And, while many less-fortunate Germans were left behind in the east to suffer a punitive neglect throughout the reign of communism in the Cold War, the public purpose of military occupation in the west was to restore a nation through representative democracy and a free market. These were the basic tenets of a policy that would eventually become known as the "Marshall Plan," and all U.S. military personnel in Europe were frequently reminded of both its political and humanitarian objectives.

Upon Renate Renk's return to Nuremberg, she would have found the city serving as a major logistical base for American military operations. The Palace of Justice was bustling with excitement, in particular, as the international spotlight fixated on the frequently dramatic proceedings of the Nuremberg War Crimes Trials. And, after a year of prosecuting the most high-profile Nazi defendants, the Allied Nations were honor-bound to deliver an indisputable sense of justice for a world in dire need of healing, and to affirm mankind's redemptive qualities in the future judgment of posterity. A worn copy of *The Stars and Stripes* military newspaper (European edition) has since survived among the Whitney family documents to report its historic headline:

Court Leaves Faint Hope for Twenty-One Nazis: Judgment Blames All for Crimes

Nuremberg, September 30 [1946]

The International Military Tribunal, today, set the seal of justice on the civilized world's damnation of Nazidom and its lust for conquest.

In so doing, it served notice to the twenty-one bored (but tense) defendants that, when sentence is pronounced tomorrow, they can expect the sternest punishment.

For seven relentless hours, the high court—each of the eight judges, reading in turn—piled up a condemnation of the Nazi regime so strong and so all-embracing that none of the twenty-one remnant of the Nazi elite could hope for better than a term in an Allied prison. Few could hope even for that. Death, sixteen days from now, faced the majority.

[…] The drama today was the drama of human justice, branding the Nazi system for all time with crimes against peace and humanity.

Perhaps it was all the stronger for its impersonality. Save for differences of language or accent, the eight judges read in almost the same voice, at almost the same speed, cataloging the crimes of Hitler's system. […] The courtroom quickly sensed the stern mood in which the high court had reached its verdict.

[...] In finding Nazism guilty of aggressive war against each of the countries it overran, and against the Soviet Union on which the Wehrmacht broke its strength, the court castigated Nazi leadership for conspiracy, crimes against peace, war crimes, and crimes against humanity—the four counts of the indictment.[1]

This article was published early on October 1, 1946, just ahead of the expected sentencing announcements, later that afternoon, when 12 Nazis (including Hermann Göring) were condemned to death.

Thereafter, jurisdiction over the Nuremberg War Crimes Trials was relegated to U.S. authorities for the next 12 overlapping rounds of indictment, averaging eight months each, until 1949. And while a few war criminals would evade justice for many years, such as Adolf Eichmann in Argentina, the vast majority of the civilized world was soon transitioning from grief to a more enduring mindset of rebuilding. Although still learning English and adjusting to the new status quo, Renk was happily employed in Nuremberg as the U.S. army began its widespread and systematic denazification of West Germany. And, among those early days of understandably awkward interactions and semi-suspicious glances, there was one German-speaking ARC official who wandered into her office for some minor physiotherapy (and an inevitable friendship). It was the gregarious Katharine Whitney Curtis, having just recently returned from America.

So This Is Germany!

KWC during her final year with the American Red Cross (1947). Courtesy Donna Dorn, International Academy of Aquatic Art.

Since the lift of military censorship after the war, Curtis started writing far too many letters to exhaustively reference. Therefore, it's sufficient to start with her final 1946 carbon newsletter, written on December 14, which broadly summarizes the period between her leaving New York and arriving in Nuremberg:

Here, it's almost time for Christmas, and, of all places, this one finds me in this ancient city! Last year, I was in Marseilles; the year before, in Caserta; the year before that, on the Isle of Capri; the year before that, I celebrated in Chicago. It seems a lifetime ago!

After a short stay in Camp Kilmer [New Jersey], we sailed for Bremerhaven on the [USS] Admiral Coontz from New York on November 6. The trip took only nine days, and, in spite of some wind [and large waves], was very pleasant.

[...] We were in Bremerhaven only overnight, [...and we] went "sight-seeing," the next day, but all there was to see was "rubble" and ARC clubs. The people, as such, were the same type that one always sees around port areas; and, certainly, none of them were smiling! [...] We had sleepers [overnight

9. Rebuilding

train cars], the next night, for Wiesbaden. [...] We watched the scenery race by, and all the cities seemed to be mostly rubble and hollow walls! Such <u>awful</u> destruction! [...And] Wiesbaden has been bombed too!

[...] I was on the train for Nuremberg, where I was to take over as area-club supervisor. [...] We rode on a civilian train, which reserved two cars for the military, and I found a seat in a compartment with two GIs returning from their Swiss tour: a sergeant, [who was] a member of the *Stars and Stripes* staff, and a young lieutenant, who gave me all the "dirt" on the Nuremberg ARC gals! I got into their compartment by offering to share my sandwiches and candy bars with them, and we laughed, all the way to our destination, mostly over the wild "black market" stories of the two GIs.

[The previous ARC supervisor] met me at the [Nuremberg train station] in the rain, and we drove in our German sedan to the little three-room apartment, which she has since turned over to me. I have a living room, bedroom, small gas-stove kitchen, and a large bathroom with steam heat. Only, the furnace broke this week, and, at present, I have <u>no</u> heat! I have a little German woman who takes care of my every need. So, when the furnace works, I am perfectly happy!

I have two rooms (and a store room for office space) in the Provost Marshal Building, right next door to The Palace of Justice, where all the trials are being held. And, I hope (sometime soon), to be able to drop in on them for a "look-see." For office staff, I have an ARC secretary and a German girl (typist). To handle my "motor pool" of two jeeps, in addition to the German sedan, I have both a German driver and a grand GI, for which I am very grateful (since I have long ago outgrown the desire to do a lot of "road work" over here alone)!

My territory includes two clubs here in Nuremberg: The large "Linde Stadium Club," [...] and the "Lincoln Club" (Negro). [...I also have clubs] in Fürth, Schwabach, Ansbach, Erlangen, Herzogenaurach, Hamburg, and Coburg. I have been on the road almost continually, since my arrival down here, [...] and I must say that there hasn't been a dull moment. I feel as though I had lived here all my life, as far as being adjusted is concerned. I have one of the choice assignments, I feel, and I am perfectly happy and love my job. I have about forty ARC gals in my clubs.

The city of Nuremberg is the worst-bombed city that it has been my misfortune to have been in. Much of the residential section, and almost one-hundred percent of the old walled city, has been almost totally destroyed. It makes me fairly sick, every day, when I drive past the ruins on my way to work. Although most of the sidewalks and streets have been cleared [of rubble], there are high piles of it on all sides. And this was <u>such</u> a beautiful old town!

[...] It's nice to be here for Christmas, and we are all head-over-heels in plans for all sorts of parties. For the first time, we are being allowed to have them for the German children, and all the DP (displaced) children that we can reach. My latest personal problem is that my ARC secretary and I have just taken over six-hundred DP children in a nearby town, which doesn't seem to have any military unit that's close enough to help them. So, we are going to "take them on" with the help of our "office staff," and the surplus of ARC candy and gum.

[...] Today seemed to be "Christmas Tree Day" in Nuremberg (and vicinity), and all the German people on the streets were carrying their trees home in the light sprinkling of snow. [...] I decorated a huge tree in the front lobby of the Provost Marshal Building, this week, with a great deal of the silver shreds that the air corps used in their war against flak. It makes a gorgeous decoration!

[...] This will about catch you all up with me. It is way past midnight, and Lord knows when I will again find time for even these few details. I think of you all, often, when I see some of the peasant women along the roads, in their gay-colored skirts and aprons, riding bicycles; or when I see them patiently trying to make order out of a pile of rubble, which had formerly been a home. I will try to write more after I have experienced Christmas in a war-torn Germany.[2]

Three weeks prior to this letter, on November 26, Curtis was issued an official security ID by the "Office of Chief of Counsel for War Crimes," who designated her as the ARC "Area Supervisor."[3] She was clearly fascinated by the ongoing Nuremberg War Crimes Trials, "right next door" to her everyday office in the Provost Marshal Building. Furthermore, the Whitney family's oral history recalls that Curtis casually assisted the *Stars and Stripes* military newspaper with some "reporting" during the trials, whether as a freelance contributor, or perhaps in a more unofficial capacity.

On January 11, 1947, she wrote to Estelle with the first mention of her romantic life since Paris.

Dear Estelle,

[…] My work here has been so all-consuming that I haven't missed the "heart interest" so far, and I'm only hoping that it will continue to be so.

I had a marvelous telegram: "Happy holidays, darling. I hope your work, housing and pleasures are deserving of your wonderful self. Love, from your Bill [John]."

He's managing the El Conquistador Hotel in Tucson [Arizona], and it would be nice if we ever got together again, even in a business way! Bill was the staff sergeant that I was engaged to in Casablanca (through Palermo days), and who is such a lousy correspondent that I broke our engagement when Colonel Brock started to "snow me under" [WWII slang for strong, persistent persuasion in a dubious cause]. Bill is about my age; unmarried, to date; an "intellectual," nice companion. But, at that time, I thought that I wanted more than companionship. However, it's a long way to Tucson, and I'm no longer "eating my heart out!"

[European] conditions here are every bit as bad as I had anticipated. […] Two of the greatest errors our politicians have made are the rapid demobilization and the sending over of "babies" to be the army of

Curtis about to return to Europe (September 1946).

occupation. Then, too, the occupation forces are being reorganized into communities, and, until such time as they "settle," everything is in a state of confusion. And I mean everything! No plan to place responsibility for anything! And troops moving around, like hop-scotch, with no apparent rhyme or reason! […] And so, we "bumble" along. Nobody knows how long the ARC clubs will be necessary, and the struggle to keep them going is just as bad (maybe worse) than it was in combat times!

Add to this, a very severe winter (with much sub-zero weather); rivers and canals frozen, so that transportation of supplies is at a standstill; failure of electricity; low gas pressure, and pipes freezing; furnaces breaking down, due to use of coal; […] radiators busting; cars freezing, due to lack of (or improper distribution of) anti-freeze; etc. And you have a partial picture of the "glamour" of this job! […] Aside from that, life is a "bed of roses!"

[…On January 4], I forgot it was my birthday, when I got up [for work], and, when I pushed open my office door, I was startled to see a "spread of gifts" on my desk, and my whole office force beaming! Then, during the morning, Regensburg friends kept phoning in, and, when I landed at Coburg that night for dinner, the gals sang "Happy Birthday," and presented me with a lovely wood carving. Later in the evening, we went to the Officers Club, where the orchestra played "Happy Birthday," and we drank six bottles of champagne (which I can't stand!). So, it was a gay birthday, too!

So, you can see, there are ups and downs. But it is interesting. And I've done so much in the seven weeks that I've been here that it seems as though I'd been here forever. What used to be a mere spot on the map of Europe has taken on real character and personality.

[…] And, as you say, there are worse things than being alone, just as I have learned that there are many things worse than death.[4]

9. Rebuilding

Among those most affected by the difficulties of that particularly severe European winter, there was one German teacher (an acquaintance of Curtis), named Gretl, who wrote to her American benefactors from Hamburg on January 13.

> My dearest friends,
>
> This is the first letter in [1947] to you. Believe it or not, conditions are so terrible. We had a terrible cold spell, twice. Our kitchen got hardly a little warm, and it was impossible to write with cold hands. Twice, during the week, the electricity was cut off, and we had no lights, and candles are not to get [sic]. You cannot imagine what a hard winter this is. The people have no heat, and no food. [...] Many people, who live in huts and barracks, have been frozen to death. And many people committed suicide. It is terrible, terrible.
>
> Last night, the cold spell was broken, and the ice and snow started to melt. Our kitchen is a little warm again. It certainly feels good.
>
> I could not go out teaching, [recently], because transportation was bad, and the homes of the pupils were too cold. I sometimes went to bed to keep warm. But, for three nights, it was so cold in my bed that I didn't know what to do. I suppose you have read all about it in your newspaper.
>
> I certainly was very happy to have gotten your [care] package. So many nice things have been in there. Oh, dear friends, it has helped me so much, ever so much. I could make our Christmas a real Christmas. [...These were] all nice things that I have not tasted for a long time. [...] Let me thank you, again, for the package. It surely came at a time much welcomed.
>
> [...] I had quite some trouble with my teeth, and I could hardly get a dentist to attend to them. But, believe it or not, a little coffee from you has helped, and I got my teeth all fixed. [...] I had to buy six grams of gold. I got it on the black market for six-hundred marks. I make about two-hundred marks a month, so you know what it means. I had no gold, as all I did have was destroyed in July, 1943. [...] There are a few things that I have given away, and, believe me, I am giving them to people <u>very much in need</u>.
>
> [...] I shall close my letter for today, my dear friends. You know, it is not easy for me to write an English letter, and time marches on. It is already 11:00 p.m., and it is getting cold again in our kitchen—no more coals for today! I say good night to you all, and I shall be writing soon again.
>
> God bless you all,
> Gretl[5]

Curtis encountered many other dismal situations in Germany, such as the population of homeless orphans living in "caves" under rubble, or the case of local girls prostituting themselves with U.S. soldiers to buy food.

While Curtis suffered similar living conditions (with frozen pipes and a broken furnace), she eventually caught a cold (and a 102°F fever) while "jeeping" in between various ARC obligations. After recovering, she wrote to her mother on February 12 with further details:

> This is just a "stinkin' mess," over here, and I'm just "riding the gravy wagon" and trying to "brighten the corner" where I am! I'm spending money "like a drunken sailor," sending care packages to [European] friends whom I've found since I've been overseas. I'm having [an American friend] send me wool so that I can give my newly found DP friends some work to do, and pay them in "supplies" so that they can make something for themselves. I'm taking all the "stuff" my friends send me to such places as the TB [tuberculosis] hospital for displaced children, etc. My <u>latest</u> [project] is to send home for art supplies for the marvelous artists I found in the workshop of the Latvian camp near Nuremberg. They have so little (practically <u>nothing</u>) with which to work.
>
> [...] I am making a trip to the TB hospital (125 beds), this week, and to the "convalescent home," which the UNRRA [United Nations Relief & Rehabilitation Administration] gals have "cooked up" in order to get some extra rations for the poor little starving DP kids, who now have <u>no</u> fats and no milk in their rations. Because of this, the UNRRA gals "made up" a "convalescent hospital," to which they send the most undernourished kids for a two-week stretch, feed them the special "hospital" diet, [... and] then send that batch of kids "home," before taking in another group for two weeks. They have

nothing, in either place, for recreation. And I'm supplying some "extras" from my supplies, plus whatever friends have sent from home, to date. At least I can do that much "good" while I'm here!⁶

Curtis's altruistic mindset was readily shared by many Americans, and, on March 12, 1947, the "Truman Doctrine" was announced with the new foreign policy of "Containment." Truman argued that helping to rebuild these nations would also help contain the spread of communism. On June 5, the new secretary of state, George C. Marshall, announced his long-term plans for a wider rebuilding of Europe. This program (approved by the U.S. congress in 1948) would hence become known as the "Marshall Plan," which treated communism as most virulent when left alone to fester among otherwise hopeless living conditions.

Later that summer, on August 5, Curtis wrote to her mother about another particularly stark aspect of post-war Germany:

I have started several times to write the following item to you, but, since it is not for general consumption, please don't pass it around. Use discretion, because I really shouldn't write it. But, I think you'll get a bang out of it, too.

When my supervisor [and my other colleague, Virginia], were last here, I took them out to my Negro-staffed club […] because I had promised myself that I would, at long last, get out there to check on a "Kiddie's Party" that I had seen appearing repeatedly on their [club] program since Christmas.

As we pulled up to the club, I had a "funny feeling" about the whole thing. And, at the front door, I found a row of baby [strollers], and I said to myself, "Kay, you've had it!" And, sure enough, in the front hall and a small "waiting room" were several white women with colored babies, the cutest things you've ever seen, and you know me! Tears came to my eyes, and a lump in my throat, and I stopped to speak to the little one (in a GI outfit) in the front entrance hall. His mother spoke to him in German, he kissed my hand, and I thought I'd die, right then and there, I was so mortified! I went ahead into the snack bar, looked in, and came back out saying, "The party is in there. Let's go on in!"

In we went, and I couldn't bear to look at my supervisor's face when there, in front of us—[as we sat] at the ARC snack bar tables, facing a stage—[there were] three colored GIs acting as judges [for] forty white mothers with forty of the cutest pickaninies [sic] you ever did see! They were having a "baby contest," for the largest and for the smallest; for the most bow-legged, etc. After about five minutes of just looking, I turned back to the other two [ARC colleagues] and said, "Well! This is it!"

Virginia said, naively, "Some of them are here with nurses, aren't they?"

And all I could say was, "Now, Ginny, don't try to be funny! These are just poor little black bastards!"

Whereupon she said, "Oh no! Kay, oh no!"

And [our supervisor] just about burst a blood vessel over [the idea of] a "black bastard baby contest" in an ARC club! For the sake of argument, I took the "dark side of the question," and we went up to the club director's office, where my [local (African-American) club director], Alma Bailey, told us that it had all started at Christmas time when the field director in her building had six or seven such cases, and the staff thought it would be nice to help them. The next month, there were sixteen, then thirty-seven, then fifty-six. And then, the day we were there, they numbered eighty, and Alma had had to restrict it to only those German mothers living in Nuremberg proper! She said that the mothers were proud of the babies, and that while she wasn't interested in the mothers, she was interested in helping the children in any way that she could.

She had "her [GI] boys" doing the judging so that they would be cognizant of the results of the folly of other Negro soldiers, who had caused such suffering. She said that the fathers of many of these children had American families, already, and couldn't be expected to break up their American homes for these German women!

Well, you can imagine the conversation that was held, and I felt so sorry for Alma, who said to me (when we were alone), "If it hurts you people to see this, imagine how we colored women die, each time we see it!" The matter of these parties was taken up by our headquarters, and, of course, she was told that although her purpose was a worthy one, the ARC could not permit it. And Alma said, quietly, "Oh, well. It was getting so large that I didn't see how I could handle it any longer, anyway."

9. Rebuilding

And I said, "Why don't you write to [former First Lady] Eleanor Roosevelt, and see if she can put you in touch with some US organization that will help you to stay over here and try to help these poor little misfits," which Alma had seen in England, France, and (now) Germany. I also thought to myself, Lord! If there are this many black ones, think how many white ones there must be!⁷

During this period, about half of all U.S. soldiers remaining in Nuremberg were African American, and Curtis made several other mentions of Alma Bailey and their ARC "Negro clubs."

The ARC was soon handing over all of its regional responsibilities to the Special Services branch of the U.S. army, and Curtis was also looking to transfer. She wasn't planning on returning to America for various reasons, the most practical of which concerned basic financial pressures inherent for any (non-traditional) woman working in a male-dominated job market. And, with her mother's unwavering preference for an "independent" life at Ferda Lokin (on a fixed income), Curtis was naturally obliged to help maintain the island property.

She submitted her transfer request by September 8, and, on September 20, she wrote to her mother with a significant update:

No more "ARC" on my address, just "K. W. Curtis, Tours, OCSS, EUCOM."
[…] I'm finally out of uniform, and does it seem strange! The job I have is "Director of Tours (Special Services) for the army, its dependents, and for the entire [European] theater." At present, I have a feeling that "all that glitters is not gold," and I may have to become a "rubber stamp" to my chief. It's too soon for me to draw any real conclusions, but, even if I am, I can still gather all the information and make a lot of valuable contacts (if I'm smart). I thought I'd have to sign a two-year contract, but I did not. They made it for one year, and I'm sure I can renew it, if I want to.⁸

Although Curtis had originally applied to the assistant director position with the Special Services, she was just made full director of tours, and told to relocate to their new headquar-

Curtis at her office in Nuremberg (undated).

ters in the German town of Bad Nauheim, about 160 miles northwest of Nuremberg. She would remain there until 1949, when their headquarters would change again, but only after gathering a few more immeasurably worthwhile friendships and experiences along the way.

Director of Tours

As Curtis settled into her new environment around Bad Nauheim, she continued writing about her transition and extensive traveling throughout the surrounding region. She eagerly started learning about the business of their numerous (and expanding) tour programs across Europe, as represented by the many colorful posters in their travel office. She was given a former ARC woman as a Special Services assistant, in addition to a British secretary and a German typist. She exclaimed on October 3, 1947, "I am very happy to move away from the rubble of Nuremberg, and I'm sure that I'm going to be happy in my new 'trade!'"[9] She continued to report that her mother was keeping as busy as ever, and that Gaylord was still visiting Washington Island regularly, and "growing like a weed." She soon also wrote that she had arranged an "experiment in international goodwill" by encouraging Gaylord to send a care package to a local German boy, "To have Gaylord get interested and tolerant early."[10]

Upon adjusting to her new work environment in November, Curtis confessed that she was struggling to build her self-confidence amid the various bureaucratic "road blocks," including some frustrating meetings with her male supervisors. She was planning to depart on a Mediterranean cruise over the holidays to explore additional tour prospects, and this trip would be her first opportunity to forge important business contacts, not only for the Special Services, but also for the promotion of her recurring passion. She wrote to her old Chicago friend, David Clark Leach, in this regard on December 9:

Dear Clark,

I am sticking my nose back into synchronized swimming again, and I wanted to ask several favors of you and the synchronized swimming committee.

Anne Townsend Whitney on Washington Island (c. 1950).

[…My new] job takes me into many of the European countries, and, in each of these, I would like to contact the leading swimming authority in an effort to spread the synchronized swimming "gospel."

Last week, when I was in Copenhagen, I had a meeting attended by [about five local coaches and swimming authorities]. We had a copy of my book, and I attempted to interpret the work to the audience through the ten girls [including two Danish swimming champions] in the water.

The music was unsatisfactory, but I think we managed to at least create an interest. I am hoping to return, after the first of the year, to see what they have been able to accomplish in the interim.

Here in Luxembourg, where I am drafting this letter, I have not been able to contact the swimmers (in this short trip), but I shall send back a copy of "Synchronized Swimming," to be delivered through my hostess here.

My request to you and the synchronized swimming committee is that:

I would like copies of the AAU book containing rules for competitive synchronized swimming, at least twenty to thirty copies, if I may have them for distribution to the countries I contact (free distribution I hope?).

Can the US send one duet to next year's Olympics in England to demonstrate synchronized swimming? I think that it would be a great feather in our USA cap. And, of course, I'd love to see it done while I'm here in Europe to attend the Olympics. I think it would really "cinch" the event for European interests.

Let me know what you think of the whole thing that I'm doing, please.

[…] Hastily,
Katherine W. Curtis
Director, Tours Section[11]

Curtis was effectively serving as the ambassador (emeritus) of synchronized swimming abroad, helping to establish an international groundwork that would lead to the sport's Olympic acceptance in 1984. By Christmas of 1947, she was en route to Cannes (France), where she embarked by sea toward Algiers, and throughout Italy thereafter.

She was also promoting synchronized swimming on January 27, after returning to her office in Bad Nauheim. This letter was addressed to Avery Brundage, president of the USA Olympic Committee, who would eventually become the chairman of the International Olympic Committee, from 1952 to 1972.

Dear Mr. Brundage,

A world of welcome to you, from an old Chicagoan, and then to some synchronized swimming business.

[…] I wrote to Clark David Leach, before Christmas, asking him if there was any chance that the AAU might send a pair of synchronized swimmers to the [1948] England Olympics for demonstration purposes. As yet, I have not heard from him, and I don't want to miss this opportunity to contact you while you are [in Europe and] so much nearer than the States.

In my present position, as director of tours [for Special Services], I have been attempting to "spread the gospel" of synchronized swimming in any country that I visit, and where I am able to contact the coaches and swimmers. For instance, while in Copenhagen, recently, I met with the coaches and women swimmers […] to explain "swimming to music," and left them to develop a group, which I promised to "inspect," this spring. I am planning to do the same thing in Luxembourg, at an early date, and I think that I may be able to get to Stockholm also.

[…] I have felt that the future of synchronized swimming would be assured if I could stimulate the interest in this form of swimming in Europe through my personal efforts; and, also, if there could be a demonstration by finished performers at this year's Olympics, so that the Europeans could better understand the possibilities of development and progress in this type of swimming.[12]

On March 6, just over a month later, Brundage was courteous enough to personally respond to Curtis's petition, but with a seemingly neutral attitude:

Dear Miss Curtis,

Your letter reached me at St. Moritz [Switzerland] during the Winter Games, but I had no opportunity to reply. There has been some talk of having a demonstration of synchronized swimming at the

Olympic Games, but the decision rests with FINA, and I have not been informed of their attitude. If you are particularly interested, you might write to Secretary R. M. Ritter [at FINA].

[…] I am happy to learn of your activities, and wish you success in your work.

Sincerely,
Avery Brundage[13]

An opinionated retrospective of Brundage was later written by Esther Williams, an Olympic competitive swimmer and Hollywood movie star who started popularizing synchronized swimming through her films during World War II. In her autobiography, *The Million Dollar Mermaid* (1999), Williams chronicled her account of Brundage's negative reaction to her otherwise successful movies:

> Despite the growing interest in synchronized swimming, the International Olympic Committee [IOC] refused to certify the sport because of [their] ill-tempered, old chairman, Avery Brundage. Although I never spoke to him directly, I was told that time after time he would reject appeals for synchronized swimming. He complained that the swimmers wore sequins in their hair, makeup, and pretty bathing suits, as if that should be sufficient reason to dismiss it from consideration. "They're just clones of Esther Williams! That's not a sport!" he was reported to have said. The athletic component of what I did was still unrecognized, at least by the head of the IOC. After all these years, I was still being condemned as "fluff."
>
> Whenever I tried to help the appeal for synchronized swimming, there would be items in the media, and my efforts backfired. As far as Avery Brundage was concerned, my name was a stigma, so I stayed out of sight. For all those years, I couldn't even attend a meet, or give out a medal, without attracting Brundage's ire. Perhaps I inherited his leftover grudge against Eleanor Holm, who had preceded me in Billy Rose's Aquacade. Eleanor had qualified to participate in the 1936 Olympics in Berlin, the infamous "Nazi Olympics." However, she had been so bold as to be seen quaffing champagne in public, and Brundage sent her home without allowing her to compete. Fifty years later, he was still giving women athletes a hard time. Finally, the grouch died, and a new Olympic sport was born.
>
> […] I was proud to be there when it came into the Olympics. I was proud to be an inspiration, a godmother to the sport. It was a very emotional moment for me. Tears came to my eyes on camera, and I thought, "I love every one of those girls in the water."[14]

Although it seems that Curtis never encountered this particularly antagonistic version of Avery Brundage, the rise of Esther Williams' glitzy performances apparently polarized the "grouchy" IOC chairman against synchronized swimming. Nevertheless, Williams was faithfully embodying the most idealistic qualities of synchronized swimming, as only a "fairy godmother" could (back in the U.S.). And, just as importantly, Curtis was fighting to "spread the gospel" for an aspiring Olympic sport (overseas), as only a more elder and authoritative matriarch could.

The early part of 1948 provides rare insight into Curtis's marital history, as she wrote to her mother (also divorced) on February 22, "I am amused at you and I, and our wedding anniversary dates. I never remember mine, which was December 29, I think. I, too, feel that even if I had to 'do it over again,' [that I] probably wouldn't do anything much different, and it might have been much worse." And, in regard to the assassination of Mahatma Gandhi (only a month prior), she commented further, "Yes! [Life] does seem strange without Gandhi. So many strong individuals gone, [which] makes one think that a certain good era of philosophy is over. And Lord knows what this next one will hold!"[15]

She continued to speak her mind on March 4, revealing her increasingly negative emotions and surroundings:

> Dearest Moth,
>
> Your nice long letter with the newspaper clipping finally came through, this morning, and I'm surely glad that it did. I'm in one of my periodic "low" periods, completely frustrated from a "business"

standpoint, and fed up with army procedures and stupid men! I walked to work through the park, this morning, and the trees are starting to bud, and their tops were filled with birds twittering away, and I got so homesick for family and [Washington Island] that I had to blow my nose real hard. I'm not fooling when I say that, if only I had enough money, I'd be home in no time. But I just can't seem to see how I'd ever live in the States, at present.

[…] This feeling that I must stay over here indefinitely (or until the Russians push me out) is beginning to pall [and affect me]! It may sound silly to you, but I can't think of anything which would appeal to me more than crawling into a hole on Washington Island. All of this, over here, may sound glamorous to you folks at home, but you should know me well enough to know that living is living, no matter where one is trying to live. [Add to this], never being able to get away from being surrounded with suffering and privations—now, with no apparent possibility of solution—and this horrible feeling of the closing in of the pincers of communism (they seem to move like a glacier, with no way to stem them!). Well, suffice it to say that enough is enough, and I'm feeling more and more that I've got to be able to look forward to some other financial solution in the future. And, between you and me, it doesn't look as though old Europe has much of a future.

And let's not let you get too smugly satisfied with the idea that you are just contented with the idea that you are an American. The same elements in the average American that I object to (and find boring) are the very same characteristics that you have been the first to criticize all your life: lack of informational background, which is available to all in the written word, if not by actual contact; lack of common courtesy, kindness, and consideration of "the other fellow" (tolerance, I guess, is the word); not being able to "do as others do" when outside of the USA, but always demanding American bars, American service, etc.; and such braggarts as we are! What has ever made us believe that what [works] for Americans in America is going to be best for every other human being in every other country?

For heaven's sake, as I've said before, don't get the idea that I've become un–American. If anything, I've become more American-minded. But I can look at us objectively, now, and it hasn't made me any happier! I, too, believe that we have more good qualities than any other nationality, but we have plenty of objectionable qualities, too, due partly to our youth and struggles, as you've pointed out. But such fundamentals as I've mentioned have nothing to do with the "culture of upper-class Europeans" that you mention. I've found that class to be the epitome of decadence, and I have no tolerance for them, since they have made no effort to better general conditions (sounds like Bob Whitney, doesn't it?) for all classes.

It's really terribly painful to have all your illusions ripped away over here. I, too, agree that, somewhere down deep, there always seems to be another little one, hidden away, that you hope like the dickens won't be dug out. But I'm growing thinner and thinner, over the last year!

You see, the last blow came when [my supervisor] came back from England, having done his usual "messing up," and has said nothing but "no" to everything this whole week. For the first time in my life, I have accepted being a "rubber stamp," and will (from now on) just "coast," as long as [this supervisor] is in office. Nobody with an idea in their head has a chance. And that's that![16]

This ideological disillusionment seems to have surfaced only a week after the communist coup of February 25 in Czechoslovakia, where Curtis had personally travelled since arriving in Europe. The coup removed any common doubt for the Marshall Plan's necessity, and it was officially signed into law by President Truman on April 3.

One of the more immediate objectives of the Marshall Plan was to prevent communism from spreading to the Italian elections of April 18. Two days before, Curtis wrote to her mother, "Much will depend on the elections this weekend, and we have an Italian representative due in our offices Tuesday to complete details for extended Italian 'tours.' Maybe, some way, I can promote [acquire] some 'free' transportation, down that way. […] Did I tell you that I heard a broadcast of the President's speech, and got such a bang out of it? He certainly has grown in his job, hasn't he?"[17] She continued describing the conditions of Europe to Estelle (who was still sending care packages for local Germans), reminding her on May 5, "You said in your Easter letter that you were 'almost thoroughly disgusted with humankind.' Sister! You can be thankful that you're not over here, living in the midst of where things are supposed to be going on to make the world a better place in which to live. [...] Living in Germany is like living in a vacuum of despondency, despair, and frustration. Nobody who hasn't been here can understand it, but it is something 'out of this world.'"[18]

Throughout the rest of May 1948, the tour program was officially approved after Italy's positive (pro-western) election results, committing Curtis to personally travel the prospective 11-day route for the acquisition of all necessary contacts with local hotel managers and travel agencies. The trip began on June 4, starting from Bad Nauheim to Munich, where they were joined by representatives from the Busseti travel agency. In her travel notes, she chronicled that "such rapid-fire conversation took place in Italianized English, and such use of hands!" They departed together across the French occupation zone of Austria, passed the Italian border, and continued through Bolzano, Verona, Bologna, Florence and Rome, where an official VIP greeting was waiting for Curtis at the local Busseti office. It was here, she describes, "As a special gesture to 'the guest of honor,' you see, all of my stay in Italy, I was dubbed '*Il Colonella*' [The Colonel]. And it was quite a comedown to get back to Germany [as] a mere 'civilian' again."

Curtis and her party were eventually brought to St. Peter's Basilica for an audience with Pope Pius XII, who had been staunchly anti-communist during the recent elections. "Everyone was thrilled to pieces, and he was so charmingly informal, speaking to each individual in the group. [...] He is a most astounding person!" And, while the tour was passing through Naples, Curtis took a personal day to visit Capri and her old community of friends, including the elderly Russian princess and her daughter, Olga Kartzow. The Italian tour contained many other local diversions, with Curtis concluding that "Italy is as beautiful as ever. And, most surprisingly, is rebuilding much more [quickly] than any other place I've seen; perhaps, because her life's blood is in the stream of the tourist trade; perhaps, because of all the US help. [...] I can hardly wait to return!"[19]

Curtis arrived back in Bad Nauheim with the increased respect of her male supervisors, who soon entrusted her with additional projects across Europe. Among the Marshall Plan's many other economic surges, the Italian automotive industry was particularly revitalized, and Curtis was personally interested in Fiat's small "Topolino" model, which she acquired that summer. When asked again about the status of her romantic life on July 4 (1948), she declared to Estelle that there was "no masculine companionship of any kind anymore. If I can keep up my job, my clothes, and my correspondence, I consider myself lucky. But, with all this travelling of late, my correspondence is shot to pot."[20]

After a summer full of various travel ventures, Curtis took another Mediterranean cruise in October for the usual acquisition of tour contacts and materials, while also having to suffer the obnoxious American tourists, cockroach-infested cabins, and all "these Italian men with their hand-kissing!"[21] By November 2, she was back in Bad Nauheim and writing to her mother about how "it's such a pity that we have such stupid men over here. One reason why I'd better come home is that I'm really becoming anti-social! And that ain't good, particularly for one who has her own living to make!" She also detailed some recent troubles with her boss "and the Swiss, over our grand tours. He's such a jackass, and I can't help hoping that this mess will finally 'hang' him. [...] Today was spent 'with the Swiss,' to say nothing of screaming over the phone to Rome and to Copenhagen, where neither office understands English well enough to know what I'm driving at! Glamour, did you say? Phooey!"[22]

One of her more significant and recurring travel destinations was the German town of Biedenkopf, which she wrote about with great fondness on November 22.

9. Rebuilding

Dearest Moth,

Remember how the saying goes, that if one stays long enough in the South, how the black ones begin to look white? Well, this is the tale of me becoming part of a German family, members of which were members of the Nazi Party, and the young husband, [Heinz Gottfried], [...who was] an officer in Himmler's crack panzer division (the African one) for nine years. He's now only twenty-seven years old! Their home in Biedenkopf, near Marburg, is the only home in Europe where I have really felt "at home," and this includes American houses, too. And I want you to get this complete picture!

The first time I went up to [Biedenkopf, in July (1948)], we visited the Military Government office. And, while there, I saw pictures of the various commodities produced in that *Landkreis* [district]. Among these were some very attractive dolls, [...] and I asked to be taken to the home where the dolls were being made. Here, I found Frau Frost [...and] her daughter, Annemarie, [who's] now married to Heinz Gottfried, a concert pianist and artist in watercolors and oils, who had formerly spent nine years with the panzer division!

They were charming people, just like all our old Milwaukee Germans. [...] Frau Frost could speak a little English; Annemarie understands a little, but speaks less; and Gottfried neither understands nor speaks. So, most of our communications are in German, and mine is improving! I have returned to their house repeatedly. Gottfried plays his beloved piano by the hour, and we women talk, mostly about Annemarie's baby, due in March [1949], and how we can make a living for the family through the sale of her dolls. They are adorable, and I have helped them to sell many to the Americans here, in Bad Nauheim.

[...] Annemarie is an artist, and has taught herself this doll-making as an expedient [source of income] since both her brothers (beautiful boys) were killed in the war (by the Russians, thank heaven!). One was just eighteen, and the other nineteen! The American officer who first entered their home village confused the boys' [black] insignia (panzer division) with that of the [more infamous] SS, and confiscated the furnishings of their home. And, then, the first troops through that area were American Negros, who busily dug up the back garden and stole most of their silverware, etc., which had been buried there for safekeeping! Now, they are back in their own house again, but are allowed only three rooms and the bath. Other Germans live in the rest of the house, and they share the kitchen, which they had been using, also, as a workshop for making the dolls.

[...] It is a relief to have found them. Only every once in a while, I have to pinch myself to see if it's really me! We sit and look at Gottfried's war pictures of all those leading war-masters and his panzer advances, just like I've listened to so many US soldiers' stories. [...] Gottfried's tales are as follows:

Strasbourg [in France] had fallen to the Americans [in November (1944)], and the Germans, including Officer Gottfried, had retreated across the [Rhine] river. Gottfried received orders that he was to gather his eight panzers (tanks) and four-hundred men to retake Strasbourg (Himmler's orders). Gottfried thought he was much too young to die, but, since chances were that he would, he'd like to spend his last night doing something he'd enjoy. So he got into his staff car and whizzed back to Heidelberg, where he spent the entire night playing piano with old student friends. In the early morning, he drove back to Strasbourg, gathered his eight tanks and [four-hundred] men, and started his offensive.

The first American tank that he came [across] had been struck by a shell, but not demolished or burned. "Aha!" he thought, "This [is] my chance to pick up some cigarettes and chocolate, of which we have none!" So, out of his own tank he climbed and approached the US tank. Just at this moment, out popped the head of a US soldier. The two men stared at each other in utter dismay, and Gottfried reached for his gun, pointed it at the American soldier and said, "Hands up!" At this point, the American disappeared back into his tank, and so reappeared with his gun, pointed it at Gottfried, and also said, "Hands up!" For some unexplainable reason, Gottfried decided that he'd had enough, and dove for some bushes alongside the road. The American calmly retired into the tank, gathered together his supplies and rucksack over his shoulder, climbed out of the tank, and ambled down the road—nobody bothering to take a shot at anyone!

Gottfried was finally injured and taken prisoner at Cologne [Germany], where the Americans, in searching him, found his school of music graduation papers. Being true to GI form, they couldn't see how such a person could also be an officer of Himmler's panzer division, so they commanded him to play [piano] for them. And, true to GI form, they were so thoroughly impressed, that they fed him, praised him, and filled his pockets with all their candy, gum and cigarettes. Then they sent him on "back" [to surrender] while they all went forward!

The next batch of Americans to pick him up found all this American stuff on him, beat him up, and threw him into prison. And [now] we can sit, in the one room that they can afford to heat, and laugh together nowadays! Once, his division exchanged an American officer that they had captured [...] for a set quantity of gasoline, cigarettes, and chocolate—all of which they had none! And such stories go on, hour after hour! [One] time, his commanding officer was forced to commit suicide because he refused to attempt to capture a certain "mountain" (as a present to *Der Führer* [Adolf Hitler] for Christmas), because it would entail a great loss of men. Such stories don't bear repeating in detail here!

On one of my recent trips, I took a new young hostess along with me. She was a graduate of Vermont University, and had been one of the groups of US students [sent] over here to study the functioning of the Marshall Plan. She was such a swell college kid that I wanted the Frost's to know her, in contrast to many of the army personnel that they had seen here.

[...] So! Now you have the history of how I "turned native," and I hope you aren't too horribly shocked! They are such nice people, and only wish that I could put all three of them into my pocket and bring them all to the United States! Or that you were here to visit them with me! You will hear more of them from time to time, and now you will have a bit of background![23]

The Frost-Gottfried family in Biedenkopf would continue to be one of Curtis's closest German contacts in Europe, and this letter effectively portrays the complex ethical landscape of post–Nazi Germany, where—aside from "true believers"—their shameful association with swastika-stained regalia was happily discarded for the prospect of a better life.

On December 12, 1948, she wrote about returning to the "Biedenkopf family" for the holidays: "And you should have seen their eyes when I presented them with a banana apiece, the first they'd seen since 1936! Of course, that's almost the same way I felt when I saw my first ones in Switzerland in 1946!"[24] By Christmas, three care packages arrived from Estelle, and Curtis distributed them before departing to spend New Year's Eve with tour associates in Bolzano, Italy, where she sang "Auld Lang Syne" and danced the night away. "When we reached the little square," she continued to describe in January 1949, "with its carpet of snow, we met two angelic young Italian boys with colored 'tassel caps' on the back of their curly heads. One wore a bell on a strap around his neck. This he would ring, and then the pair would carol out some old Italian chants like a pair of angels. I'll never forget that picture!"[25]

The first few months of 1949 would be Curtis's last in Bad Nauheim, as the Special Services were soon returning to Nuremberg. It was before this move that she reunited with an old friend, Major Walt Libbey, who, she wrote on January 24, "Was in the inspector general's section of the fifteenth air force when I was in Italy with them, and knew Colonel John [Brock] well." It was then fortuitously revealed, "The colonel was living in 'married' billets in Baltimore, these days, but Walt didn't know whether he'd gone back to his first wife or married the girl from California. And so it goes!"[26] These surprising details confirm that John Brock had indeed left Curtis for another woman, potentially a "girl from California," who had been curiously unmentioned until now. But, with her final words on the matter, "And so it goes," she seems to have accepted this long-awaited answer as her final emotional closure, after the pain of being abandoned in Paris had either fully healed or merely silenced itself. She never heard of him again.

Nuremberg for Good

On March 8, 1949, Curtis wrote again from Bavaria, regarding both her recent Special Services transition and the status of synchronized swimming:

> Dear Estelle,
>
> Yours is the first letter I will have written from our new location! I drove down here, yesterday, in the little Fiat [with my] bag and luggage—up hill, and down dale—and, about thirty kilometers out of Nuremberg, I made the horrible discovery that I had no foot brakes! So, I drove the rest of the way in low gear, praying that the handbrake would hold 'til I reached my destination—which it did! And today was spent in my new offices. Yep, I have two nice rooms now, thank heaven. [...] On the whole, it's sort of fun being back here on my first German assignment territory! I think I'm going to be happier here!
>
> [...Coach] Ellen Murphy Wales just wrote a long letter about AAU synchronized swimming, and the fact that it will soon be international. Canada is now using it for competition, and our rules. Ellen is national chairman of rules and nomenclature, and is working her head off. It all seems sort of remote, now. Although, I'll try to keep something going in Denmark and in Luxembourg. Maybe I can even start a "spark" in Italy![27]

Her return to Nuremberg would last until 1960, and her recommencing of this assignment is generally associated with the founding of a new (West) German government, later that month, on May 23.

On March 13, 1949, Curtis wrote about her new post, describing, "Here I am, all safely tucked away in a tiny single room, with one window looking out on the dilapidated old *Bahnhof* [train station] and the noisy street cars." She reveled in finally having the luxury of hot water and a working radiator, in contrast to her previous (ARC) assignment in Nuremberg, while declaring overall, "I have never seen such disgraceful billets as this post has provided the Special Services headquarters." But the highlight of this letter was ultimately in regard to the Frost-Gottfried family: "The Biedenkopf baby arrived last night, and was [described as] a 'little Katharina'—so the cable said."[28] Annemarie and Heinz Gottfried had apparently decided to name their daughter after Curtis, who explained this to Estelle on April 6:

> I took last Friday and Monday off, and drove up to Bad Nauheim and Biedenkopf to see the new spring countryside, to get away from headquarters atmosphere, and to visit my new godchild. [Katharina] was very well-behaved, and is really a remarkably healthy child. [...] The christening is to take place [this summer (1949)], and will be quite an occasion. Between now and then, I'll have to learn the etiquette of becoming a German godmother! Queer world, isn't it?[29]

Also in this letter to Estelle, she mentioned being "awfully lonesome for old friends and some intellectual companionship," mainly because of her limited financial options in Europe. She elaborated on her social life to her mother on May 11:

> The past two weeks, I have suddenly blossomed out, socially. Nothing personal [or romantic], I'm always the "unattached female," but I have been out to dinner in various houses (and usually been bored to death!).
>
> However, last night, I took [some local friends] and a young Swedish "tycoon" from Stockholm out for cocktails and dinner, and then we ended up in a nice German nightclub, rebuilt on the spot of the old bombed and burned one (open only one month). [The] men were good dancers, and we had a very pleasant time.
>
> Tonight, while I was eating dinner here (alone at the hotel), in walked [two couples of friends], and the five of us went over to a German hotel and danced a couple of hours. My German is good enough to "pass" in general conversation, and I found the evening a pleasant diversion.
>
> I can't say that I enjoy drinking as much wine as the Germans drink (and last night it was champagne, which I really dislike), but the company and the flattery of the European men is always gratifying. You couldn't hire me to live with one of them, though! However, one seems to be able to establish a friendship with them on a purely platonic relationship, which seems impossible to do with Americans over here. I don't know what's the matter with them. All they want to do is sleep with you! It's disgusting![30]

On May 29, six days after the formal establishing of West Germany, she wrote to her mother with a renewed sense of purpose in Europe:

> The "changes" over here just come and go, and my "tours" struggle along "forever." As I've said before, the military is a law unto itself, and it never even bothers to talk or think about anything else (a stupid lot). And what the European political changes will mean, God only knows.
>
> The "little" Germans are paralyzed with fear that the Americans will leave, and that the Russians will crowd over Germany. Most of them are prepared to kill themselves, rather than endure Russian rule. And, from experience, I'm rather inclined to agree with them. At present, there is much talk like that, whenever one gets into German groups. I called on my friends [recently, and talked] until 1:00 a.m. with nothing but stories of Russian brutalities, [and] my hair dresser did the same this week. They feel that the day the Russians come into Germany, that day is the end of the world for them!
>
> Personally, I don't believe the Russians are trustworthy, or ever will be. And I hope that there are some men, outside of Russia, smart enough to outguess them and their destructive beliefs. I'm not a big enough thinker to know how Russian thought can be overcome, but, as long as they keep that "iron curtain" preventing their masses from knowing how the rest of the world lives and thinks, I don't think the rest of the world has a chance. And, when I think of the similar masses in China [in regard to their 1949 communist revolution], I could give up myself! But, since I continue to live and exist, I shut out as much thinking as I can, and concentrate on my silly little tours—hoping that, perhaps through them, I can give a few Americans a better understanding of a tolerance for the wide, wide world, and humanity as it really is! Amen!
>
> If the Germans ever agree among themselves, and support each other in a liberal government, it will be a miracle. They're really a pretty "ratty" lot, it seems to me! But maybe I'm just "depressed!" [I] have sort of a Swiss cold, which I'm planning to "sleep off" this weekend.[31]

This May 1949 letter is crucial for understanding Curtis's idealistic concerns during this period, when political harmony was most at peril between east and west.

She conducted a successful French tour in the latter part of May, and wrote about visiting the famous Normandy beach landings, where Colonel John Brock's only son had died. She also saw Josephine Baker perform in Paris, "Which was a treat, after all, because the last time I had seen her was in Casablanca in 1943, when she was entertaining 'the boys' in Red Cross clubs. She's carrying a bit more weight, these days, but is just as energetic as ever, and wore gorgeous costumes. The most startling number was when she sang 'Ave Maria,' with the stage made into a cathedral, and the whole theater decorated with 'projected' stain glass windows."[32] Curtis was also able to visit the Frost-Gottfried family for their baby's christening on August 7, and "the baby Katharina looks like a chipmunk, her cheeks are so fat." She further exclaimed, "Thank heaven she has two German godparents besides me!"[33]

On July 22, she sent one of her first serious and heartfelt petitions for her mother to relocate to Germany:

> Dearest Moth,
>
> I've been up to see the "Dependent's Section" of the army, and they say that we should have no trouble at all, meeting in New York and coming back together. The army pays your transportation over here, and back to the USA again, and it pays mine (both) ways for "inter-contract leave." [...] And, as soon as Jane sends me a statement that you are my "dependent," I can file papers applying for your shipping data from New York. [...] In other words, you could be ready to sail from New York in October [1949].
>
> [...] I'm sick to death of being so lonesome over here, and this eternal living in a hotel room, and eating hotel food. If you will only come over and save me from being the "social outcast" (all single women over here are that), we can have a nice house or an apartment of our own. [...] You'll not have a "darned" thing to do, except the things you want to. And, having the car, we can go wherever we want in Europe. And to hell with all these stupid people over here. We can choose a few of the nicer ones to spend an evening or so with us.

I know what an effort you'll think it has to be, but just pretend you're like I am. What difference do the [material] things you've got around you really make? Store away what you want to find when we come back, pack yourself a suitcase, [...] and get yourself to New York as comfortably as you can. [...] I could plan to reach NY first, to meet you, and the two of us could go directly to the camp, where you will be processed, and we can sail right back here. [...] If you don't want to stay more than one year, you don't have to, but I think you'll really be crazy about it all. [...] So please say yes.

[...] It's all up to you, now, [...] and all for free, Annie. A nice modern place to live, all by ourselves! [...] So hurry! The later in the fall that we sail, the colder and windier it may be. How soon could you be ready? Maybe Bob could come back to Ferda Lokin 'til you got back. Or maybe Jane, George and Marion will "take care" of it.

[...] Annie, do come. We can have such good times, "peaceful" ones. If you think I'm still "gay and giddy," I'm not! [...] You think you'll feel far away from Jane, Gaylord, Speed [George], and Marion, and all the rest. But, you'll be surprised to find that you won't feel any farther away than you do on Washington Island. And, you'll find everything here so vitally new and active! Gosh! We could have wonderful talks about this poor old world of ours. I'm choking over here with no one to really speak to!

[...] Tell me what month that you will meet me in New York. For Pete's sake, Moth, make it early, and don't try to struggle through another Christmas there! We'll have a high old one, over here, with German carols and everything!

[...] Heaps of love, and hurry! Hurry! Hurry![34]

When her mother's answer arrived by August 12, Curtis responded with a particularly somber and practical tone:

Dearest Moth,

Naturally, I'm awfully disappointed at your decision. But, if that's the way you feel, then that's it. However, please don't plan on any additional money from me, because things become tighter and tighter, over here, and it's all I can do to get the insurance and my regular allowance over to you all. [...] And let's not have Bob there [at Ferda Lokin] unless he has cash in-hand. None of the rest of us has enough to take care of any other, these days.

But I must admit that I am able to live here much more cheaply, and on a higher level, than I could in the USA at present. [...] Although most of my "tours" are "free," there is always some additional incidental expense involved, but I feel it's almost compulsory that I make use of every opportunity offered. And, when I was so insistent that you come over here, too, I thought it would be pleasant for both of us. But you know what you want, and what you'll be getting. As for improving Ferda Lokin, there just isn't any more money. And, if it becomes unlivable, we'll just have to sell it, sentiment or no sentiment. And you know me only too well, that, as long as I have a roof over my head, you'll have one over yours, too. But, you'll have to come to where I find it possible to earn enough to keep the roof over our heads.

Now, let's consider the matter closed. When you feel you want to come over here, you tell me. The offer stands as long as the government allows it.[35]

The following month, on September 3, Curtis provided an explanation for her mother's rationale:

Dear Estelle,

[...] I haven't been too happy, since last spring, so couldn't write real letters. This headquarters is quite a mess, and, unless something happens pretty quickly, it's going to fall apart from dry-rot! My job is one of the things that's been kicked around a lot, and isn't settled yet. Maybe, by Christmas, I'll know something definitive. [...] My one hope, right now, is that [an old friend] will fly over here for the first two weeks in October. [...] I'll certainly be glad to see someone from home. I find that I get lonesomer and lonesomer [sic] for old friends.

I tried to get Mother to come over here this fall to live with me, but she said next year [1950] was Washington Island's one-hundred-year anniversary, and that she didn't want to miss it (wanted to finish her book, etc.). So, I guess that's that! I'm sorry because I'm getting tired of living in one room, in a hotel, and eating army food![36]

Curtis's feeling of financial restriction also came across in her subsequent correspondence with a YMCA (Oregon) coach, who initially inquired about the progress of "water ballet," and how to get it started in the pacific northwest. After referring the coach to a local swimming authority, Curtis wrote, on October 5, "I envy your work with synchronized swimming. The only opportunities I have had in Europe, [so far, have included] an aquacade for AFHQ in Caserta in 1945, a meeting I have had with some women swimmers in Luxembourg, and a similar meeting with the women's Olympic swimmers in Copenhagen. Europe has not as yet done anything with that type of swimming. I only wish I had the money and time to promote it!"[37]

And So It Goes

The year of 1950 began with a series of health problems for Curtis, following her report to Estelle on January 15: "I, myself, seemed to have ceased menstruating last August—so I'm getting a good medical checkup."[38] It was during this routine exam on January 30 that her doctors made some timely but problematic discoveries, which she further described to Estelle from a military hospital on February 10:

> All of a sudden like, [...] the MDs here decided on a cutting party on February 2. They cleaned out my "basement," even up to my appendix (uterus and both ovaries), due, they said, to a family of soft tumors which were taking over. The [initial test] indicated no malignancy, and they seem to feel that, when the lab test comes back, it will show the same. [...] I was out of bed, Saturday, and have been out more than in, ever since, and I leave the hospital tomorrow!
> [...] And the most unbelievable part is that this whole thing isn't costing me a cent! It's worth staying over here the rest of my life![39]

It was during this medical furlough that she was inspired to start planning one of her first return visits to America, after her June 28 payday, for about a month's vacation with friends and family to alleviate her growing homesickness.

The first time that Curtis wrote about her German physiotherapist, Renate Renk, was in a relatively happy letter to her mother on April 18:

> I decided I was too tired to drag down to Capri, [...] the first week in May, when I am taking a week's "sick leave." But I've found a wonderful substitute. I am going down to the Black Forest in the little Fiat, and I'm taking my German physiotherapist, Renate Renk (who is about twenty-five to thirty years old) with me as a companion and guide. We are going to take a holiday like the Germans do, and walk all over the *Schwarzwald* [Black Forest]. I can't think of anything which will do me more good. I'm so sick of American army people and their hotels and their tours. Renate is well-read, likes good music, etc. And, before the war, she was a physiotherapist in a children's hospital in the Black Forest, and loves it.
> I phoned her tonight to see if she could and would go, and was I surprised to hear her say, "Of course, I'd love to go. But I must ask my mother first, you understand. Then you come out to my house, where I have maps, and you can meet the family, and we can make plans!" So, she will call me at the office, tomorrow, and I really hope she can go. Boy! A whole week in the woods and hills, with plain food and plain living![40]

Despite her lapse in mentioning Renate so far, the history of their friendship can be traced back to Curtis's original (1946) arrival in Nuremberg, shortly after Renate was first employed by U.S. occupation forces.[41]

Curtis was feeling particularly "low" in the period before her month-long furlough in America, and, after spending that time with additional efforts to convince her mother to come to Europe, she wrote from "on the Atlantic" in regard to her subsequent emotions on August 21:

> Dearest Moth,
>
> [...] I'm sorry that I didn't get a letter off to you before I left, but I sort of "pooped out" by the time I got to New York [via Chicago], and I didn't do much of anything. I got sort of despondent, too, and I didn't much want to go back to Germany. Therefore, it didn't seem smart for me to do much letter writing. See? The one bright light is the thought that you will come over with me, even if for just a short time. I know it sounds infantile, but I do get so damn lonesome over here that I just dread the thought of two more years of it.[42]

A few days later, Curtis wrote to Estelle on August 25, after discovering some potential pitfalls (mid-voyage) for this tentative plan to bring her mother over from America.

> My latest upset is that I heard a rumor, that, due to shipping shortages on this side, no more dependents would be sent to Europe. So, maybe Annie won't get here after all! I will have to check into that as soon as I hit Nuremberg. [...] And so it goes.
>
> While I think that I'm lucky to have this job for the next two years, I must admit that I wasn't too enthusiastic over returning to Europe. [...] But, maybe when I get behind the desk again, I'll be OK. Word reached me in New York that our [Nuremberg] Headquarters had been reorganized, and my offices moved again. Never a dull moment![43]

After Curtis returned to Nuremberg, she sent a final "ultimatum" letter to her mother on October 22:

> Dearest Moth,
>
> When I was home with you, I thought that you had agreed that you would join me over here, next spring [1951], in order to make our future living conditions more comfortable and agreeable for both of us. But your recent letters have led me to believe that you have no intention to come over here, hence this letter, which I am sending via Jane so that she can also see the future as I see it.
>
> First, it seems to me that it is becoming more and more difficult for you to live alone on Washington Island with comfort and safety, with help so difficult, no indoor toilet facilities or running water, and with the slippery walks. [...] Every winter, I worry that you will fall and break a hip, or have a serious pneumonia attack, all alone up at Ferda Lokin. And I never feel that you are having the proper medical care, to keep you as physically fit and comfortable as you can be. You will have to admit that your teeth and eyes both need attention, not to mention your arthritis and high blood pressure discomforts. Living alone, as you do, makes it necessary for you to do many things which irritate your physical condition, and make you unnecessarily uncomfortable.
>
> As for me, I have lived for seven years as the army dictated, in one room with all the army discomforts and bad food. As long as I am alone here, that is all I am entitled to, and the occupation laws will not allow me to rent an apartment from the Germans, even if there was one to rent. But, if I had one dependent here, the army would be forced to provide me with at least an apartment (with one maid) or a small house (with a maid and a house-man). This would mean that you and I would have enough space to have our own bedrooms, as well as enough living space, [...] and help [staff] to keep it clean and to take care of the furnace. Thus, you could do exactly as you please, with no housekeeping duties at all, if you didn't want them.
>
> As for social obligations, you could have as few or as many as you wish. I have none. Whenever I go anyplace, it is usually to have a meal with someone who has taken pity on me because I usually eat alone, either in a German restaurant, or at the army "Mess," located in this "dormitory" where I now live.
>
> The long trips that I take are no longer compulsory, because I have an assistant who can take them, and if I had a home to which I could invite my chosen friends, I would not tour. As it is, I do not get so lonesome if I travel on holidays. When you chose to travel, we could quite cheaply. When you'd rather sit, you could.
>
> As far as [international] safety and security is concerned [with the Cold War], you would be just as

safe here as in the US. And here, the army would take care of you in an emergency. At home, you'd have to look out for yourself. At present, I would say that living conditions, here, are much less hysterical than they are where you are [about the risk of war]. We are not worried!

[…] As for what will happen to Ferda Lokin, I am sure that it will be cared for by friends. And, if somebody steals something, well, I guess we can live without anything there is in the entire place. Things, really, don't count a great deal in one's lifetime. Even though they are fun, for memory's sake, they should never become a burden.

[…] If you can't bring yourself to decide to stay over here for the balance of my two year contract, then why not pretend you are coming for six months only. When you leave, I could go back again to my one room.

I am sorry I didn't insist that you return with me, but I thought it might be easier for you if I waited until the end of winter. And, so, whenever you would choose to come in the spring, I could ask for transportation. But I must know now, once and for all time, what your decision is to be. If you choose not to come, then I will cease worrying about your local comforts of living. And you, Jane and George will have to work out your future as best you can. Ferda Lokin will remain, as long as you want it, and I will try to keep it up as best as I can, so that it will be as livable as possible. I will continue to send my fifty dollars per month [over $500 in 2020], and meet any special bills that I can, but you will have to be responsible for your own wellbeing.

I hope that I don't sound cold and calculating, but, for the past year, I have been hoping that you would decide to help me solve my problem of how to make future life as comfortable as possible for both of us. Remember, when [my friend] went to Hawaii, I even suggested that […] I could look for a job there, so that we (you and I) would have mild weather and congenial companionship as we both grew older. And you said "no" to that, also.

I am sure that life would be much more pleasant, comfortable, and healthy for you over here with me, but I will leave the final decision to you. And I'll never ask you again. […] So, Annie, make up your mind (for the last and final time), and please let me know as soon as you can, so that both of us can settle down peacefully and live according to the Fates from now on. I realize how difficult and unpleasant this is, but I can't make this decision for you.

Heaps of love,
Katie[44]

She continued sending letters to her mother unilaterally throughout the following month, including this particularly informative job description on October 29:

I don't know whether you realize it or not, but I have under my supervision ninety-two Special Service tour booths (in the clubs), and fourteen military post travel information offices (in the military post headquarters buildings). Through them, I influence all of the Americans connected with the armed forces, in Europe, in their travel and tour interests and habits. I also do a great deal of promotional and publicity work through our headquarters publication, called *Spotlight* (a weekly affair), and the *Stars & Stripes* (daily), which runs a travel column called "Furlough Facts" several times a week. All in all, I (and several other people) think that I'm a pretty important person, not only to the armed forces, but as a sort of liaison worker between the armed forces and civilian organizations of the countries to which we travel.[45]

Curtis finally received an answer by November 19, to which she responded, "Your 'ultimatum' letter arrived, and, of course, I'm disappointed; as are many of my co-workers who had also hoped that you would see your way to joining me. However, as I said in my letter, you make the choice, and I'll not mention it again. Although, it does seem a pity that both of us live alone."[46]

In truth, Anne Townsend Whitney was simply proving faithful to her unique community at Ferda Lokin, and perhaps most faithful to the remaining time that she had with her only grandchild, Gaylord. At 75 years old, she would have naturally felt an impending sense of her own health's decline, and, therefore, an overriding sense to maximize as many of those precious summers on Washington Island as fate would allow. It was unquestionably a painful decision for her to make, being caught between her matriarchal duties at home, and the repeated pining of a lonesome daughter overseas.

With her mother's final choice on the matter, Curtis would have to look elsewhere for local camaraderie. And this was most likely the motivating factor behind her "adopting" of various German families, including that of Renate Renk. Curtis decided to stay with friends again for the winter holidays in Bolzano, from where she wrote to her mother with a renewed sense of congeniality on January 4, 1951:

Dearest Moth,

This is my first letter of the New Year, and of my fifty-fourth year! And it is being written to tell you, again, what a rolling stone that you gave birth to on January 4, 1897! And to regret that you are not with her at this moment. I had expected to be back in Nuremberg by now, but we had an enormous snowfall here, the day I arrived, and that's all I need to encourage me to telephone the office for an extension of my leave time. And I'm enjoying it thoroughly.

[…] Over the rooftops facing me, I can see huge snow-capped mountains, for Bolzano is snuggly tucked into a cup of the Dolomites. […] There must have been eighteen inches to two feet of snow, all over everything. It was a <u>beautiful</u> sight, but it didn't predict comfortable travelling. […] It was lucky that I decided <u>not</u> to go back in the morning, because, when the guide returned here after conducting the tour back to the Brenner Pass, he said […] that they had been delayed three hours by an avalanche of wet snow sliding down onto the track.

[…] I am now one-hundred percent European. I own a pair of those huge ski-shoes that look so "smart!" I could have bought some ski pants, too, but couldn't find any that were large enough to fit me. […] Not that I ever expect to <u>ski</u>, but they become an essential part of European wardrobe.[47]

It was shortly after this letter that Curtis received word that her mother had broken her left arm, and would have to stay with some Wisconsin friends on the mainland for eight weeks. She sent her mother a short (and restrained) Western Union telegram on January 8, saying, "Thank heaven it was not your hip. Have a good rest. I hope food is good. [More] letters mailed [to the] island. Love, Kay."[48]

10

Passing the Torch

"The Great Easter Tour," as named by the Busseti Travel Agency, began on March 23, 1951, and was bound for Spain, Portugal, Morocco, Egypt, Israel, Turkey and Greece. Curtis typed up 21 painstakingly detailed pages to chronicle her trip, which began with a flight from Bavaria over Switzerland and France. They landed in Madrid, where Curtis was accompanied by a courier and the local Busseti agent with special VIP accommodations, including a private car ride to the Emperador Hotel. They arrived amid the massive Good Friday processional, a religious parade that packed the ancient streets with uniformed police, candle and flower-decorated floats, with holy figures walking in high-pointed robes of various colors. Curtis remarked, "There wasn't a sound, except the drums and that weird bugle call, and I can't begin to tell you how reverently serious the atmosphere was." The tour group was then treated to some authentic flamenco music at the "Great Gypsy Tavern," before they joined the roaring crowds of the Easter bull fights.

Curtis first saw Lisbon, Portugal, by moonlight with the help of a particularly knowledgeable tour guide, who later brought them to Pena Palace, a location of personal significance to him, in the city of Sintra. She explained, "Our [Oxford-educated] guide lived there [in the palace] as a boy. He showed us his part of it, described the incidents that happened, and we got lost in the past history. The guide's father was a member of [King Manuel II's] court, was a very good friend of the king, and lived in this castle [...before] the king was compelled to flee Portugal [to England] during an uprising."[1]

The (1951) Easter tour continued to Morocco, which had developed considerably since Curtis was last there in 1943. She excitedly went looking for all her familiar sights in Casablanca, and also throughout Rabat ("as beautiful as ever"), where she found her old ARC club building repurposed as an art gallery. "I even found the garage where I used to keep the car!" She then described her arrival in Egypt, where, "Before the plane doors opened in Cairo, there were shouts of, 'Where is Miss Curtis?!' And, as soon as I stepped out, the reception committee's cameras began snapping. And that was the start of the 'royal treatment,' which I was accorded by the [local Busseti representatives]." Among other diversions, she was eventually brought to a local shop, where the guide "tied a face-veil on me, [...] and off we went to visit everyone that he knew in the bazaars!" The tour group departed for Giza, that afternoon, while Curtis stayed behind temporarily to catch up with an old British major from World War II that she'd befriended in Rome.

> [My guide] accompanied me, and then rushed me out to mount my camel and ride from the Sphinx to the Pyramid. I think that I'd reduce my middle rapidly if I took up camel riding as a serious exercise! [Not to mention] that back-breaking crawl through the low corridors to the queen's tomb! And down an inclined ladder, backwards! I was certainly glad of my early PE training. We stopped for tea [...] and watched the sun set behind the Pyramid, and then [my guide] and I went for a sail for an hour on

Katharine Whitney Curtis (*center*) with representatives of the National Egyptian Tourist Office, Giza (Easter 1951).

the Nile in one of their big, heavy, strange-sailed ships. [My guide] and the Arab boat boy sang weird Egyptian songs, and I kept pinching myself, saying, "Really, old lady, this is you!"²

By April 2, Curtis was en route to the Old City district of Jerusalem, which was then partitioned between Israel and the Kingdom of Jordan.

The U.S. tour group was met by another eager welcome committee, which included Dr. Musa Husseini, director of the Arab Tourist Agency, who would later that year be executed for participating in the July 20, 1951, assassination of Jordan's King Abdullah I.

We arrived in time for lunch, and then [...] we went to the Mount of Olives first, and from there to the Garden of Gethsemane, where eight olive trees still stand and are alive that once sheltered their Creator. [...] We entered the city through St. Stephen's Gate, [...and] it was all very impressive, due to the excellent guide, who created a dignified, reverent atmosphere, and certainly knew his bible. I am ashamed that I knew so little that I couldn't ask intelligent questions, but I "soaked up" a lot of the general information and "atmosphere." [...] We tiptoed around, spoke only in whispers, and it was awe-inspiring to find oneself standing on the spot where Christ was crucified.

[...On April 3], we stopped at a hotel in Jericho to get something cool to drink, because it was blistering hot. [...] And, on the way back, we passed again the huts of thousands of Arab refugees who were thrown out of Israel by the "illegal" occupation of certain areas by the Jews. There they sat, baking in the blistering sun, and Jordan with no means to develop an economy capable of absorbing them! Upon our return to the hotel, I had cocktails with the governor [of Jerusalem, Ihsan Bey Hashim], and Mr. [S. Roger] Tyler, the American consul in Israel. [And then we] visited all the hotels with Dr. Husseini, and had dinner with him and Father Eugene Hoade, a Franciscan who wrote the official *Guide to the Holy Land* [1946]. By that time, I was completely confused and ignorant, and I welcomed the opportunity to seek some information from those worthy gentlemen.

After dinner, Father Eugene gave us the historical background of the area, and Dr. Husseini gave us the present-day situation, and then the meeting was thrown open for questions, all of which were most stimulating, and opened our eyes to the need of a better understanding on our part of the present

Israel-Jordan question. [...] The governor and I accompanied Dr. Husseini to his home for the rest of the evening, and, during that time, I collected a list of books to read, to help clarify my thinking.³

While the 1951 Easter tour consisted of many other interesting stops throughout Turkey and Greece, it's more important to understand the surrounding historical context of Curtis's visit to Jerusalem.

Since the United Nations' two-state partition of Palestine in 1947, the Arab rebellion in 1948, and Israel's wartime expansion in 1949, the "Green Line" border of Israel and Jordan now ran along the West Bank (of the Jordan River) and through the Old City district of Jerusalem. It was during this latter wartime expansion that many Palestinian refugees

Curtis looking up at the Great Sphinx of Giza (1951).

were displaced into makeshift settlements, with some of these many "huts" ending up between Jerusalem and Jericho (West Bank) for Curtis to witness firsthand. And it's clear that she received her initial political education on the "Israel-Jordan question" from a distinctly Palestinian perspective: the doomed Dr. Musa Husseini, who, "When faced with evidence and proofs [after the assassination of King Abdullah I], admitted to his part in the crime, and confessed that he held meetings with the conspirators at both his house and at the offices of the Arab Tourist Agency."⁴ After the details of Husseini's criminal involvement were reported by *Time* magazine, Curtis exclaimed to her mother on September 9, "When I read about his [death] sentence, I got gooseflesh all over me! What a world we are living in!"⁵

Curtis had returned to Nuremberg by the start of summer, and made a special trip to Switzerland with Renate Renk, who "had never been outside of Germany before, and it was quite an experience for me to observe her while she discovered that there were good things outside of Germany!"⁶ They continued growing closer as friends, in and around Nuremberg, and Curtis departed for another Special Services tour on October 19 to France, England and Ireland. She wrote about feeling like an old lady after visiting a local hangout for existentialists in Paris that was "crowded with young men who need haircuts, and girls in [masculine] 'George Sand' trousers."⁷ She then traveled to London, just in time for the October 26 reelection of Prime Minister Winston Churchill, whom she spotted with "Mrs. Churchill [as they] came out of their Conservative headquarters in the same building as the Cosmos [tourism] office. And she looked very happy, but he did look weary!"

In Ireland, she was greeted by more local travel representatives, who "dubbed me 'Katie Darling' at the first handshake." They spent some time exploring the capital before ending up at the Gresham Hotel, "The most modern in Dublin, quite deluxe! Here, there was a marvelous lunch prepared, and maybe you think that I wasn't proud sitting at this grand table with four good-looking Irishmen, right next to the luncheon table of the new US ambassador to Ireland [Francis P. Matthews]!" Curtis explained further, that "one of [these] Irishmen was a newspaper writer, and the following quotation appeared in his 'Tatler's' column of the *Irish Independent*," Dublin's daily paper, on November 5:

Curtis balancing against the wind.

Mrs. Katharine W. Curtis is a friendly, unassuming, and informed American lady with a winning way, a wise head set on experienced shoulders, a warm heart to offset it, and an unusual job. It was that job, and a dash of Dublin blood [referring to Francis and Arabella Rankin] that brought her on her first visit to Ireland [...] to [eventually] help and encourage the American solider in Germany to take the opportunity to see and meet his new neighbors in Europe. [...] It is Mrs. Curtis' duty, determination and hope to make him take a wider and more intelligent interest in the countries around Germany.

Most of her time, [Curtis] spends at a desk dealing with army papers. Whenever she gets a chance to travel, she does. [...] She believes in seeing a country before she tries to sell it.[8]

This "Tatler" article continued describing Curtis's tourism strategy, and how much she enjoyed Ireland and planned to return. She was later assured, by a local colleague, that "not everyone can be so fortunate as to make the grade with the 'Tatler,' [so] congratulations!"[9]

Curtis stayed in Nuremberg throughout the winter holidays, and wrote to her mother in early February 1952 about not planning to visit the U.S. because of the upcoming summer Olympics in Helsinki, starting on July 19. She also commented on current events:

As for [General] Eisenhower, I personally don't think that he will ever run for the presidency. I am sure that he knows that he will be of far greater value to the world welfare in his international position than as president of the US, in spite of all the wishful thinking of the politics at home. [But] I don't see presidential timber any more than you do, Mom. We're certainly in a queer status! Many other "army folk" feel as I do over the idea, [...but] I can't speak for the [average] GIs because I'm never with them anymore![10]

The Helsinki Olympics

In a Valentine's Day card to Estelle on February 11, Curtis revealed that "synchronized swimming will be demonstrated [for the first time] at the Helsinki Olympics, in the latter part of July. [...] I'm terribly thrilled, and I only hope that I can stretch my leave-time to include a trip there, too!"[11] Two days later, an article was prepared by the EUCOM public information office "for immediate release," and all those local "army folk" were educated on Curtis's unique background, going all the way back to the 1934 Chicago World's Fair.[12] After this summary was published, she wrote again to her mother on March 9, commenting, "Now that the folks around here think that I am a character, [ever] since the article in the *Stars and Stripes*, I find that (at long last) I have been 'accepted' (and that I'm inclined to think that it's going to be a nuisance!)."[13]

In the same letter, she provided her mother with an equally revealing remark, "I did tell you (didn't I?) that I was never further from matrimony than I am at this date! [Although, I recently told my human-resources colleague] that I was thinking of it, so that she would let me turn in one of my policies, so that I would have a few pennies in the bank somewhere if I ever had to leave this job suddenly. She wouldn't let me convert it unless I told her some such story."

By this point, it's worth noting that Curtis seems to have fully embraced the lifestyle of an "unattached female," in spite of all the social stigma and institutional inconveniences of her day. And, regardless of what she pursued (only six years prior) with John Brock, it was the lack of any overruling relationship commitments that afforded her the flexibility not only to travel the world, but to operate as independently as she instinctively preferred.

Three months before the summer Olympics, Curtis returned to Greece for another Easter tour in April, flying with a group to Athens on Good Friday. They arrived at dusk, and were thrilled by the unexpected sight of countless Greeks carrying candles throughout the city. Curtis affectively described, "As we peered down through the gathering shadows, each city square was proceeding with its own celebrations, and the streets radiating from each square were crowded with tiny glimmering candle flames. The scene looked like a huge ant hill, with lines and lines of ants, with each bearing a shining grain of pure gold! Never will I forget it!"[14] Among various other religious events, the most important of them involved King Paul of Greece, such as the Easter egg-cracking ceremony that Curtis witnessed. She ended her trip by flying through Naples to stop in Capri and reunite with her old ARC secretary, Olga Kartzow, and the "little old [Russian] Princess Elizabeth [von Wittgenstein], Olga's mother."

By May 11, Curtis was starting to complain about chronic stomach pains, explaining to her mother, "At present, it aches at odd intervals, usually about 3:00 a.m. So I just allow myself more hours in bed, and call it a night! When the ache comes, I rise and walk the floor until it subsides (about an hour), and then I crawl back into bed."[15] She initially

A publicity photo from her office in Nuremberg (1952).

attributed this discomfort to her diet, or perhaps her gallbladder, but wouldn't discover the true cause until after the Olympics.

One month before departing, she typed up a letter on June 30, 1952, with an important update: her close German friend, Renate Renk, had married a local Waldorf schoolteacher named Wolfgang Dullo.[16] And, although this might have altered the dynamic of their camaraderie as two single women, Curtis supportively used her travel connections to send the young couple to Rotenberg on a special (and otherwise unaffordable) honeymoon. Also by this time, the Marshall Plan's funding was concluding, after four years, with western Europe having made indisputable progress toward a full economic recovery. As expected, this new strength among the western democracies provided a stark contrast with their more bitter Soviet neighbors, who—along with Israel (and a new aquatic sport)—were soon expected to make their first Olympic appearance in Helsinki.

On August 9, Curtis wrote her public newsletter about this important historical landmark for synchronized swimming:

> I had received word from Mary Derosier (national chairman of synchronized swimming) that there would be a group of American and Canadian girls there [at the Helsinki Olympics] to demonstrate and exhibit synchronized swimming, in the hope that the International Rules Committee would accept it for future competition. And I felt that I must get there somehow.
>
> I finally left Nuremberg on Thursday morning, July 31, […] arriving at the end of my journey, midnight of that same day! […On] Friday morning [August 1], I called Mary and made a date to meet her at noon, then I gathered up my maps of the city and set out on a walking tour of the city to get my bearings. […] The linden trees were all in bloom, and the air was filled with their sweet scent, mixed with the odor of the ripe strawberries and raspberries in the market! And the gay, international flags, flying from their standards along the avenue, were most exciting! I found Helsinki to be a very clean, cordial and gracious city.
>
> […] I met Mary and several of her girls for lunch, which we had in an open-air place, set up specifically for Olympic service. […] Friday afternoon, I went out to the Olympic pool with the girls, and met the whole group. There were four girls from Detroit […] who were present as the "outdoor champions," I believe. Beulah Gundling represented the solo, and three girls were there from Canada. […] They were a grand group of girls, who swam like real "synchro kids." They were allowed to perform each day before the scheduled swimming program, both the afternoon and evening programs. And, at the final FINA gala—staged by the International Swimming Association after the end of each Olympics—there were two fifteen-minute spots allowed for "synchronized," with an audience of fifty-thousand, including all foreign swimming teams and their coaches. I found that the spectators [including Prince Phillip of Edinburgh], as well as the swimmers, were enthralled and very enthusiastic. And the girls were excellent!
>
> Saturday morning, four of us took a sight-seeing bus trip of the city, […and] back to the pool we went for the afternoon events, which included the woman's high-diving, with Pat McCormick. By the time that I had gotten something to eat again, I was so dead tired that I fled to my comfortable room, and I was in bed and asleep before 9:00 p.m. I guess that I'm not as young as I once was!
>
> Sunday morning, I went out to the pool so that the girls could show me all of their routines, which I had not already seen. […] After the closing ceremonies, we all fought our way from the stadium to the pool, where the FINA [gala] was scheduled to start almost at once! And, at the end of this affair—almost midnight—we (the girls and Mr. Gundling) went to a nightclub restaurant to eat, and it was 3:00 a.m. before I finally got back to my room.
>
> […] The International Rules Committee met and decided to accept the rules, as proposed, for all three events: the solo, the duet, and team numbers. So, synchronized swimming has come of age![17]

Additionally, Curtis would later recall to her family that, somewhere among all these Olympic ceremonies or casual meet-and-greets, a ceremonial Olympic torch was lit in recognition of her presence in Helsinki for these demonstrations. But, in another sense, she was joyfully "passing the torch" to a new and vibrant generation of swimmers and coaches, especially Beulah and Henry Gundling, whose invaluable contributions of time (and significant resources) would build upon the sport's collaborative efforts toward Olympic acceptance.

Shortly after Curtis's return to Nuremberg, her chronic stomach pains worsened to the point of landing her in the hospital. She explained this situation (and other recent events) to Estelle on September 25, 1952:

> Sure enough, there was a big, fat gastric ulcer in almost the same spot the other one was, two or three years ago [in the summer of 1950]. As a result, this letter is being written from a bed in the sixteenth field hospital, here in Nuremberg, where I have a nice little private room. […] I hadn't had any pain for the past week, so I don't anticipate any more, here, on that monotonous "sippy" diet. I am told that I must remain in bed for the next week. […] In the next ten days, I should show definite signs of healing.
>
> […] As you probably read in […] my newsletter, I got to Helsinki. Personally, I wish that I had been in charge. The synchronized swimming itself was OK, but it certainly could have been much more attractively presented, I thought. However, the point was accomplished, in that the sport was accepted, and that everyone liked it very much. I had a nice chat with a woman coach from Rio, and saw [various other important officials]. I'll finish this tomorrow! Here comes the pill!
>
> […Saturday…] Jane writes that Annie is aging. She's now seventy-six, and she won't follow the doctor's suggestions. Her legs are quite badly swollen, and she's apt to "pop off," any day. I only hope that she doesn't have a stroke, up there [on Washington Island], alone. She still plans to spend this winter up there again, and I hope that it's not too severe![18]

Despite the initial prognosis, Curtis was actually bedridden for over a month. She wrote her final hospital letter on October 31 with some rare words about her outlook on religion and politics:

> Dearest Moth,
>
> The Doc has just been here, and I am to leave tomorrow morning. The ulcer is completely healed, […] and everyone is very happy over the whole affair; me most of all, because I've heard so many sad, sad stories since I've been here, that I'm full to running over [with tears, figuratively].
>
> And a funny thing happened just now, when I was in the office, phoning. The Episcopal chaplain (a handsome captain) was in, making arrangements to give some woman communion in the morning, and I up and said, "I'm one of your backsliders,

Curtis en route to Nuremberg (1950).

Captain. I bawled so loudly when I was being baptized [as an infant] that none of my brothers or sisters were baptized. And, sometimes, I really feel guilty about it!"

And, Lord bless him, didn't [the captain] say, "Why don't you join us for communion tomorrow morning?" Whereupon I almost fell in a dead faint, and told him that I'd never had communion! So, one of these days, I'll drop into his office and "talk religion" to him. His office is right in the same building that I'm in, so it won't be any great trouble. And I've never discussed religion with anyone. And he's right good-looking (wouldn't he be if he's an Episcopalian?), about thirty [years old]. I think it will be quite an experience, because all that I seem to believe in is the good old "golden rule." What a time he'll have, trying to make me believe in "religion." Don't you wish you could listen in?

At any rate, five weeks in a women's ward of an army hospital is enough to sour anyone. I never knew there were so many American women in the world with nothing between the ears—with everything for a happy life, right in the palm of their hands, they sit around griping and letting it slip through their fingers. And so many of them just can't adjust! Thank heaven "adjustment" has always been comparatively easy for me!

[…] I'm so pleased. I got my [absentee] ballot from Chicago, after all, [to] cast it for Ike Eisenhower, in spite of all [the rhetoric] that ass, Truman, has been sounding off about. I can't tell you how much damage to the US that this mudslinging has done, as far as Europeans are concerned. They just can't picture the president of the great USA stooping to what Harry T. has done. And I can't, either! I, too, don't understand McCarthy. But I guess that there must be fire where there's smoke.

[…] I must stop now, as I have several notes to get off before I get back into the swim of things again. I'm feeling fine, but know that I get tired quickly.[19]

Curtis soon returned to the office and reported feeling better (after losing some weight), while never mentioning whether she actually talked religion with the military chaplain. She wrote to Estelle on December 14, 1952, revealing, "I got a letter from Jane [during Thanksgiving week], saying that Mother was hospitalized in Sturgeon Bay as the result of a slight stroke on November 24."[20] As feared, Anne Townsend Whitney's health was sharply declining (at almost 78 years old), with new evidence of "a palsy of some sort" in her handwriting after the stroke. With these new considerations, Curtis started considering a return visit to Ferda Lokin much earlier than expected, "To look over the whole situation personally. […] And should Mother die, I would have to pay my own transportation if I wanted to come home [for the funeral]."

Curtis spent New Year's Eve quietly at home in Nuremberg, and wrote to Estelle amid the ambient atmosphere of celebration:

You couldn't have sent me anything that I'd have liked more than that very excellent likeness [of you]. It stands on my dresser, affording me such a fine feeling of comradeship. […] Tonight, the whole neighborhood is filled with banging firecrackers and screeching fireworks! I never knew Germans celebrated that way! It's quite nerve-wracking! I've decided that there's no better way to start a new year than in chatting with old friends, so here I am! My friends can "guzzle" all they want, but that's not for me. I had to "fight them off," and I suppose they think that I'm just "queer," which is OK by me. […] Maybe, if I start [1953] with this chat with you, it will auger that I'll write to you more often. At any rate, I can now talk to your picture![21]

Kite Without a Tail

On January 20, 1953, the newly elected president of the United States, Dwight D. Eisenhower, addressed his country with a particularly stirring summary of the times, including the perils of Soviet communism in the Nuclear Age, with an emphasis on America's new role as the leader of the free world. President "Ike" swore his oath upon George Washington's bible, and the Cold War continued along its precarious course. Meanwhile, a much-affected

Katharine Whitney Curtis—who once shared a World War II Christmas with Eisenhower (and 200 Italian children) on Capri—switched off her radio in Nuremberg and started writing, "Dearest Moth, I just listened to the direct broadcast of Ike's inauguration (7:30 p.m. here!), and even more thrilling than the ceremony was the thought that you were listening to the same thing on Washington Island. [...] Life can be thrilling, can't it? Did you weep, too?"[22]

A week later, she continued her discussion with her mother about returning home in either spring or autumn (1953), depending on when she could be granted leave. She regarded this upcoming furlough as another opportunity to bring her mother back to Europe, and, in the same letter, she responded to her mother's standing counteroffer, clarifying, "I haven't any desire to come home and teach [in Chicago], Moth. I don't want to live in a city any larger than Milwaukee. And I don't want a job with a lot of financial responsibility." Curtis was intent on staying to work in Germany for at least five more years, in preparation for retirement. And, while attempting to assure her mother about the relevant pension details or her ideas for supplementary revenue streams, she concluded by saying, "Don't let my future worry you. It will all work out somehow. It always has."[23]

The likelihood of returning home before 1954 wavered throughout the next few months, until she received word that her mother had a second stroke, by late April 1953, when this news was passed along to Estelle:

> This time, her eyes and her legs were affected, and she was in bed for two weeks with neighbors taking care of her. She refused to go to the hospital! And she won't leave the island, either. She seems to be convalescing satisfactorily, and Jane has written to say that I should not plan to come home, that there's nothing I could do, that Mother may last a long time (or that she may go suddenly at any time).
>
> [I am just sitting tight and waiting] because money will become more and more essential, particularly, if Mother is invalided (I must think of my own future also). It's a pity that Mother must be alone, up there, but she has chosen it that way, so she can't be too unhappy. Mother seems to be "crawling around" well enough to prepare her own food again, and she has written to me, long-hand [with even more obvious signs of a tremor]. It's too bad that her attacks always come at holiday times, because Jane always has previous plans that she hates to have upset—so she's never very nice about going up to see Mother, or to bring her down to Milwaukee for a change! Oh well! There's nothing that I can do to change their personalities![24]

It was with this reluctant plan of "sitting tight and waiting" that Curtis returned to Ireland in May 1953 for another travel tour. It was on this trip, among other cultural activities, that she kissed the famous Blarney Stone to acquire the "Gift of Gab" in County Cork, while also traveling through the town of Cashel, the ancestral hometown of her (4X) great-grandfather, Archdeacon Daniel Hearn.[25]

By mid-summer, she was assembling more concrete plans to return home in September. On June 9, she wrote to her mother, explaining, "I'll do whatever you'd like to do. But I won't be able to get home again 'free' for two years."[26] She continued saving up leave-time through August 20, when it was revealed to Margery Turner, "I just received orders today that I would be flown home 'on about August 30.' I'm going straight to Chicago, [...] then to Washington Island through Milwaukee. I'll have only two weeks, and what I do will depend on Mother's desires. I think that my return trip will be by ship from New York [in October]."[27]

Indeed, the next letter of significance was written from New York on October 9, after Curtis had already visited with her mother:

> Dear Estelle,
>
> The die is set! I board the army transport, "General Patch," on Monday morning to start my return voyage. I wish that I were just arriving, but I don't regret any of the wild scrambling that I have been through. I only wish that I'd had more time.

[…] I got to New York when it was clouded over and "misted" (a "soft day," as the Irish would say!). Carl [T.] had planned a small cocktail party at the gorgeous modern apartment of one of his friends. […My] old ARC friend came to the party and spent the night, here, at the Shelton Hotel with me. The next morning we spent gossiping, and Carl joined us for lunch; […] after which, Carl and I walked to "the apartment," where we […] met some friends, had dinner, and "did" some of their favorite "spots."[28]

While still in New York, on October 11, Curtis described this portion of the trip more explicitly to her mother, who was more progressive than Estelle:

I'm pooped out today. […] I've not had a second to relax, after [some friends] and I "did" the UN building, yesterday afternoon, and "The Village," last night. […] I called Carl [T.] and told him that I couldn't take another cocktail party ("gay.")

[…] All of Carl's friends are gay, and they took me in like a long-lost relative. I'll write the details from the ship, but I can't seem to burn a candle at both ends as I used to![29]

Her friendly host, Carl T., was most likely part of her mother's extensive network of "interesting characters," all of whom Curtis admired and naturally got along with. As promised, she wrote more about this from "aboard the General Patch" on October 19 (1953):

Dearest Moth,

I've been on board one week to today. […I'll] be back in the old rut again, wondering if I really ever was "back in the States," and wishing that I'd had enough sense to take the whole leave-time right on Washington Island. But, I'm always so afraid that I'm going to miss something that I rush around, trying to see everyone that I miss. As a result, I really was dead when I finally reached New York.

[…] Carl [T.] has found his "real love!" in the form of a young Jewish dress salesman, Max [R.], who has an ultra-modern apartment that cost him $10,000 [or over $94,000 in 2020] to have it decorated! […] We spent much of my New York time there, looking at his [new] television or listening to his records. Carl gave a small cocktail party there for me, the day I arrived (the usual types attending). These happened to be the personal secretaries to individuals who had penthouse apartments, so the conversation was quite interesting. Then, Carl and I "did" some of the "gay" bars [in "The Village"].[30]

Curtis wrote about exploring Greenwich Village from what were the earliest days of the underground LGBT cultural revolution, a movement (including Beat poets like Allen Ginsberg) that was responding to the wider social repression of homosexuality throughout the 1950s. This letter from New York was ultimately one of the last sent between Curtis and her mother, just after their September-October 1953 visit. Curtis continued describing the details of her relatively peaceful voyage across the Atlantic, and also wrote about wanting to reserve "wire space" for an international phone call with her mother around Christmas. She resumed her regular work schedule in Nuremberg, among continuing visits with Renate, and left for Capri in late December to spend the holidays with Olga Kartzow and Princess Elizabeth von Wittgenstein.

Anne Townsend Whitney died on a Sunday, February 21, 1954, and this news was confirmed to Curtis in Nuremberg on February 23. After fighting for a free moment at work, she wrote a cathartic letter to an old friend, Dr. Victoria Vacha:

It was certainly nice for me that your valentine letter arrived, today, […] because Jane's cable about Annie's death came late this afternoon, too. And, no matter how long one's been expecting it, the pit of one's stomach squirms a bit. Of course, it's a blessing that she didn't become a bed-ridden invalid, but how difficult it must be when one's mind remains clear, while the body falls apart. I don't think that I could stand medicine, Vic. Death just tears me apart when folks struggle against it. I certainly hope that, when my turn comes, I can accept it, relax, and let nature take its course!

[…I'm] actually glad that I got home in September! Since my return [to Germany], we are no longer given free transportation to and from the States on our inter-contract leave, so I'd have been "stuck" to pay all my expenses if I chose to come home. However, Jane and I had settled that, while I was home, there was no need for me to come home for the funeral. Now, I hope that somebody will sit down and write me the details. I'm sure they'll all have ideas about what I should do with Ferda Lokin, too. [...] I'd really <u>love</u> to come back, right now, if I could <u>afford</u> to, and just sit up there doing just whatever I <u>wanted</u> to, <u>when</u> I wanted! But, no! I'll struggle along over here for at least five more years, I guess, and try to build up some more "retirement." I hope the health holds out![31]

Curtis also reported this news to Estelle on March 2, with some additional details and reflections:

> If you have not already learned of it, this note is just to let you know that Annie "moved on." [...She] was bedridden, the last three weeks, in a nursing home on Washington Island, and Jane was good about keeping us informed of each change. Finally, I phoned Jane on [February 21] to <u>hear</u> what was what. At that time, they told me that it was only a matter of hours, and the end came that same day [with a confirmation cable on February 23]. The only word that I've had from Jane <u>since</u> then was a cable, stating, "Funeral Wednesday [February 24] on Island. All going."
>
> I guess it's lucky for everyone that she didn't have to linger as an invalid, but I'll sure miss her correspondence!
>
> I've had so much work to do that I haven't had any time "to think." But, today, I am home with a nasty cold, so I thought that I'd best catch up on some correspondence.[32]

Curtis received the full story of her mother's passing by March 14, when a more emotionally revealing letter was written to Estelle:

> Jane finally got around writing me the details of mother's death. Her last three weeks in the nursing home on Washington Island were at her request (instead of the hospital), and were filled with one stroke after the other until she was completely helpless, when she slept herself away. I'm very glad that she was [buried] on the island. It gives me more of an anchor there. Right now, I feel like a kite without a tail, but I know that I'll strike another balance soon.[33]

Anne Townsend Whitney's obituary was published around the time of her funeral, stating, "Anne Whitney (née Townsend), seventy-eight years old, Washington Island, died at her home. [...And] before moving to Washington Island, about eighteen years ago [in 1936], her family lived for many years in Chicago, where Mrs. Whitney was a social worker and library worker. She was one of the founders of the Washington Island Garden Club and the Community House, and she was very active in many island activities and projects."[34] Curtis made arrangements thereafter for a public memorial fund, and also for the Italian "St. Francis Stone" (that she once salvaged from the rubble of World War II) to be placed by her mother's grave on Washington Island.

Although it's impossible to know what private words were shared by Curtis before her mother's death, it may be significant indeed that one of their last conversations was about Curtis being taken in "like a long-lost relative" by the LGBT community in New York. Perhaps Whitney was already aware of her daughter's potential predisposition, despite the inherent awkwardness of addressing the subject matter directly. But, regardless of anything spoken or withheld, their bond of unconditional love was certainly reaffirmed in unshakable truth before the end. And, as a fitting testament to their relationship, there's one particularly beautiful, honest and encouraging letter that Whitney wrote to her daughter, just over ten years prior, when the uncertain storm clouds of World War II had finally arrived:

> Dearest Katie,
>
> I got your letter from Washington [DC] after I had talked with you on the telephone. It is all very exciting, and exactly what I would do if I were your age. We do have a lot in common, don't we?
>
> I wish that you could profit a little by my experience, but I suppose each one has to have his own [experience] to fit into his own personal case. [...] Don't be <u>too</u> motivated. Old age <u>will</u> creep on, so

call on the privates, corporals and sergeants to lift heavy things where you can—they will love it, anyway—and you just use your brain. Then, when you get back, you'll still be able to fit into some necessary place, whereas you couldn't if you're too worn out physically.

I have in mind two people who went over with the Salvation Army, last war [WWI]. They just had to go back to an old [and boring] grind, because, somehow or other—lack of proper plans, I think—they didn't seem to have anything constructive to offer [afterwards] where it would be interesting and alive.

I am hoping that, in the next ten years, you will have made a name for yourself that will be of use to human beings. You have a swell start, just the way that I would like to have done myself. But, you will do it better, and it will be a great satisfaction to me. There are a few women, all over the world (in every country you will find a few), who have taken the initiative and helped along the road of human progress. More power to you.

It has rained ever since Wednesday, and nothing [productive] has been done on the outside nor the inside, for that matter. There is a tremendous north wind, today, and the west is black enough to satisfy a murder-mystery for Gaylord's best murder mood [imagination].

[…I'm] off to the mailbox. I bet that no big [military] boats crossed today, and that even the little mail boat [for this letter] will have to go to Rowleys Bay, [a more southerly harbor on the mainland].

[…I'm] sure that you are tremendously busy. So do not try to write, if inconvenient. I will take the will for the deed.

See you soon,
Love,
Moth[35]

The Boy Named Wolf

It was on April 11 that Curtis first revealed to Estelle that Renate Dullo (née Renk) was pregnant.[36] Indeed, Renate was actually just about to deliver, and Wolf-Christian Dullo (nicknamed "Cuckoo") was born on April 24, with Curtis later reporting that "he's a sweetie, and the world of the Family Renk-Dullo revolves around him! They still do everything as their great-grandmothers did, which takes an awful lot of personal effort, it seems to me!"[37]

After the death of Anne Townsend Whitney, her youngest daughter, Jane Whitney, was intent on purchasing some Smoky Mountain property around Gatlinburg, Tennessee, from Wiley Oakley, a famous Appalachian mountaineer and storyteller. This enchanting retirement plan also appealed to Curtis, who wrote to ask her sister if they could both live there and grow old together, with the open possibility of selling Ferda Lokin in exchange. But it was soon after reported, "[Jane's] answer was [actually] what I really had expected, but rather hoped it would not be. 'No,' of course!" In truth, Jane was completely exhausted, after having to deal with her mother's practical affairs for so long, so it was bluntly explained to Curtis, "I have no desire right now to live with anyone. In fact, I am just beginning to get a taste of what it means to relax without responsibility for two people, and I love it. […] I want to try to build a place like I have wanted all my life, and that I never expected to have." Somewhat embarrassed, Curtis confessed to Victoria that it was all unlikely to begin with, and "I'll just have to continue my present [short-term] policy, 'Life by the inch is a cinch, by the yard is awful hard.'"[38]

Estelle was quick to mitigate Curtis's feeling of abandonment, and a generous new retirement strategy was proposed (and excitedly responded to) by November 18:

Dear Estelle,

[…] If I didn't think that I'd scare you to death, I'd cable my acceptance of your proposal to join you in retirement. Do you really think that you could stand me and my erratic independence? If you'll promise that you'll tell me whenever I am getting in your hair, so that I can attempt to mend my ways (or we can take a brief holiday from each other), I do believe that we should be able to work something out together. I'd sure like to try it, if you haven't changed your mind in the meantime! So, if it's OK with you, let's start planning together, huh? By the way, don't forget that I'm not very religious, though. But who knows how I can develop in the years ahead?

[...] It's well after midnight, but I wanted you to know (as soon as possible) that I think you are a darling to have thought seriously about us living together. Don't take that "sleeping pill" yet, it's just starting to look as though we might have some fun together after all. Let's hear some more of your good ideas. This one was a honey![39]

Curtis's spirits were clearly lifted by Estelle's offer, and, with a new and exciting familial relationship starting with Wolf-Christian (who would soon become her godson), her definition of "home" was clearly changing. However, that upcoming Christmas (1954) would still be particularly difficult, without her mother, as Curtis wrote to Victoria on January 30 (1955): "I missed Annie more than I ever thought I would, [...and] the remaining family ties are pretty weak!"[40]

For the past few years, Curtis had been working directly out of the Palace of Justice in Nuremberg, and she was soon being featured again in such newspapers as *The Overseas Weekly* on March 13 with her usual résumé of synchronized swimming history and accolades. And, despite "a few inaccuracies and omissions," Curtis exclaimed to Victoria that this particular article (in the aforementioned) was "still pretty good. And what a difference it makes in these snobbish military circles! 'I never knew you were so famous,' etc. etc."[41]

Curtis wrote again to Estelle on April 4—about a week before Easter—asking, "How did you know that I've been looking longingly at that version of the Bible for some time? You must have been a mind-reader. And now, may I suggest (without offending you) that I'd like to send a check to cover its cost; [...] OK by you?"[42] Estelle was a practicing Christian, and would have naturally had an evangelistic mindset toward Curtis, who was indeed becoming more open to that type of conversation with age. Although Estelle's offer to join her in retirement was not likely to expire, it was probably Curtis who made the decision against the arrangement, perhaps because of her admittedly "erratic independence." Estelle would ultimately leave Chicago for Arizona, while Curtis was still destined to retire at Ferda Lokin.

In early June, Curtis mentioned some recent travels in tandem with her plans to become Wolf-Christian's godmother on June 20:

If I'm not careful, I'll have so many of the younger German generation "on my back" that I'll never be able to straighten up! I'm planning to drive up to see the other godchild (in Biedenkopf) over the July 4 weekend, then that's done for this year! It's funny how involved one's life seems to get, no matter how simply one tries to live! I seem to get so cluttered up with people tugging and pulling me every which way.[43]

She was also starting to plan her next U.S. furlough—spring 1956—to be spent entirely on Washington Island. She wrote to Estelle on September 27, 1955, reporting that there was still "no news from George and his family, or from Bob. Everything must be OK, or I'm sure I'd have heard. Gaylord must be about to graduate from college, but I'm not sure!"[44]

In lieu of these family connections, Curtis commiserated in a letter to Jane on December 31 with a summary of community life in Nuremberg, including the night after Christmas that she "spent with Renate, Wolfgang, and their darling baby, Wolf-Christian, [who] calls himself 'Ging-Gang,' and me, 'Tata!' We have great fun together!"[45] She wrote about this again to Jane on January 10, 1956, reporting, "I had a real nice [fifty-ninth] birthday, with lots of flowers. And Renate even brought the baby to the office so that he could deliver a paper lace-trimmed bouquet with a speech, '*Ich habe dich lieb* (I love you). *Ich bin dein Herzlein* (I am your loving little heart).' And he looked like an angel!"[46]

On May 13, Curtis continued to delight in her new German family in this letter to Estelle:

> Renate and I so often speak about you, and wish that you could join us over our coffee cups or soup bowls. The baby [Wolf-Christian] continues to be a darling, and his vocabulary is astounding for a two-year-old. [...] You can imagine how I melt, when that baby voice calls out his greeting, "Dear Tata." We love each other very much, and have established quite an understanding for a pair [that doesn't even] speak the same language.[47]

After Curtis's summer 1956 furlough to Chicago and Washington Island, she wrote again to Estelle on July 18, while passing through New York: "[I've] heard from Renate regularly. She evidently wrote to me every Thursday night, which [is usually] our night to have supper together."[48]

In October, an international crisis began in Budapest, the capital of Hungary, which is about a seven or eight-hour drive from Nuremberg. The Hungarian people had grown restless under the harsh yoke of communist rule since World War II, and, when the state security police fired upon a peaceful student demonstration on October 23, the whole nation rose up in a wildfire revolution that brought down the Soviet-backed government by October 28. But, when it was formally declared on November 1 that the new democratic government of Hungary intended to withdraw from the Warsaw Pact (Soviet satellite states in opposition to NATO), communist military forces invaded Budapest under Soviet orders to set a punitive example. The democratic revolutionaries resisted briefly through November 9, but their skirmishes ended with both a bloody capitulation and the expulsion of approximately 200,000 Hungarian refugees. Overall, this chain of events comprised one of the first substantial rips in the Iron Curtain, and the 1956 Hungarian Revolution would be remembered as one of the most violent and precarious international incidents of the Cold War.

Despite the aftershocks of this crisis, underscoring just how quickly chaos and warfare could erupt anywhere in the world, Curtis remained undaunted. She wrote to reassure a more concerned Victoria Vacha on November 18, 1956, "As for the international situation, things go on here in Europe as usual."[49]

Curtis would eventually write her last letter of that year to Estelle on December 31, describing, "The weather was the most beautiful we've had in my ten years overseas (in Germany). We had a fall of soft snow, covering the trees and ruins 'til everything looked exquisitely unreal. It was heaven itself for the children—with their skates, sleds, and skis—as you can imagine. [...] I had the baby (my two-year-old godson, Wolf-Christian) from 10:30 a.m. 'till noon on Christmas Day, and we went calling together, which was lots of fun because he's really a little angel!"[50]

Her first letter of the new year on January 14, 1957, provided a unique window into the everyday domestic life surrounding her Nuremberg residence at #14 Karl von Linde Strasse:

> Dear Estelle,
>
> I'm sure, by now, that you should have received my Christmas letter. [...] If that's gone amiss, please take this note in its place.
> Renate just came into [the apartment] to put some "bushers" [*sic*] on the legs of my furniture so that they won't scratch the parquet floor! Over here, it seems to me that they spend half of their days taking

General Hastings, wife, aide, and Curtis (*second from right*) touring West Germany (November 1956).

care of the floors! But, while she does this, she insists that I go on with my letter-writing. So here I am, back again.

You see, last week, I had an acute attack of some sort of gastric-intestinal difficulty, which, I think, is due to fatigue. But, I went to the doctor, who started a series of tests. […] In the meantime, I have taken today and tomorrow "off" on "sick leave," in order to make myself rest for four consecutive days. […] And Renate, who can see my apartment windows from her house, watches me like a hawk to keep me from doing anything. And you know me, not being accustomed to being "waited on." It's quite a game! But, I am resting!⁵¹

On March 17, Curtis wrote about another cheery interaction with Renate and Wolf-Christian:

And a cheery St. Patrick's Day to you, my dear Estelle!

[…] I went up to Renate's for dinner, today, and what do you think is the baby's favorite pastime on rainy days (as it was today)? "Doing" a jig-saw puzzle of a map of the USA! And he'll be three [years old], next month! Don't you think that's pretty smart? It's a scream to watch him seeking the pieces that "match," and he does it so quickly!

When I arrived today, he said to his mother, "Please go and lie down and rest, or go into the kitchen and cook, while Tata and I play!" And, when [Renate] persisted in talking, he calmly gave her one of his picture books, saying, "Please look at this book. Don't talk!" And he and I have such good times together. This summer will really be fun! Renate sent her best regards today, as always, and hopes that you've stopped your "falls."⁵²

In August 1957, Renate insisted that Curtis visit a specialist regarding her stomach complaints, which had been growing more frequent and intense. A broad array of medical tests were eventually scheduled, and Curtis wrote to Estelle on October 7, "I [went to the ninety-eighth field hospital] because I was fed up with what my herniated stomach was doing to me and my way of life, and Vic (and the medical staff over here) agreed that surgery was the last resort, but should be successful." During this surgery on September 18, her doctor fortuitously discovered "that I had come in 'just in time,' because the [inflamed] esophagus was all messed up with adhesions, and there was an immediate danger of perforation." She recovered at the hospital after two weeks, and soon reported back to work in Nuremberg, where she concluded her report to Estelle:

> [...] Poor Renate is so upset. She had planned to "take care" of me upon my return from the hospital, but both the baby and her husband have "Asiatic Flu." Upon my return yesterday, I drove up to see her, for just a moment, but I don't want the flu, for sure. So I'm staying away until the family is better. And I am able to take care of myself completely, even if I'm so lazy that I don't want to! One of the girls from the office had planned to spend nights with me [socially], and she has had the flu, too. So, "the best laid plans of mice and men…"[53]

Curtis was writing about what would in fact become known as the (1957) Asian Flu Pandemic, the second major outbreak of influenza in the twentieth century, following the 1918 "Spanish Flu" and preceding the 1968 "Hong Kong Flu." The (H2N2) "Asiatic Flu," although the least severe of these three pandemics, claimed between one and two million deaths worldwide.

The Dullo family would recover well enough, but Curtis reported her own onset of symptoms by October 30, 1957:

> Dear Estelle,
>
> [...] On top of everything else, I've been home (since last Thursday) with a light case of the flu! Just enough to make me feel "sick," so I can't do all the million-and-one things that I'd like to do while "forced" to be at home! Phui! But, by the time that I feed myself, take all my medicines, and straighten up the place, I'm pooped! I can't even enjoy writing letters, because that goofy old left side of mine gets "the twitches" [ever since the surgery], and that's the end! Enough of my griping! Doc said that I shouldn't go back to work 'til next Monday.
>
> [...] P.S. Renate sends her best. She was in bed over the weekend; exhaustion, we think![54]

She then wrote to Dr. Victoria Vacha on November 4 with a more focused account of medical symptoms:

> I'm still carrying around that darn flu bug, but I'm back in the office, and will try to get out to the Doc again. [...] Last night, I had one of those drenching sweats, and had to change the nightshirt and sheets. So, maybe now I'll get well. I'm certainly looking forward to the first day that I can say, honestly, that I'm "well" again. I really can't complain about the operation discomforts. They're coming along just fine. You should see me and my hot-water bottle [stuffing into] bed each night!
>
> [...] Anything that you can send Renate, in the line of clothes, will be most welcome. I'm now having my travel coat made over to fit her. I hate to part with it, but she has no winter coat (except a "shortie"), and I don't need two coats. So it goes! What she can't use herself, her family will be happy to have.[55]

On November 20, Curtis wrote to Victoria with another mention of the Dullo family in Nuremberg:

> [I recently] stopped in to see Renate, and found them busy with Christmas gifts. Renate was making an Advent calendar for Wolf-Christian, and Wolfgang was carving a whole set of farm animals and a toy village! Did I tell you that I was having Christmas dinner with them on December 25?
>
> [...] I went to work all day, today, but it was a German Protestant holiday, and I had no girls there. So, I got bored and came home at 4:30, and Renate came over to give me an excellent massage. [...]

Saturday, Renate and I go shopping. [...] I have to get some ski pants for the godchild in Biedenkopf, and some for Wolf-Christian, too. And so it goes.[56]

Curtis's gift-giving, as part of their local community life, was fondly remembered by Wolf-Christian, many years later:

During the first years of my life, she supported the young family of my parents by organizing goods from the American stores. This is why I was presumably the first German boy living in Nuremberg wearing classic blue jeans. It is very funny, by the way, that Levi Strauss (the inventor of the blue jeans) was born in Buttenheim, about [twenty-seven miles] north of Nuremberg. [And in addition to] her support, Kay also shared the idealism of my father [toward] helping children get a better education. They had vivid discussions.[57]

After Curtis had fully regained her energy and good health, she wrote to Victoria on December 11 about their upcoming holiday season:

My three-year-old [godson] is so noisy! Are all boys that age apt to be? He sure keeps Renate busy! Right now, he's sewing things for Christmas on [Renate's] sewing machine, and her stories of how he "fits" the scraps to her are so funny. I stopped by there, last night, hoping that she'd give me a massage, but they were much too busy. Wolfgang has made a village with gobs of animals (of wood) for "Ging-Gang" [Wolf-Christian], and [Wolfgang] was painting them all! There must have been at least six or eight horses, the same number of cows, and of sheep!

This noon, I ran out to see if they wanted to go to the weekend music [concert], and the father and son were sitting at the dining room table, upon which was a pile of dried peppermint leaves and stems. [Wolfgang and Wolf-Christian] were busy separating the stems, and "bagging" the dried leaves, because they drink "peppermint tea" as a substitute for expensive real tea! While the father and I were discussing our plans, the baby kept looking and looking at me, and finally said (in German), "Tata, do you have new glasses?" And he was right, the observant little devil!

Wolfgang Dullo, Wolf-Christian, Katharine and Renate (c. 1956).

His mother took a great deal of trouble to make him a rather elaborate Advent calendar, one of those things where you open a little window each day of December, and a big window on Christmas Eve. She had carefully cut out little angels, which she pasted behind each window on a gold background. When I arrived, [Wolf-Christian] at once pulled me to see this masterpiece, and watched my face intently, as much as to say, "Are you as enthusiastic about those darn angels as my mother?" And, when I asked him what he thought he'd find behind the big window, he said at once, "A truck!" Poor Renate almost collapsed![58]

On December 30, 1957, Curtis wrote her last letter of the year to Victoria, reporting, "Christmas dinner at Renate's was quite successful. The goose was very tasty, and their tree very gay with its white candles and homemade trimmings. The baby was overwhelmed with all his gifts. This is his first real Christmas. [...Also, Renate] insists on me coming to the house for my birthday dinner. [...] I tried to convince her that a birthday was just like another day to me, but you know how these folks are. So, off I go to a celebration!"[59]

A Second Wind

Curtis wrote her first letter of the New Year to Estelle on January 7, 1958, confirming a full recovery of health: "I'm feeling like I used to feel, years and years ago. I'm just raring to go, all the time, and I can (and do) eat and drink anything and everything at any time. As a result of the recent holiday binge, I've added considerable weight. [...] But, I can't tell you how thrilling it is to feel so well again! Thank heaven I rebounded so well!"[60]

She resumed her typical daily routines alongside the Dullo family, while also traveling sporadically for work. She reported an upswing of social events, including "a monthly dinner meeting of the famous Skål [International] Club, of which I am one of two women members, here in Nuremberg." She continued to Victoria Vacha on February 13, describing that "the rest [of the Skål members] are men, representatives of various travel organizations (and most of them do not speak English). It really is a God-awful bore. They treat me with such respect and deference that I feel like Queen Victoria, but no warmth!"[61]

On March 14, Curtis revealed some exciting details about a new project at work:

Dearest Vickie,

[...] On top of everything else, a short AFN [American Forces Network] radio program that I broadcasted recently was so successful that it "sold" a series of five-minute spots, one every week, starting immediately. So, I had to squeeze in the preparation of scripts. And, today at 11:00, we'll cut two more tapes to last 'til I get back, March 28. These "spots" should be interesting to work on, and I'm fortunate in that our technical information office has an excellent, interested young girl script writer, who has some radio and TV experience.[62]

Throughout the following months, Curtis continued writing about her AFN travel programs, before departing with Renate on a long-expected vacation to Austria. Her job performance was evaluated upon her return, by June, and the administrative officer wrote, "Mrs. Curtis is very competent in the performance of her duties; [...] is extremely interested in her job, and enthusiastically supports her program by training service club directors to encourage the enlisted man to travel while in Europe. She has a keen sense of humor, and a charming personality that radiates enthusiasm."[63]

On June 20, Curtis wrote to Victoria with some more AFN details, and also about a landmark synchronized swimming update:

[I'm] leaving here, next Friday morning, to go to Munich and cut some AFN tapes for my radio program. Did I tell you? I now have a regular five-minute program on AFN (Europe), every Thursday night (8:55 to 9:00), called "Travel Time," and it's quite popular. We cut at least one month's tapes [per taping session].

[…] I had a copy of the *Synchro-News*, and it was the news that the National AAU Synchronized Swimming Committee had offered two names to the Helms Foundation board of directors for their 1958 award for outstanding service to synchronized swimming (the first awards in this field): the names of Annette Kellerman and Kay Curtis!

What do you know? "Sainted" before I'm dead! Even if the directors don't accept these names, I'm quite touched, and will drop Norma Olsen (chairman of the AAU Committee) a note of appreciation! Nice, isn't it?[64]

Also in this June letter, Curtis wrote about now planning to retire in 1962, which would be her final timeline. Interesting circumstances continued to unfold for her in Nuremberg throughout September and October 1958 as she befriended an opera tenor named Cesare Curzi, who would host social gatherings after his local performances. Additionally, Curtis's evening radio program would start airing between *Suspense* (9:55) and *The News* (10:00) on AFN, the whole process of which she continued to find very stimulating, despite the "nuisance" of having to record everything in Munich (a long drive away).

Regarding the Helms Hall of Fame nomination, the aforementioned "note of appreciation" was sent by Curtis to the AAU chairman, Norma J. Olsen, on October 22, 1958. She also made sure to mention her recent brainchild: "spreading the gospel" of synchronized swimming in Israel, where another Special Services tour would soon be sent in December.[65] She then wrote to Victoria on November 22 about recently attending a special synchronized swimming event in Europe:

[A colleague] and I flew up after work on Friday, November 7, to Amsterdam. […] We were met by a representative of the Rotterdam tourist office, with flowers for each of us, and we drove to Rotterdam. […] Sunday, we were "given the sights," […] before going to the synchronized swimming show, which [was the purpose for] this Holland trip.

They were waiting for us, and had saved seats, good ones. The pool was a huge one, [with] one end set up with canvas scenery. […] The chairman of the International Swimming Committee (whose wife coaches the Amsterdam girls' team) met me at the door, and the secretary (who wrote the letter inviting me) soon found us out to welcome our arrival. The chairman conducted the evening program, and gave a brief history of synchronized swimming, announcing my presence in the audience. After the show, [he] gave me a strange little metal "plate," struck off because their club had been in existence for twenty years.

The program, as always, was twice as long as it should have been; first half was vaudeville swim acts, and the last half was "Swan Lake," done very well! […] The swimming was much better than the French and Germans that I have seen to date, and I'll be very interested to attend their first competition in Amsterdam, the weekend of December 13. […] It's a good boost to my morale, and worth the day's leave and expense. It's amazing how worldwide the interest in synchronized swimming has become. […] FINA will be asked at the 1960 [Rome] Olympics to include synchronized swimming in the next Olympics [Tokyo, 1964]. Wonderful, huh?[66]

Despite the fact that synchronized swimming would not be included in the Olympics (officially) until 1984, its growing international interest throughout 1958 was certainly inspiring for Curtis as she prepared to go on the December Israel tour (instead of the aforementioned competition in Amsterdam).

Curtis's strategy was to rendezvous with some potential synchronized swimming contacts in Tel Aviv before spending Christmas in Nazareth, from which she wrote this letter to Victoria on December 24:

I am sitting in a strange little room in the Galilee Hotel in Nazareth. The two younger girls, who are in this room with me, wanted to climb to the top of the hill to see Nazareth bathed in the moonlight. But, somehow, this old carcass just didn't want to push enthusiastic sentimentalism any further tonight. I'm sort of like a squeezed sponge, I guess.

[…] We contacted the man who coaches the swimming team for the Olympics, and I was astonished to find that they have done nothing with synchronized swimming since Beulah Gundling and her husband had a clinic here! They want a teaching clinic, elementary methods, and movies, so I said that I'd let him know all that I could find. And that was that, except that Bob Kiphuth is having a clinic here, next May [1959], and I think I'll write and ask him what "arrangements" the government was making for him. Maybe I could pull somebody over from the States, who knows?[67]

During this Christmas trip, Curtis wrote about visiting many other interesting locations throughout Israel, including the nomadic dwellings of a (cigarette-smoking) Bedouin sheik and his household, "on the desert" around Beersheba.

Some of her first words for the new year were written on January 8, 1959, joking to Victoria, "Now, I wish that I'd been born rich instead of so beautiful, so that I could retire this very minute [instead of in 1962]!"[68] Curtis's next important letters were all written to prospective allies for the cause of kickstarting synchronized swimming in Israel. The most comprehensive summary of her involvement was written on January 22, 1959, to the director of the Israel Government Tourist Office, with these highlights:

Curtis (*center back*) visiting a Bedouin sheik (*front*) and his son (*right*).

Dear Yohanan [Beham],

It was indeed flattering to have you meet us on our arrival in Tel Aviv.

[…] Do you remember that (when I knew that I was returning to Israel) I asked if there was some way in which I, as the creator of "synchronized swimming," could help the Israeli swimmers to develop this sport in their country? While I was in Tel Aviv, I had a conference with Mr. Gyl, of "Hapoel" [an Israeli sports association], who told me that, two years ago, Mrs. Beulah Gundling (US champion in this form of swimming) had been in Israel with her husband, and had given an elaborate demonstration of this sport. Following this effort, the rule book had been translated into Hebrew, but no efforts had been made to teach the activity. [Mr. Gyl] said that he would like to have a clinic on synchronized swimming for the teachers of this sport, and would be interested in any concrete suggestions I could make for such an event.

[…] As you know, my chief interest in this matter is to prevent Israel from falling too far behind in this new aquatic field, which I know they will receive enthusiastically. At present, I understand that there are teams existing in France, Spain, Holland, Belgium, East and West Germany, the Scandinavian countries,

Austria, Hungary, Czechoslovakia, Russia, The United Kingdom, Canada and The United States. The Gundling's have also presented the sport in Asia and Latin America. I understand, too, that the question of including this sport will be considered at the 1960 Olympics.

Because I believe that this sport has a very wide appeal, far beyond the competitive field, I am most anxious that it be presented by a "teaching" staff rather than a "coaching" staff, if you understand the different approaches. The sport has a strong entertainment appeal, and I am sure that it will be of interest to your Israeli hotel owners with pools, and to the recreation centers with swimming facilities, because of this unique entertainment feature. The competitive field can be developed later.

Upon my return to Nuremberg, I wrote to Mr. Gyl [on January 12, 1959], giving him the names of books on synchronized swimming which could be of assistance to teachers, as well as the name and source of the first teaching film on the subject.

[...] If you have managed to live through [reading] this letter to this point, please accept my gratitude for your patience. And I'll appreciate hearing your opinion on this, my latest "brainchild," when you have the time.[69]

In addition to continuing correspondence for this international side-project, Curtis resumed her other activities in Nuremberg throughout the following months: hosting Israeli tourism officials, attending the opera with Cesare Curzi, writing radio scripts for AFN, and entertaining plans for a reunion of the 1934 Modern Mermaids (between other engagements) upon her upcoming stateside furlough in May.

After her return to Germany, she wrote again to Yohanan Beham on July 13, reporting, "I wrote, today, to *The [Jerusalem] Post*, calling their attention to synchronized swimming and its unusual values. I thought that it wouldn't hurt, and that it might help. I suppose that I'll be considered another 'crackpot,' trying to sell my personal project!"[70] Indeed, her letter was published, soon thereafter, in *The Jerusalem Post* with the following pitch:

Synchronized Swimming

Sir, in the Friday, June 6, edition of your newspaper, there appeared an excellent article [...on] "Women and Veteran's Play," which I found very interesting. This letter is a direct result of that article.

In enumerating the sports best suited to Israel interests, the article omitted one which I feel would bear close scrutiny on the part of the sport leaders of Israel. That sport is a form of swimming called "synchronized swimming," of which I am the originator.

[...] This form of swimming synchronizes the swimming movements of the individual members of a team with each other, and the movements of all of them with the accompaniment—be it an accordion, the singing voice, beating of tom-toms, an orchestra, or a recording. It is a type of swimming that has great entertainment value. It offers endless opportunity for creativity.

It is my opinion that it is a "natural" activity for the people of Israel, no matter the age or the sex. I hope that some of the Israel swimmers or representatives of the Wingate Institute of Physical Education will be interested enough to discuss this form of swimming with Mr. Kiphuth, who recently conducted his second swimming clinic in your country.

[...] I, too, will be happy to answer any questions on this matter, should anyone wish to contact me. I am stationed with the US army in Nuremberg, Germany.

[...] I am sure that every individual who participates in synchronized swimming (actively or as an observer) will never regret it! Here's hoping that Israel will find some way to include it in the play of its women and veterans![71]

Not long after this publication, Curtis's invitation was cordially answered by an Israeli swim coach on July 27:

Dear Mrs. Curtis,

In answer to your letter in *The Jerusalem Post* about synchronized swimming, I wanted to inform you that this [sport has been] on the list of activities in the YMCA Jerusalem since 1952.

Mrs. Beulah Gundling performed in Israel [in 1952...and] she was kind enough to teach some of the

Israeli girls her wonderful art. [...] We have here a very enthusiastic team, which will confirm every word that you said about synchronized swimming.

As you kindly offered your help in developing this branch of activities in Israel, we would be very thankful for new literature about synchronized swimming. Our books are at least five years old.

Thanks for your interest in our country, anyway.

Yours, very sincerely,
Dr. [Bella] Wirz [Thannhauser]
Leader of the synchronized swimming group
Jerusalem YMCA[72]

Curtis soon made the requisite inquiries to confirm this information with one of her other Israeli contacts, who wrote to assure her on September 14, "We are well aware of Dr. Wirz' work, [...and] we do not give up hope that [synchronized swimming], to which you devote so many efforts, will find its respectful place in our sports domain."[73]

On September 16, just after it was announced that Curtis's nomination to the Helms Hall of Fame was successfully moving forward, she wrote back to Dr. Wirz with the following updates and response:

> Please forgive my long delay in replying to your good letter of July 27 [1959], telling me about your group of synchronized swimmers in the Jerusalem YMCA. I greatly regret that [none of my other Israeli contacts] told me of your existence. I should so much have liked to see the group and to talk to you personally.
>
> But, to today's matters, if you will let me know what publications you already have on synchronized swimming, I will do my best to see that others reach you.
>
> I have already communicated with Beulah Gundling, who is a very old friend. She has written that she will send a complimentary copy of *Aquatic Art* to me, to send to you. [...] Do you have Betty Spear's [book], *Beginning Synchronized Swimming*? Beulah also asked if you had heard of the loop films put out by Don Canham, [...] showing basic, intermediate and advanced standard-figures in mainly underwater shots, and some in slow-motion, so that details of execution are clearly observed.
>
> [...] Does your team perform in exhibitions in various pools in Israel? Is synchronized swimming taught any place beside your YMCA? Does the Wingate School of Physical Education do anything with synchronized swimming? Does Israel support a series of community, recreation pools where synchronized swimming could be taught? Is there a government office for recreation in Israel?
>
> I don't want to be a burden, but I would appreciate answers to these questions, if and when you have the time. Again, thanks for your kind letter. And greetings and best wishes to your swimmers.[74]

As some of the official announcements for the Helms Award were starting to be published in October 1959, Curtis wrote to Jane for a family update, which was then conveyed to Victoria on November 18: "[Jane] phoned George to find out what was happening to Gaylord, that he now has his master's degree. [But] it looks as though he might end up in the navy. And, also, that he might get married if he goes into the navy! I'm really glad that I'm not a 'young-one' in these hectic and unpredictable days and years!"[75]

On March 30, 1960, Curtis revealed the emergence of an exciting opportunity, which, in retrospect, would provide an appropriate ending to this "second wind" period of her overseas life:

> Dearest Vickie,
>
> [...] Some time ago, the Gundling's wrote to my headquarters asking the Army to send me to the Sixth Annual Aquatic Festival of the International Academy of Aquatic Art [IAAA] being held in Tallahassee, Florida—April 6 through April 10—so that they could make a fuss over my Helms Award. Of course, the Army said that I could [only] go on my own expense, [...] so I turned down the offer. Well! At 1:30 this afternoon, the phone rang in the office, and it was Air India in Stuttgart calling to say that they had just received a single ticket for the whole of West Germany on the inaugural flight

Curtis posing with her Helms Hall of Fame certificate (October 1959).

of their new jet, flying from London to New York, […] and they'd like to offer it to me. […] Boy! I almost died from surprise, […and] it dawned on me that this <u>could</u> mean that I could go to Tallahassee.[76]

After this IAAA event, she was en route back to Nuremberg by April 12, 1960, and wrote to Victoria with a fresh summary:

> Here I am, back here [in a German airport] already. It's raining, as usual, […] and I feel as though I've been on a merry-go-round! And, while I sit here on this bench, my body feels as though the bench were <u>flying</u>! I can hardly wait to fall into my own bed, tonight, for a good night's sleep!
>
> <u>After all</u>, I finally got to Tallahassee, and it was really worth all the efforts of everybody. […] Marge Turner and Bernice Lorber Hayes were there with the Gundling's, and, between [the financial contributions from] all of them, I got space on [a plane] leaving New York (Saturday afternoon), and reached Tallahassee at 9:45 p.m.
>
> Marge rushed me up to the swimming pool, where the kids were <u>still</u> performing. I saw three <u>excellent</u> numbers before we all went to the banquet, where 150 kids (some as young as three years) and their coaches gathered. There were no speeches, but it took some time to award the trophies. […] Then, Henry Gundling called me—from where I had been eating with [Bernice] and Marge—to the main table, awarded me their first-degree trophy (their highest honor), and asked me to talk to the kids. And, when I looked out at those 150 shining faces (with their 300 starry eyes), you can imagine how touched I was! It surely was a once-in-a-lifetime experience.
>
> The team from Canada was there with Pansy Forbes (and many more of the old-time coaches), and all of them were <u>so</u> nice in expressing <u>their</u> appreciation of what I had begun. And it was after 2:00 a.m. when I finally got to sleep. […] At 8:00 a.m., we were back at the pool, where five of the best numbers were performed for me. And the kids took it all so <u>seriously</u>, Vickie, I could hardly <u>stand</u> it.

[…] Briefly, what the kids are doing <u>now</u> looks more like <u>dancing</u> than swimming, but I suppose it will all eventually balance out.[77]

Curtis's remarks about the need for counterbalancing synchronized swimming's historically "artistic" nature would prove especially perceptive, as this issue was key to assuring the sport's ultimate acceptance by the Olympic community. But, despite the ever-critical eye of synchronized swimming's undoubted "mother" and leader emeritus, this April (1960) IAAA festival was nevertheless a satisfying experience, as she expressively reported to Air India on April 25:

> It certainly was an answer to a prayer, and I wish that you could have seen the eager faces of the 150 young swimmers and their coaches […] when the IAAA awarded me their highest trophy in recognition of my creation of "synchronized swimming" many years ago. Both they and I will be eternally grateful to you for making my appearance at the Tallahassee Aquatic Festival a reality.[78]

Auf Wiedersehen

On April 29 (1960), Curtis wrote to a travel colleague, "As you have probably seen in the papers, our USAREUR Special Services headquarters has finally been scheduled to move from Nuremberg to the Heidelberg area by mid–August 1960. This move, among other things, has convinced me that I have served with the army about as long as I wish to, and that I am definitely planning to retire to the States in the fall or winter of 1962. Because of the speed with which time has flown by in the past, I am starting now to 'plan ahead' to this retirement date."[79]

Two days later, the U-2 incident occurred on May 1, 1960, when a U.S. pilot, Francis Gary Powers, was shot down during his top-secret aerial reconnaissance over the USSR. This triggered a swell of Soviet outrage toward Americans as the Kremlin propagandized this undeniable act of espionage, and a major U.S. embarrassment. Powers was eventually sentenced to ten years of imprisonment (combined with hard labor), and he would suffer increasingly intense interrogations. Curtis had been planning an idealistic bridge-building tour to Russia for American servicemen and their families, but shortly after this

Curtis admiring her IAAA trophy in "Fedhaven," Florida (1974).

major upset, she remarked to Victoria on May 18, "Present international conditions certainly don't look good for the Russian trip! I certainly don't <u>want</u> to go!"[80] She continued this dialogue on May 28, concluding, "As for the Russian trip, I still don't really <u>want</u> to go. But, if the <u>tour</u> goes, so go I (from June 20 to July 1). We'll see what the State Department says by then."[81]

Despite the U-2 controversy—or, perhaps, all the more because of it—the Special Services "Russian Tour" began as expected on June 20, and Curtis later wrote a nine-page summary of her personal glimpse behind the Iron Curtain. Their tour group consisted of 30 American civilians in a "deluxe" motor-coach that crossed from Bavaria into Czechoslovakia, as described in the following highlights from Curtis's summary:

> It was 5:00 when we reached the border-town of Waidhaus, and the area of "No-Man's Land," with its electrified barbed-wire fences and guard-houses. The Bavarian guard's radio was blaring, "Walkin' My Baby Back Home," and ["Button Up Your Overcoat"]. We had been warned not to take any pictures.
>
> Ten minutes later, we were cleared by the Bavarians, and were reporting for entrance into the first of our three socialistic republics. [...] During the next three-and-a-half hours, [a guide] told us of the history, geography, and heavy industry of the country, while we noted piles of "Tank Busters" [airplane debris] left from the last war, and red stars on top of all of the industrial buildings.

Four hours later, the tour group arrived at their hotel on Wenceslas Square, Prague, where a crowd soon gathered to watch the unloading of that "luxurious" coach. On Tuesday, June 21, the tour group crossed into Poland, where "it was very depressing [especially in Warsaw], like the whole of Germany at the end of the war: skeletons of buildings staring, empty-eyed, at the sky." On Wednesday, the tour crossed the Polish-USSR border and arrived at the Hotel Minsk, Belarus, where Curtis stayed in a single room, "And, when I entered it, the radio was already blaring out its propaganda. When I couldn't turn it off, I quickly unplugged it from the wall."

She woke up on Thursday, June 23, to "a giggling announcement over the phone, 'Time you to get up [*sic*],' and we were greeted with smiles in the dining room at 8:30 breakfast." Later that day, the tour group had lunch in Smolensk, Russia, where another "crowd gathered around us, in front of the hotel, and gazed at us with sincere curiosity." By midnight, Curtis was in Moscow at the Hilton Leningradskaya Hotel, "Where I retired to my quiet single room (with bath) and its blaring radio, which I quickly unplugged from the wall!" And, after various other diversions, it was on Sunday afternoon, June 26, that their group was first confronted with signs of the recent political controversy:

> After lunch at the hotel, we journeyed to Gorki Park to see the exhibit of the remains of the U-2, [...which] was in a chess club building of the park. [...] In spite of the presence of a line waiting at the entrance, our (obviously) American group of fifteen was allowed in, ahead of the line. We were met at the entrance to the exhibit by another guide, who spoke excellent English, and who described (in minute detail) every section of the exhibit, which was already explained on signs (both in Russian and in English). At the end, she said, "One [member] of your delegation has said that [Francis Gary] Powers should not be punished. I am sure that if one of our men was caught [flying] over your country, doing the same things, that <u>you</u> would punish him. We feel very badly over this, because we always welcome you cordially to our country and treat you well, while you are here as our guests."
>
> I'm afraid that I didn't listen very carefully to her descriptions of the exhibits, because I was conscious that the [badly-disguised] "French person" was standing behind us, attempting to take [propaganda] pictures of us, and that another member of our party saw a man in front of us taking pictures. [But] at no time was there anything else that could have been considered offensive to us.

Curtis's chronicle of the Russian tour was full of many additional details, including their return trip through Warsaw on June 29, where, "Most of us were emotionally affected on our visit to the old [Jewish] ghetto, some of which still remains as it was at the end of

[WWII.]" And her final comments were for July 1, describing that "the Czech-German border crossing was uneventful but dismal, with its 'No-Man's Land' and barbed-wire '[Iron] Curtain.' By 8:00 p.m., I was once again safely home, breathing the air of freedom! My one observation is that the more one sees with one's own eyes, the better position one is in to understand modern political situations."[82]

The last letter before Curtis's transition to Heidelberg was written on July 16, 1960, from a friend's apartment in Lazise, Northern Italy. Curtis highly recommended the Russian tour to Victoria. And, upon being asked about living away from the Dullos, she answered, "I guess we'll adjust OK. It's a strange situation, and too difficult to try to write about it. Renate is to attend a physiotherapy course in Stuttgart, so won't be in Nuremberg when I finally leave. […] As for me, I find that I am becoming more and more selfish, and inclined to 'take care of me' first!" She was also frank in revealing her mindset for the upcoming U.S. presidential election: "It seems to me […] that [Vice President Richard] Nixon would be the best man. But, who knows? [John F.] Kennedy seems so young, […and with] so little 'practical' international experience. However, I really don't put much weight on my personal preferences!"[83]

Curtis's fears about moving to Heidelberg were confirmed by August 16, when she finally wrote to Victoria, "I'm terribly behind on correspondence, but I'm so damn discouraged that I just can't make myself write. I know that I'll get over the shock. I know that I'll once again get into a rut, but I also know that I'll never again be the same person that I was before this move!" She continued to describe the chaos of trying to move "without one [scrap] of help from anyone, except Wolfgang, who helped me the very last week." The new Special Services headquarters gave her an office "worse than a chicken coop (right next door to a smelly old men's latrine)," and a single-room apartment with a shared bathroom. She concluded, "Never have I experienced such conditions, and not one single person in our newly-formed headquarters cares a tinker's darn! No fooling. I've seen a lot in my years over here, but never anything like this."[84]

Curtis managed to adapt to her new environment by September 14, when she wrote her first (relatively) positive report from Heidelberg to Victoria: "Things are shaping up slowly, and I'll soon find a more-or-less comfortable rut into which to settle, until [my retirement in] 1962, if our present regime doesn't wipe out this entire headquarters before then. Things are really being undermined. However, I seem to have become quite 'slap-happy,' and I feel that I'll outlast 'them,' no matter what happens." She was able to seize upon a last-minute opportunity for a different apartment, "The same size as the one I had (but with my own bath)," and her spirits were further lifted when the AFN requested to resume her five-minute "Travel Time" radio programs, which were soon being broadcast (again) across Germany, France, England and Italy.[85]

On October 10, 1960, Curtis reported to Victoria, "Gaylord sent me a nice photo (their wedding picture). I told you that he was in Navy Intelligence School in Pensacola, didn't I? The gal [Caroline] is such a sweet-looking youngster. I do hope everything works out well for them. I hate the Intelligence, but I'm sure that they have no idea what's ahead of them. So, 'where innocence is bliss, 'tis folly to be wise' still holds, and I won't offer any words of wisdom."[86] She also wrote to Victoria about "Travel Time" on October 26, revealing, "My radio program is on again, only, now I'm [writing the scripts] alone. […] I sure hope that it isn't a flop! I only have a five-minute spot, once a month, so I can't do very much. The first one wasn't too good. I'm hoping that the two that I am taping tomorrow will be better; [there's] always some new responsibility in this job, but I guess variety is the spice of my life!"[87] Finally, she proudly reported to Victoria on November 14 that Wolf-Christian had become the best English-speaker in his class; also, "What a pity that Nixon lost. I will watch with great interest, now, to see what Kennedy can really accomplish. Today's radio implied that, in his planned meeting with Nixon in Florida, maybe some cooperation could be expected. We'll see!"[88]

She later revealed that, after spending Christmas Eve in Heidelberg alone with her candles and caroling records, she took the train to Nuremberg and visited the Dullos and some other friends. By January 6, 1961, one of her earlier radio scripts, "Travel Resolutions for 1961" (timed at just over four minutes long), was broadcast with this typical example of her on-air persona:

> Hi, fellow travelers,
>
> Now that the holiday rush is a thing of the past, let's resolve to plan ahead for this year's travel!
>
> Let's not travel like the man who jumped on his jet and dashed off in all directions. Keep in mind these three guides: First, don't expect to do and see everything. Second, don't turn yourself into a zombie by planning every minute over every day and night. Third, don't confine your visits to big cities.
>
> The rewards of travel are gained by osmosis, not by exposure. Remember, always, that the basic purpose of your holiday should be diversion and relaxation.
>
> With this in mind, here are a few 1961 highlights [and attractions, coming soon…][89]

This broadcast also included Curtis's personal recommendations for various countries throughout Europe, from the seasonal carnivals in France and Italy, to the upcoming "Shakespeare Season" in Stratford, England. She concluded by referring her listeners, mostly American servicemen, to the Tours Office at their local Special Services club, before signing off: "Don't forget, that a suitcase in the hand is worth two in the barracks."[90]

She wrote again to Victoria on April 22, referring to a number of important family updates and world events:

> Gaylord's baby arrived ahead of schedule on April 10, and both mother and son are doing well. Christopher was to be christened today, and George and Marion were taking their holidays to drive up for the festivity. […] Gaylord and Carol seem to be very happy, and—for a change—are keeping in contact with me! Carol wrote that the baby looked like his [twenty-six-year-old] father, and I'd say he had his father's "shape."
>
> Carol wrote, "Dear Aunt Kate, the Whitney name will carry on for another generation. Our little boy resembles Gay a little, and I hope that he will continue to grow up looking like his father. Everyone is getting along, even our Pussy Cat, in spite of Gay's 'once-a-day' feeding. We're all so happy that everything seems to be normal. Love, the Whitney's."
>
> [Curtis] Doesn't that sound nice?
>
> […] I'm not even going to get started on the Cuban Situation, or the Russian Space-Man. I wish that we could just settle a few of the minor matters of this old world![91]

This letter was written only five days after the Bay of Pigs crisis of April 17, 1961, in Cuba, where the CIA had failed in an attempt to help overthrow the communist dictatorship of Fidel Castro. And it was just after Christopher Whitney's birth (on April 10) that Yuri Gagarin became the first human in history to be launched into space (in the name of the Soviet Union) on April 12.

The Cold War continued to intensify when, four months later, East Germany started building the Berlin Wall on August 13 to break the steady defection rate of its own citizens. Curtis commented on this "Berlin situation" to Estelle on September 30, which, "Of course, 'touches' the whole army, but hasn't caused the Special Services any special headaches (so far), thank goodness. They are making a lot of loud noises. But, somehow, I don't think that it's going to lead to any great big bust [or military conflict]. But that's just me speaking."[92]

10. Passing the Torch

On October 19, Curtis wrote to Victoria about feeling depressed before retirement, and how she wanted to take advantage of a special "Around-the-World" package tour, which would end where "Gaylord and his family are, on Hawaii, for a three-year [Navy Intelligence] stint. So they'd be there, too, if I hurry!"[93] And she then wrote to Victoria on October 24 about some more immediate travel plans:

> I am trying to coax [my friend (Louise)] to join me on a [1961] Christmas tour to East Africa (seventeen days), which visits Malta, Addis Ababa (Ethiopia), and Nairobi (Kenya), [...where we'd] spend six days (including Christmas) "in the bush" with all the exciting animals and birds. [...] On Saturday, December 30, we'd start the flight back from Nairobi to Khartoum (Sudan); New Year's Eve spent in Cairo. [...And], on January 1 [1962], we'd fly back from Cairo to Frankfurt.
> [...] I'll never get <u>another</u> chance like this! I only hope that Louise will go with me! Christmas holidays in a military community, when you are an unaccompanied female, are strictly "for the birds" [worthless], and I have <u>no</u> desire to go to <u>either</u> of the German families [in Biedenkopf or Nuremberg] and make the other provoked! So this seems to be a pleasant and unexpected solution! And it sure has given my morale a boost![94]

In another letter to Victoria on November 6, she confirmed her plans for an extended stay in Hawaii, while also confirming that "Louise has agreed to take the Christmas safari, and [our work associate] writes that the departure is <u>sure</u> for December 16 [1961]. So, now I'm trying to dig up some 'smart' summer clothes [...because] I'd like to look a little 'snappy' on the safari. Who knows, maybe one of the lions will like me!"[95]

Before and after the 1961 Christmas tour, Curtis would continue writing and recording her five-minute radio spots, which, by their final broadcasts in June 1962, were integrated with Johnny Morris' *Panorama* travel segment on AFN. This integration is apparent in this particularly noteworthy script, which was broadcast on Sunday, February 11, 1962:

> Hi Johnny, what are you doing in the travel line for *Fasching* excitement? [...] "*Fasching*," [...] or "Carnival," is a universal pre–Lenten celebration, primarily in Catholic countries, so it is not restricted to Germany, as I'm sure you all realize. Even <u>we</u> celebrate it with Mardi Gras in New Orleans! Did you know that "Mardi-Gras" means "Fat Tuesday," to indicate that one must use up the fats which are taboo during the Lenten season?[96]

This script is interesting mostly because of the day that it followed—Saturday, February 10, 1962—which is when Francis Gary Powers was swapped for Rudolph Ivanovich Abel on the "Bridge of Spies," Glienicke Bridge, between Berlin and Potsdam, East Germany (within range of Curtis's regular radio broadcasts).

Curtis celebrated her 65th birthday with the Dullos in Nuremberg, and remarked to Estelle on January 15, 1962, "Nuremberg is still 'home' to me! It's really a shame that we had to move to Heidelberg."[97] She also visited the Frost family in Biedenkopf (early March), before being treated to a special farewell by her colleagues, sometime in April, when an American GI escorted her on stage (by the radio microphone) as another Special Services woman wandered in with a "lost expression."

A piano accompanied the announcer's playfully scripted lines, which dramatically summarized the life of Katharine Whitney Curtis up to that point, from her debut of synchronized swimming at the 1934 Chicago World's Fair, to her many ARC clubs throughout North Africa, Italy, and Southern France. Her post-war position as chief of the Leave Activities Office was then chronicled by her various administrative innovations, which "have taken American servicemen and their families on jaunts to the nearest castle, to the word's best music festivals; from the snow-capped mountains to the desert plains, and across Iron Curtains." The crowd acknowledged her more recent Helms Hall of Fame Award, and their ceremony was concluded with a gift from all 24 "Com-Z" service clubs, which presented Curtis with sponsored vouchers for her "Around-the-World" voyage. They "leid" a custom garland of flowers and interwoven travel brochures around her neck, and tied a memorial bracelet around her wrist. Finally, she looked out upon that crowd of grateful smiles and excited bystanders—some of whom were just now realizing who she truly was—before being hailed in German: "*Auf Wiedersehen und gute Fahrt!*" (Goodbye and good journey!).[98]

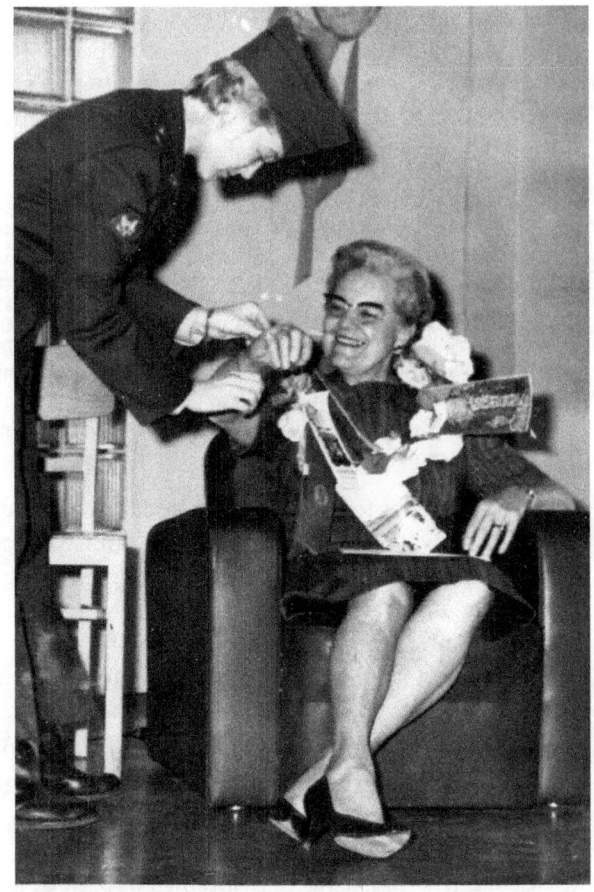

Receiving a gift from her Special Services colleague (April 1962).

11

A Rolling Stone

At the beginning of the 1965 John Wayne film *In Harm's Way*, the camera pans left toward a black-and-white shot of a Navy officers' club in Hawaii. The scene is set as the night before the attack on Pearl Harbor in 1941, and a gathering of officers and guests is revealed next to a pool with some period music and polite dancing. This atmosphere is disturbed by a particularly intoxicated woman, who starts dancing sensually through the crowd. Tom Tryon's character complains on the sidelines of this display and soon petitions the bandleader for a less provocative song. After expressing further indignation, he's consoled by his wife, played by a 26-year-old Paula Prentiss, as they resume their slow dance among the other couples. Prentiss gave her lines at the end of this elaborate sequence, but with one mistake too many, and the director yells out in a thick German accent, "No, no, no! Won't you ever get it right?!"

All the weary extras (local military personnel) returned to their starting positions as Otto Preminger continued expressing his late-night frustration, and Paula Prentiss soon ran off to the adjoining tennis court, crying in the dark. Lieutenant Gaylord Whitney, a few years older than Prentiss, had just returned home from a 12-hour shift at FICPAC (Fleet Intelligence Center Pacific), and was now watching all of this extra drama with his new neighbors on Ford Island. After Preminger calmed down, he fetched the distraught actress himself, and apparently offered a private speech of encouragement. They returned to film what would become the final take from the opening sequence, which still pans across the front lawn of Gaylord's former Navy housing.

The members of this Hollywood production were billeted nearby, and each of the big-name actors were now accepted as just another regularity among that community. Before going to work, Gaylord would often observe "the morning crowd" gathered around a large banyan tree, which was just across the road from the officers' club, and in clear view of the Arizona Memorial on the water. Mrs. Caroline Whitney was frequently chasing after their energetic three-year-old son, Christopher, who would disappear as often as their family's prize-winning Dalmatian. And Christopher's one-year-old sister, Lenore, was also starting to walk by that time, and she was once picked up by John Wayne himself for a brief encounter as he talked with Gaylord about the beautiful Hawaiian morning. On other such occasions, a less-fortunate production assistant was apparently trying to sober up Burgess Meredith at 8:00 in the morning. And, after Patricia Neal accepted the offer to use another couple's bathroom, one afternoon, Gaylord's neighbor comedically fetched that "freshly consecrated" toilet seat and boasted to the crowd, "Nobody's ever going to sit on this again!"

Lieutenant Whitney's work at FICPAC regularly involved classified, high-resolution (U-2) photography, which he specifically used to evaluate potential nuclear targets among hostile nations. Indeed, this was the prospective utility of Francis Gary Powers's clandestine reconnaissance over the USSR. The Cold War had already reached its most extreme tensions during the Cuban Missile Crisis, a couple of years back, when (Ensign) Whitney experienced an eerie and unforgettable week as all the major "ships-of-the-line" began departing from Pearl Harbor. Unnervingly, this precaution was designed to mitigate the cost of an all too possible nuclear exchange with the Soviet Union.

Curtis was traveling between Indonesia and New Zealand during the crisis, which occurred just a few weeks before her mid–November 1962 arrival in Hawaii. Both Gaylord and Caroline remember attending an "Aloha Party" aboard Curtis's ship—a Swedish freighter, named the *Vaasa Leader*—which was apparently allowed to carry a small number of discounted passenger cabins without being considered a cruise vessel. Curtis stayed four months in Lanikai-Kailua with one of her old Special Services friends, and they attended various social events around Honolulu together. They made sure to visit the Whitney family on Ford Island, and it was later recalled (in humor) that she was "always talking," whether it was about her remarkable acquaintances that Gaylord and Caroline would never meet, or about some exotic destinations that they'd probably never visit. She loved "observing the kids," and she'd frequently accompany Christopher on his wacky escapades. Caroline remembers being maternally frustrated, one day, when Curtis encouraged Christopher to keep a shiny old pop can with which he'd become momentarily fascinated. She called it his "treasure," but this romantic attitude toward "trash" just wasn't something that Caroline appreciated, inside the house or otherwise.

The fact that Curtis was prone to long, one-sided conversations was undoubtedly caused by a natural desire to explain herself, after 20 years abroad. But she also made sure to offer several sincere gestures of generosity, including, upon her departure, a sputtering "lemon" of a car that she had purchased for her four-month stay on Hawaii. Most importantly, this was the period in which she gifted her family with that invaluable "General Patton" story, not to mention many other noteworthy tales of adventure. She would continue sharing her stories with as many friends as there were chance diversions before her journey's end. And, luckily for everyone, she managed to write a few more things down along the way.[1]

Prodigal Return

Regarding Curtis's retirement correspondence, most of her surviving words are from general newsletters, which, while being far less frequent, should by no means be interpreted as a sign of inactivity. After returning home to Washington Island in May 1963, she finally managed to chronicle, by December, her extensive "Around-the-World" voyage:

> As many (but not all) of you know, I left Europe at the end of September (1962) and started my long-anticipated "retirement." My German and army friends provided me with two send-off's. One, when I flew from Frankfort to Munich (where I caught my plane for Israel), and the second one, when I left Munich. I admit that it seems strange to think that I might never get back to those places again, but I had so many "dreams" ahead of me that I wasted little time with tears.

Curtis joined with an old work friend in Rome before flying to Israel, and then connected with another traveling companion in Beirut (Lebanon) to explore the Roman ruins at Baalbek.

> Our "magic carpet" trip continued (by air) across Pakistan, up to Kashmir [India], down to Delhi (by car), and around the regular "tourist circle" of Agra and Jaipur. We saw monkeys "on the loose," and

we rode an elephant, just like Jackie Kennedy (and at the same temple). We [were] thrilled over the Taj Mahal in the moonlight, the gay colors of the pink buildings, and the women's *sari* [drape-garments] in Jaipur. I was very much impressed with the memorial to Gandhi, with the golden marigolds strewn over its surface by "the faithful." We thought that we were actually in heaven when we [were living out of a] houseboat in Kashmir. [...] We even saw (and partook of the food from) a Kashmir wedding feast.

[...] It was the festival season in India, and we saw many interesting customs. The most unusual was our trip to Benares on the Ganges River, where, in the early morning, we took a hand-rowed boat out onto the river to see the pilgrims bathing in their religious ritual. This was indeed a never-to-be-forgotten experience.

She flew up to Katmandu (Nepal) for a brief stay in the Himalayas, before continuing from India to Rangoon (Burma), where she marveled over the Shwedagon Pagoda. She then connected with the rest of her official tour group in Bangkok (Thailand), and they all flew to British Hong Kong for some shopping and a visit to the Chinese border, where "the atmosphere was much as the same as the [communist] 'borders' in Europe, pretty bleak."

Curtis traveled through Singapore and various Indonesian cities, before exploring New Zealand (via Australia). It was in between these destinations that the Cuban Missile Crisis occurred, starting on October 16, 1962.

After this encounter with western civilization, we headed for [the islands of] Fiji, where we loafed for almost a week in modern, thatched huts on a sandy shore, making local tours. Then, part of the group (including us) flew to American Samoa, fell in love with it and the simple people, and then rejoined the rest of the party in Tahiti. This was everything that we had dreamed about, and I am sure that none of us will ever forget it.

Curtis wore a traditional Tahitian *muumuu* dress, feasted at a sumptuous *luau*, and witnessed a display of local dances "in a little village, deep in the forest of coconut palms." The tour group took an aquaplane to the neighboring island of Bora Bora, where they "were met by local boats filled with ukulele-strumming young men, with flowers behind their ears, and leis around their necks." She then confessed that she arrived in Hawaii in November 1962 "like *The Man Who Came to Dinner*," a Christmas comedy in which a notorious celebrity becomes stranded in Ohio among conventional locals. Appropriately, this character outstays his welcome as he obnoxiously dominates their household, but the story eventually draws out his more redeeming qualities as he manages to inspire the younger generation to follow their dreams.

In March 1963, Curtis left Hawaii to visit her friends in the Pacific Northwest, before driving down the coast (through Los Angeles) to meet Estelle in Arizona. She continued eastward (through Texas), north (through Chicago), and made it back to Ferda Lokin on Washington Island (Wisconsin) by Memorial Day.

I found [everything to be] in livable shape, and I have been busier than a cat on a hot tin roof ever since; what, with making the place into what I wanted [it] to be, and mixing up into all the island business that I could poke into. I seem to think that I can be "all things" to the Island, and I have done such jobs as to organize a "Junior Tourist Bureau," and to jack-up the Senior Bureau; to donate a "Memorial Community Bulletin Board" in Mother's memory; to act as director of the Island Booth at an arts & crafts fair in Sturgeon Bay (on the mainland); to give a slideshow [about] Washington Island at Ephraim (also on the mainland); to act as a "costumed guide" for two Greyhound Bus tours, which came up from Chicago; and I'm planning to become "Mrs. Washington Island" in the Information Hut at the ferry landing at Gills rock (on the mainland), during the 1964 tourist season. Never a dull moment!

I expect to remain here at *Ferda Lokin* (Icelandic for "Journey's End") until the middle of January [(1964), before traveling around the country again].

[...] Now you are all caught up with me. My health has been wonderful, and, if you don't hear from me 'til next Christmas, you'll at least know where I am and what I am trying to do. I'll be glad to see any of you (at any time) that can find Washington Island on the map. My phone number is Washington Island 155. And I don't think that there is anything better in life than this "retirement scheme." Be sure to try it![2]

Just after her luggage arrived from Europe, she remarked that "every flat surface is [now] covered with 'knickknacks,' and the poor little house looks like an overstuffed museum! Someday, I will weed it all out, but not right now!" By this time, the local island population had been cut in half from the decline of its mainstay fishing industry, and Curtis described how only its tourism business remained. Naturally, her professional expertise in tourism and publicity led to her immediate involvement in various island affairs. She happily declared, "I have enough 'projects' to keep me busy the rest of my life, I am sure. [...] Both the residents and the summer folks, who knew my mother well, have welcomed me as though I were the 'Prodigal Son.' [Mother] has certainly left me a legacy of friendship here, and someone is always dropping in with some little giftie from their garden or oven."[3]

Indeed, Curtis befriended many people around Washington Island, including one particularly appreciative young lad, named Carl Hardee. He later recounted the significance of his time with her in this descriptive testimonial:

> I believe that Kay gave me my desire to travel—to experience and appreciate the far reaches, the colorful peoples, and to appreciate their differences. Kay truly saw and appreciated people in a rare way. She was fascinated by different cultures and customs.
>
> Kay had a great memory, even for the seemingly mundane of details. I remember asking her the size of stones in a castle wall, and she showed me with her hands. She told me stories of eating in a tent with an Arab sheik; describing the tent, the food, [and], with humor, his intent [romantic] interest in a young serviceman she had in her company. She told me stories of crawling under the Pyramids in Egypt, and crossing Africa in an open jeep, with the natives picking the grasshoppers off the front grill and joyfully eating them. She told me of meeting [Emperor] Haile Selassie of Ethiopia, and cracking Easter eggs with the [King] of Greece; [also, about] lying on her veranda to watch the bombing of (I think) Naples, with some army official trying to get her to come back inside.
>
> I spent many days and evenings in Kay's cozy, warm cottage—cluttered with her many souvenirs of her world travels. She had a story to tell about every piece. There were many wood carvings, and, one year, she gave me a carved chimney-sweep that she had bought in Germany. There was a picture of Queen Victoria hanging in the doorway, leading up the stairs. We amused ourselves with the making of handicrafts, using as much from nature as we could. Kay loved nature, being outside, and she thought that Washington Island's economy could be enhanced by selling crafts to tourists.
>
> [...Curtis] seemed to be interested in everything. I don't ever recall her being angry. She had the greatest smile, and an almost guttural laugh. She influenced me more than any other in my life, and I truly feel blessed in having her in my life and heart. She was my "second grandmother."[4]

Carl would also remember that "[Curtis] expressed to me how living among old people both drained and bored her. She thrived on younger people's exuberance and vitality, because she needed that youth to keep herself in balance."[5] Naturally, Carl's youthful enthusiasm stemmed from the overpowering sense of magic around Ferda Lokin, including a seemingly miraculous patch of four-leaf clovers that grew exclusively by the back door. In addition to these colorful memories, Carl's close friendship with Curtis afforded him a rare perspective into some of her more mysterious complexities:

> Kay was her own woman, living a life way ahead of the times that she lived in. She was an independent thinker. Her independence precluded any strong attachment, and she valued her independence far more than any close relationship with men or women.
>
> She was gay. We never talked about it, as that was not done at the time, and it wasn't an important

part of our relationship. It did affect her relationships with others, and I think that she held a lot in that she could have shared, had people's attitudes been more open. You know, she was very briefly married at some point. I remember seeing a drawing of her ex-husband. I think that they were married for only a few weeks. But the only [substantial] relationships with men that I ever heard her talk about were professional, or with gay men.

She did admit that the only regret in her life was that she never had any children. [And I wonder] how different her life would have been, had she been "tied down" with children.

When I told her that I was interested in Buddhism, she was very supportive. She admired Buddhists because they are encouraged to think, and do not blindly accept as Christians are [arguably] required to do. She and one of her lady friends were going to take a cross-country trip in a camper, [and Curtis] was very excited about it, as she thrived on travel. They were gone for a day or two, and she abandoned the adventure because the woman had started proselytizing, and she could not tolerate or put up with that "nonsense."

I don't think that Kay felt as appreciated as she should have been, and I don't think that she was. I think a lot of islanders kept her at arm's length, for several reasons. One, being that she wasn't born there, and [also that] she had been places and seen things. She was not like them. The Island was a beautiful place to live, but a few of the "Islanders" were very protective of their special status (as such); some of them resented Kay's helpfulness, and some were jealous of her accomplishments.

[...] The fact that she invented synchronized swimming is the least important part of her life to me. She was a thinking adventurer, who appreciated life far more than most do.[6]

Carl addresses many important questions about Curtis's elusive nature, including several potential factors that would naturally estrange her from the more prudish residents of Washington Island. Carl's interpretation of her sexuality is admittedly based on implicit experience. And, although Gaylord had independently formed the same assumption, neither of them had actually discussed the matter directly with Curtis, and especially not with the knowledge of her complicated romantic histories with Bill John and John Brock. Of course, neither of these World War II engagements was any more successful than her pre-war marriage with George W. Curtis, who still remains but a "sketch" in her enigmatic history.

Overall, she never seemed too fond of subscribing to conventional institutions. And, as if also suffering from an ideological wanderlust, Curtis typically managed to keep controversial matters impersonally open-ended, from religion to politics. She nearly wrote as much to Victoria Vacha (in a discussion about the 1960 presidential election), confessing, "I really don't put much weight on my personal preferences!"[7] However, in equal measure, Caroline Whitney remembers that Curtis would later identify as Catholic, which is consistent with her previous remarks about admiring the Pope, exploring religion, and repeatedly asking for (and offering) prayers. It may also be notable, in this regard, that she later appeared in pictures with a crucifix around her neck, or happily posing with nuns. She undoubtedly entertained many differing (and contradictory) opinions throughout her life, while naturally forming her more lasting beliefs after key turning points and maturity.

In the early months of 1964, Curtis's older brother, Robert Lee Whitney, died near Prescott (Arizona), where his estate was being settled by April 20. His death was later mentioned in Curtis's Christmas newsletter, detailing another cross-country expedition from Chicago to Florida, Louisiana, Texas, Arizona and California. She listed all the friends that she stayed with along the way, and that there were just as many projects waiting for her on Washington Island by Mother's Day 1964. She concluded this newsletter by writing, "Wonder of wonders, my health has held out fine. And I am planning to hibernate right here on the Island, all winter long. Summer people will be gone, and I am anticipating a very peaceful, snug season of reading, writing, and attempts at craft projects and knitting! [...] The snow plow will keep the road to my mailbox cleared for me, so drop 'the old lady' a card, now and then, to keep our postal service working!"[8]

In October, the Whitney family in Hawaii moved to Columbus, Ohio, after Gaylord accepted a job in the private sector. John Wayne finished filming a month prior, and *In Harm's Way* was released in April 1965, around the time of Curtis's next newsletter:

> I hate to admit it, but my wonderful winter of working on my many long-planned "projects"—getting caught up on my reading, and my correspondence—has disappeared into thin air. And, now, I am considered an authority on 4-H work!
>
> In December [1964], the woman leader of the Eager Islanders 4-H Club here left the Island for a three-month trip, after telling everyone here (except me) that I had promised to take over for her while she was gone. I can't remember when I was any madder than at that moment. However, [...] they certainly needed leadership, and there wasn't really any way that I could get out from under it. So, all my lovely personal projects were shoved into the attic (where they still are), and I started studying 4-H. And that is all I have been able to do since!
>
> [...] During this scramble, I discovered that there has never been a Community Advisory Committee to help the local leader. We now have one, [consisting] of five members representing the active "organizations" on the Island. [...] And, then, there is always the problem of finances!
>
> We gave a talent show, which outplayed all talent shows of the past, with over two-hundred [people] in attendance. [...And] now that we have spent all of our club funds, we have to make some more. So, with the help of the Community Advisory Committee, we plan to have an "Island Fun Night" with the parents and grandparents joining with their kids in "family acts." There are many "Doubting Thomas'" about the feasibility of this project, but I still think it can be done. And I know that everyone would have such a good time. [...] Time will tell, but I'm not as young as I once was. And I am tired!
>
> I still have two other jobs facing me for the summer. Once again, I will be the "coordinator" for the Island Fair (August 20), and I am to be the executive secretary for the newly organized Cultural Center Commission.
>
> [...] I am sad when I think about all my lovely "projects" that I wanted to work on this winter, but I guess there will be more winters. And this one [1965] was meant to be "the 4-H winter." Maybe some other winter I might not have the health to do it. Who knows? Our winter has been a long one, with plenty of snow and low temperatures, but it has not been an uncomfortable one. So now I know that this is a twelve-month home, and that I will never be without "something to do." It will always be "how much I want to do, or am capable of doing."[9]

After the 1965 winter holidays, Curtis wrote another newsletter to summarize the recent year of varying activities and visitors to Ferda Lokin (including Gaylord and the family), where "it was almost as though new friends walked in the front [door] as others went out the back. I enjoyed every one of them, but I must admit that it was a rather 'confusing' summer."[10] She also wrote about her plans for 1966, which, in a general effort to escape her island projects, included another long trip throughout the southern U.S. between February and May.

Curtis was soon reporting that she was being drawn to the warmer temperatures in Florida, and she even managed to arrange a three-week stay in Panama with a former Special Services friend. She summarized the highlights of this trip in her 1966 Christmas newsletter:

> ### Greetings from the Old Woman Who Lives Under the Hill
>
> [...In Panama,] I thoroughly enjoyed the sunshine and heat, and I accumulated the most wonderful tan that you can imagine. The jungle fascinated me with its flowering trees and gaily colored birds. And the Panamanians reminded me of my first-love foreigners, the Mexicans. [...] We played, swam, fished, and attended a Panamanian birthday reception, where we met [Marco Aurelio Robles], the President of Panama. [...But] the highlight was an air-and-boat trip to the San Blas Islands, where the Indians by that name entertain tourists in their primitive villages on a series of very small, "coconut-tree-and-thatched-hut" islands.

> [...] While in Florida, I spent some time with a couple of former pupil-friends of mine, including Dr. Victoria Vacha, who has retired to a mobile-home court near Orlando. [...I also] spent a couple of weeks with my sister [Jane] in Gatlinburg, and I can't say that I blame her for choosing that spot for her "castle." [...] All of [the states in] this region—Georgia, Tennessee, and South Carolina—were gorgeous with the spring flowers.
>
> [...] About that time, I began to think about spring on the Island, and I high-tailed it through Chicago for the Gills Rock Ferry. [...] Then came summer, and I worked all summer long at our "best" hotel, as "Assistant Manager." It was long hours, and left me little time for anything else, but I did manage to get the mortgage paid off. And I "learned a lot."
>
> [1966] was my year to withdraw from my many community responsibilities, to patiently wait for others to take up the reins! [...] But I just had to take time to tell you all that I may be "aging," but "there's life in the old girl yet." I'll be here all winter, resting up from all the activity that I have just related to you![11]

Around the time that Curtis was working at the "best" (and only) hotel on Washington Island, Caroline Whitney gave birth to twins on October 13, 1966. The two girls were named Andrea and Meredith Whitney, who completed their family portrait in Ohio until the start of the next generation.

Curtis wrote again to her friends on May 1, 1967, six weeks after being "appointed the director of the Community Action Program for Washington Island (part of the Office of Economic Opportunity)":

> Within the first week of my "employment," it was necessary for me to go to Madison to attend a meeting of all sixteen Wisconsin CAP [Community Action Program] directors in the governor's council room. As the smallest geographical area to receive a federal grant, as well as one of the "greenest," I felt quite conspicuous, and it took me all of the first day of meetings to know what they meant by all the "alphabetical titles" that they used. [...] But, at least I met a lot of fellow sufferers, and I caught on to a few "ropes," to say nothing of collecting a lot of literature, and meeting the state "bosses." [...] Now, you must remember that none of us knows exactly what we are supposed to do, except that I am sure that we are to improve the community, if possible, through the assistance of standard federal programs that are already available.
>
> I soon started reading the government "gobbledygook" like mad, setting up a community survey questionnaire to gather up-to-date data (the last census was 1960), and getting an office set up in the 4-H room of the school. [...] I returned from Madison on Saturday afternoon, and had to prepare a report to be given at an open town meeting of the council on the following Monday! There has always been a need for some sort of "pre-school" program here on the Island, so we started on that program first. [...] Our predicament here on the Island is an underprivileged state, due to our isolated geographical location, not so much to low income. However, because the need was present, we then turned to educational channels, and (I'll spare you the minute details), it now looks as though we will have a kindergarten set up by July [1967].[12]

Her next newsletter wasn't written until June 20, 1968, while she was vacationing in Germany, and just after having resolved some serious health issues:

> This diary report is to let many of you, to whom I have owed a letter for many weeks, that I am still alive and kicking. In fact, I am having "the time of my life." I'm visiting all my "old" overseas friends until, I hope, next April [1969].
>
> [...] In November [1967], I had a session with pneumonia, and then I fell down the cellar steps and broke three ribs, which took forever (eight weeks) to heal.
>
> Then (as a climax), when I went to the MD to get my shots for a trip to Europe, I was hustled to the hospital in Green Bay, and I lost my left bosom in a bout with cancer. However, it could have been worse. The surgeon insisted that there would be no need for treatments of any kind, and that I would be able to go on with my plans for Europe.
>
> [...] I spent a lot of time with Renate Dullo and her family, visiting all the familiar spots in the area. We also spent time up at the school where Wolfgang teaches, and where my godson goes to school.

Nuremberg has changed a great deal with the modernizing of its streets, many of which are now one-way, and there are <u>so</u> many more cars!

[…] I am finding that I need more rest than I had anticipated, but I have not "suffered" as yet in any way. And, each week, I feel better. […] I must get ready to go out to dinner, so will call a halt, but now you know where I am, and that I expect to be here [with other friends in Munich] through the winter.[13]

In addition to the Dullos, Curtis visited with many other old friends throughout Europe until April 1969, when she eagerly hurried home to Washington Island for some much-needed relaxation and solitude. She wrote another newsletter in August, reporting, "I received a clean bill of health [after a checkup in July]. […] And, in spite of the fact that I swore that I would not get involved in community problems [again]—you know <u>me</u>—I have been in charge of publicity for the Center for Creative Arts and Nature Study, which has meant writing for the local newspaper and cutting tapes for broadcasting over Sturgeon Bay Radio Station."[14]

Curtis visited Jane in Tennessee for Thanksgiving, and started considering a permanent move south, away from all the responsibilities, winter snowdrifts and isolation

Wolf-Christian Dullo and Katharine Whitney Curtis in Bavaria (1968).

of Washington Island. The big decision to sell Ferda Lokin was finally made between late 1969 and September 17, 1970, when this Wisconsin newspaper article was published:

> We have all known those days when the air is humid and oppressive, and a fog lays immovable over everything. Then, suddenly, a brisk breeze springs up from somewhere, the humidity and fog disappear, and it's like stepping into a new world. So it is with communities. Everything has always been done in the same, old way for many years. Then, one day, a vigorous, civic-minded person enters the community like a fresh breeze, scattering new ideas, starting new projects, and jarring people out of their well-worn ruts.
>
> That's how it was on Washington Island when Kay Curtis retired and came home to the little house where her mother, Mrs. Whitney, had lived for many years. [...Curtis] had dreamed of [having] time to sit in a rocking chair, to read and knit and indulge in many other personal projects. [...But] Kay is an extrovert, friendly and warm-hearted. Her interest in people causes her to become involved in many civic activities.
>
> [...] In some quotations [that] Kay [has] collected, [there's] one which reads, "There are two ways to reach the top of an oak tree. One way is to climb it, and the other is to sit on an acorn." Kay is the type that would climb the tree.
>
> Kay has announced that she is soon leaving Washington Island to make her home in sunny Florida. She still has dreams of [having] a rocking chair, and leisure time to do all the things that she has always wanted to do. Such a wonderful person as Kay deserves the comfort of a warmer climate, although we would like to keep her on Washington Island. [But], being Kay, I doubt that she will be content to sit in that rocking chair for very long. I can just see her, down there in Florida, organizing a group of senior mermaids, teaching them synchronized swimming. We hope that she is happy in her new environment, and our love and best wishes go with her.[15]

There and Back Again

In December of 1970, Curtis wrote her next newsletter from "Fed-haven," a recently established retirement community for Federal employees in Polk County, Florida. She highly recommended the cleansing experience of pruning one's "materialistic possessions" down to the bare essentials, "And how I love the daily sunshine, and the lack of personal responsibilities!"[16] She soon became reengaged in civic affairs with her local Audubon Society, a national conservationist organization, just as President Nixon was establishing the Environmental Protection Agency (EPA). Curtis participated in a related letter-writing campaign to the White House, and she soon received this response: "Dear Miss Curtis, your support for my decision to halt further construction on the Cross Florida Barge Canal is deeply appreciated, and I want to thank you for your recent letter. I hope the Administration's efforts to protect our natural heritage will merit your continued approval in the months and years ahead. With best wishes, sincerely, [signed] Richard Nixon [March 23]."[17]

On May 2, 1971, a letter was written (in German) by Wolf-Christian Dullo, who thanked "Tata" for his birthday gift, while also hoping that she was happy in Florida.[18] He wrote about doing well in school, particularly in the physical sciences, and Wolf-Christian would later become a distinguished professor of paleo-oceanography at the Christian-Albrechts-University in Kiel, Germany. Curtis also received letters in Florida from Renate, who wrote on January 4, 1972, with these happy recollections:

> Dearest Katie!
>
> Your [seventy-fifth] birthday is here, and we have no idea where you are [currently traveling ... but] a small package is on its way. The main thing is [that] our warmest and best wishes are with you, my dear; not only today (January 4), no, all the time. And a heart-full of deepest thanks comes to visit you.

> [...] While [our family] sat together, today, we all talked about you, and everyone had different memories. And, all together, it [created] a very colorful picture, and, like a red ribbon, there was your love. The older I become, the more I realize that nothing counts [more] than honest feelings for other people; [these feelings are] like seeds for a far future, when we do come again on Earth. And that is our main [lesson] to our boy, to make him [aware of] other people, and to <u>do</u> something for them. You are [Wolf-Christian's] godmother, and you have always given him the best example. And he knows! What better can you do in life?[19]

Despite Curtis being particularly untraceable—indeed, like a "rolling stone"—throughout most of 1972, she resurfaced in the public eye by May (1973) for the (nineteenth) International Academy of Aquatic Art (IAAA) festival at the University of Manitoba, Canada. This grand event was witnessed by a fellow Chicagoan and synchronized swimmer, Cathy Goodwin, who later wrote this account:

> My coach, Bernice Lorber Hayes, was to present the first trophy ever awarded in synchronized swimming (won by Wright College) to the Aquatic Hall of Fame and Museum of Canada [for safekeeping].
> [...] Mrs. Hayes always said that she learned synchronized swimming from [Curtis] and her students, [...] so Mrs. Hayes felt that Kay should present the trophy with her. And that is exactly what they did.
> I was seated in an area just behind the microphone as they were introduced. Mrs. Hayes talked briefly about the beginning of synchronized swimming, standing side-by-side and holding hands with Kay. It was a very special moment for all of us watching, especially the Wright College alumni swimmers [as Curtis was acknowledged as the originator of the sport].[20]

Soon after the IAAA festival, Curtis was asked to record some of her own reflections for the July 1973 issue of the *Aquatic Artist*. While initially hesitant to criticize everyone's hard work, she offered these careful words to appraise the progressing state of synchronized swimming in relation to her original vision:

> We have both taken [to] the forms that I originally thought would prove a field of great value to many of the swimmers in the world who never <u>should</u> become (nor ever <u>could</u> become) speed swimmers. Swimmers of both sexes and all ages could enjoy and benefit from this special type of water activity.
> Even Bob Kiphuth (Yale University swimming coach), when inspecting my group of synchronized swimmers at Chicago Teachers College (to determine the acceptability of synchronized swimming as an AAU activity), said, "But, Kay, this is a new form of aesthetics. How <u>can</u> you bear to put it into competition?"
> And my reply at that time was, "But if I had <u>not</u> offered it as a competitive sport, <u>you</u> and many other well-known coaches would never have paid any attention to it." You see, I was anxious to <u>promote</u> synchronized swimming for <u>all</u> swimmers, and as quickly as possible.
> The [competitive] AAU, the [original] Kay Curtis Modern Mermaids, [...] and the wonderful [artistic] demonstrations that Beulah and Henry Gundling have [since] held, have all been [equally] part of the pattern of development of the sport of swimming, into all of its forms. All swimmers cannot become AAU champions. All swimmers cannot perform advanced aquatic art. Many swimmers will remain "dog paddlers." However, each "phase" [or form] of swimming has its [own] place in the field of this activity. There is room and place for all, and I hope that there will come a time when there will be no "feeling" [of animosity] between the contestants or the directors in all of these various interest groups.[21]

Curtis's maternal hopes for harmony are essential toward understanding her perceived role as the counterweight against any schism in synchronized swimming methodology; namely, between anyone with an exclusively "competitive" or "artistic" focus on this uniquely duel-natured sport / art form.

Also in July, *The Door County Advocate* reported the local news of a special "This Is Your Day" party on Washington Island for Curtis, as she was returning from Canada.[22] Thirteen of her old friends reunited at the community center with Curtis and Bernice Lorber Hayes, and all of their shared history was warmly celebrated. Also, on this day, July 16, while Curtis was (yet again) being acknowledged as the originator of synchronized swimming, newspapers were otherwise reporting that the White House had a secret taping system, which was suspected to contain key evidence in establishing "corrupt intent" behind Nixon's recent Watergate cover-up conspiracy. The tapes were eventually subpoenaed, and a constitutional crisis ensued as Nixon claimed "executive privilege" in his refusal to provide them. What followed was the "Saturday Night Massacre," a string of dismissals in the Department of Justice (DOJ) as Nixon moved to fire the special prosecutor behind the subpoena. These actions were met with intense public outrage, and Nixon continued defending his case through November 17 with his now-infamous tagline, "I'm not a crook." DOJ investigators were soon reinstated as increasingly more Americans demanded the president's impeachment.

At the end of 1973, Curtis finally chronicled the highlights of her recent silent period with a friendly and apologetic newsletter:

> It really is unforgivable of me to treat you faithful friends as I have, but, believe me, don't save things to do "when I retire," because something happens to "time" as soon as one stops working. Moving from Washington Island to Florida didn't help that fact one bit.
>
> [...] I was not planning to return to [visit] Washington Island after the hectic move south, but Fate decreed otherwise, and I have been back there for part of each summer. 1973 was no exception. The high point in 1972 was that I had my grandnephew, Christopher Whitney, up there with me for ten days (my first contact with a child of eleven who was a "city boy"), and I received a most liberal education, as you can imagine. It was a great time for both of us!
>
> [...] I drove up to Gatlinburg, in the Smoky Mountains of Tennessee, to visit my sister, Jane, who was living there and working with the "mountain people" and the staff of the Great Smokies National Park.
>
> [...] The holiday seasons went as customary, driving to various friends for each special day. But, in March [1973], there came a very special period, [...] visiting the Seminole areas and riding on one of the "propeller boats" in the Everglades. [Then I went] to Naples, where my brother, George, and his wife have a lovely new condominium. Here, we picked fruit in the groves, and walked the lovely beach, watching the pier fisherman before we drove to St. Petersburg to visit [other friends]. [...] We spent a day at Disney World and had dinner with Dr. Victoria Vacha, who, some of you will remember as an old [synchronized swimming] pupil, is now director of the Orange County Clinic in Orlando.[23]

Curtis listed many other friends among her recent travels before signing off for the beginning of another silent period. However, her most tangible connection to the southern USA would soon be lost, after her sister died in late 1973. According to her obituary, Jane was found lying still in her garden with "a trowel in her hand," and she was further described as "an unselfconscious woman of medium height; short, crisp and graying hair; ready laughter, and insatiable curiosity about all things pertaining to her adopted Smokies."[24]

On February 6, 1974, the U.S. House of Representatives began pursuing three articles of impeachment for President Nixon, who finally released the subpoenaed White House tapes in late July. Despite over 18 minutes of those nefarious conversations being "accidentally" erased, sufficient evidence for obstruction of justice arrived on August 5 with the "smoking gun" tape, proving Nixon had been involved in a deliberate cover-up conspiracy. Assured by members of Congress that his impeachment was inevitable, Nixon resigned his office on August 9 and flew away by helicopter from the remains of his shattered legacy. An already vengeful nation was further outraged, a month later, when President Gerald

Ford pardoned his ignominious predecessor in order to "heal the nation." He defended this decision with his first presidential declaration: "Our long national nightmare is over. Our constitution works; our great republic is a government of laws and not of men. Here, the people rule. [...And] as we bind up the internal wounds of Watergate, more painful and more poisonous than those of foreign wars, let us restore the golden rule to our political process, and let brotherly love purge our hearts of suspicion and of hate."

Once again, the average American was in particular need of distraction, and evidence of just such a timely balm arrived for local Floridians on November 15. The front cover of *The Ledger Local* newspaper read, "Swim Queen Now in Polk [County]":

> Mrs. Kay Curtis has lived a life that would make anyone's head swim. Swimming has been one of the major highlights of her life, and, some forty years ago, she originated synchronized swimming as we know it today.
>
> Now, at the age of seventy-seven, after "retiring" to Lake Wales, her energetic nature and interest in people keep her busy checking her calendar for free time between helping a neighbor, going to a Hungarian festival in Plant City, and being active in the Audubon Society.
>
> As a child, she liked all forms of athletics (especially swimming), and she swam under the water before on top. At the age of fourteen, she swam across Lake Mendota in Wisconsin, a feat that three men had failed to accomplish.
>
> In 1916, while a student at The University of Wisconsin, she had a coach who was an old Vaudeville acrobat and enjoyed teaching her diving stunts. "I was not a diver," Mrs. Curtis said, "But enjoyed performing stunts in the water instead of the air."
>
> Later, she applied these stunts in the water, when teaching swimming classes at The University of Chicago, [which both] helped in overcoming fear of the water and increased harmony of body motion.
>
> During this time, she began using music as a background for her swimming shows. "But it distressed me, no end, to have the performers not keep time to the music," she said. "And, lo and behold, synchronized swimming was born. We synchronized the body movements in the water with the rhythm of the music, as simple as that."
>
> [...] Synchronized swimming enthusiasts [now] seem divided into two groups: "Those who consider it a competitive sport, and those who feel it is an aesthetic art. All cannot become (American Athletic Union) champions. Many swimmers will always remain 'dog-paddlers.'

Katharine Whitney Curtis in her element (c. 1975).

However, there is room and place for all—the expert, the poor, and the average swimmer—in synchronized swimming."[25]

An interesting parallel can be drawn between Curtis's consistent focus on harmony within the community of synchronized swimming and the overall need for harmony in her nation's healing process at that time. She had been a willing supporter of Nixon ever since his first presidential election, and she was particularly enthusiastic about his (still-noteworthy) environmental policies, establishing the EPA. But, as with all other Nixon supporters, her trust and goodwill had been betrayed, and maintaining the "good old" golden rule was indeed the only option for helping everyone to move forward in life.

It was by July 1975 that Curtis decided to move back up north again, and she explained herself to friends in what would become one of her final newsletters:

Greetings from a Runaway!

Moving is always a traumatic experience. And this last one, to return to Washington Island for the rest of my life, has been no exception. Contemplation of this move has been going on for the past two years, at least. The continuous heat in Florida was becoming unbearable, […] and the death of my sister, Jane, removed any necessity for me to remain in the South.

[…] Last May [1974], I visited Washington Island. I had made up my mind [prior to this visit] that if anyone [would pressure me to return], I would not move back there. Fortunately, I heard no one say [anything annoying], but I did discover that my heart had been there all the time. It was my only real home, regardless of the fact that I had sold my house there, and that many of my Island friends had died since I left.

Being at the right place at the right time enabled me to locate an old frame house, the "old post office," on one of the main roads, very conveniently across from the active post office. […] The entire house was not available, […] but I am renting more space than I need; about half an acre of beautiful green grass, surrounded by gorgeous, big old trees. […] Right now, the entire area is a "golden glory," in the Indian-summer sunshine, through the brightly-colored autumn leaves. My landlords say that all of this is "mine," as long as I pay my rent!

[…] I really hadn't completely unpacked when two old friends from Hershey, Pennsylvania, arrived and spent their visiting time arranging the big living room, so that it [resembles] the living room in the old Ferda Lokin. Island friends have been saying, "It looks just like you and your old home!"

So! I think that I am lucky, lucky, lucky to have made this move. I can hardly wait to be snowed-in, so that I can catch up on reading, writing, and needlepoint. I expect to react like a big old bear, to just hibernate 'til spring [when] the apple blossoms arrive!

In the meantime, I want you to know that this message is in lieu of a holiday letter. At these times (of Thanksgiving and Christmas), I am sure you know that I will be reminiscing about each and every one of you, and of the happy times that we have had together in the past. You will know that I am, at last, anchored. There will always be a warm welcome, here, for any of you who can find me. […] I'd love that! Best wishes for happy holidays, and an armful of love for each of you.[26]

After another extensive silent period, Curtis's doctor reported (on her behalf) "Over the past week or so, since returning to Florida for a brief vacation, [Curtis] has had a mild cough […which] is resolving at present time, […and] she generally feels well. She has remained active, physically, and is quite content with her present day-to-day living pattern. She is much happier [as of March 17, 1976] in her present location, in Northern Wisconsin, than during her few years in Florida."[27]

Journey's End

By Christmas of 1977, the date of Curtis's final general newsletter, she declared (at 80 years old) the timely end of her rolling-stone period. "I'm back in my original 'home spot' in America, Washington Island, and I'm planning to remain here permanently. No more racing around, dropping in on old friends! They will have to drop in on me, personally, or via the mailman." Curtis then explained how she was starting to feel her age:

> I can hardly recognize my wrinkled *Gesicht* [face] at tooth-brushing time. I'm down to 126 [lbs.]! And I weighed 170 during the overseas period. [...But] my natural deterioration has really been a blessing. I haven't been hampered by having to diet. You'd never recognize my present body. [...] And I can do some [real] speed-sprinting on my daily walks. I don't do much swimming, however. The water's too darned cold, and I'm a bit sensitive about my appearance in the modern swimsuits![28]

Curtis also mentioned that she was featured (again) in *The Sturgeon Bay Advocate*, which claimed that she was a vital member of the local Senior Citizens group on Washington Island. She continued to describe her new (one-story) rental home, where she was comfortably wintering:

> [This house] has beautiful views from all windows. The rising sun wakes me in my bedroom. The living room opens up to the gay sunsets. The window, over the kitchen sink, looks across two acres to my nearest neighbor and their several Hereford cows (each with a recent calf). The cows and I have great neighborly contacts, every day, when the small planes—which take off from our small island airport (down the road a bit) and pass over our heads—cause me to stop and think how great it is to live in a time when humans can fly.
> [...] As soon as I got into this place, [a friend] arrived from California to spend a month with me. And during this time, my nephew, Gaylord Whitney, and his sixteen-year-old son [Christopher] spent a short time with me [among other friends].
> [...] Life on the Island has speeded up to the point that I cannot keep up with it, and I am looking forward eagerly to the "snowed-in" period, when I can really find time to experiment with my "new-found" interest of "dyeing with natural dyes," [but also with] my old therapy of needlepoint, [and to] get back into some form of letter-writing to all of you, my loving, old friends. I wish that you could join me in one of my daily walks in the woods, or [in some of my other community activities]. I am pretty well convinced that I am where I ought to be, and I hope that some of you will "come see" in 1978. [...] Love to you all, from your Country Mouse.[29]

Curtis's 1977 visit with her remaining family was also fondly remembered by Gaylord, who would stay up late with Christopher, during such trips, to watch the mesmerizing Northern Lights for some precious father-son moments.

Meanwhile, around late November 1977, a strategic letter-writing campaign was initiated by Bernice Lorber Hayes to recommend Curtis's induction into the International Swimming Hall of Fame (ISHOF) in Fort Lauderdale, Florida. The selection committee received about 20 separate nominations and personal testimonials from across the country, with most of these explicitly citing Curtis as the historical "originator" of synchronized swimming, and someone who should have been recognized by ISHOF already.[30]

Back on a snow-covered Washington Island, Curtis started writing one of her last known surviving letters on Saturday, January 28, 1978. And, as per usual, it provided her nephew with a bountiful "pamphlet" of 12 interfolded pages and scrawling, ballpoint cursive:

> Dear Gaylord,
>
> You must think I'm a louse, after you made the effort to write me two wonderful letters, and you didn't get even a postcard reply. [...] I've been snowbound, with drifts deeper than my waist, for days now. And, this morning, the snowplow dug a road out from the main road to the woodshed, where the car has been stuck in hard, crispy, crusty snowdrifts for days now.
> [...It's now Sunday, and my neighbor friend, Ted Lentz, just] dug the car out of the drifts and left it at my back door. I really haven't the courage to drive it, for fear I'll slip on the ice or back up into another drift. I guess that my age is catching up with me. I'm getting awfully lazy! Now, let's re-read

your letters for the umpteenth time. Believe it or not, one is dated November 17 (1977); think of all that has happened since <u>then</u>.

[…] I think that the whole world has gone crazy, and don't understand what's going to be the <u>result</u>! […I was recently getting a checkup] at the Door County Memorial Hospital, [where] I learned nothing <u>new</u>; no [discernable] <u>cause</u> of [my mysterious] dropping to (a presently stationary) 130 lbs.

[…] Our winter deaths have started, […and one such neighbor] has been "weak" in his head for years, and it was a relief to him <u>and</u> his poor wife, who has cared for him alone for several years up here on the Island. But, the snow was so deep, I couldn't get out of the house, and heaven knows how they handled the cemetery. <u>And</u> [another friend] fell inside her home, this week, and broke her hip. The poor thing isn't even sixty years old, and is [now] down in the Sturgeon Bay Hospital.

[…] I can certainly understand how you feel about State Government and "political garbage" [referring to Gaylord's current employment at the Ohio EPA]. Wisconsin is a fine example of <u>that</u>, too. And I'm getting sick of being [solicited] for contributions [by] every Republican committee there is, just because I [once] paid $15.00 [for] membership to the <u>National</u>! When I was playing around with the Audubon people in Florida, I was very conscious of the environmental activities, and there were several <u>very</u> active "leaders" in our local organization. <u>But</u>, here on Washington Island, I haven't located [any] such leaders. But give me another year, and maybe I'll find one or two. I'll always be interested in where and how <u>you</u> go [with the EPA].

[…] Remind me to show to you some of my [Special Services] "office material" when you are on the Island, next time. And, by the way, I'll be <u>sure</u> that I have no additional guests [like in 1977]. In going through "boxes," I found a lot of "publicity," of things that [Mother] had accomplished, and I will put them all together so that we can go over them together. She was a great character!

[…] I'm so anxious for you to meet Ted Lentz. I'm sure you'll like him. He sure takes good care of me, and if it weren't for his presence on the Island, I'm afraid that I'd be pretty bored. […] If the heavy snows hold off, this week, Ted and I are hoping to get off the Island for a couple of days to "do" Sturgeon Bay and Green Bay. Both of us have friends, in Green Bay, with whom each of us can stay, and I promised Ted that I'd "go to a movie" with him. Both of us have shopping and business to do, and I want to check on my [last will and testament], which I left with a lawyer in Sturgeon Bay (whom I haven't heard a word from since). And I also want to register with [the undertaker], who has promised to plant my ashes in "our lot."

[…] Your letters made me very happy, so do it again soon. And maybe you can coax the kids to take turns, too. Carol has already done <u>her</u> duty, and I'm still profiting on her fudge recipe. My love to you all. I promise <u>you</u> that my next one won't be so <u>long</u> (and I'll answer <u>sooner</u>).

Aunt Kate[31]

The most significant part of this letter would ultimately prove to be Curtis's mysterious weight loss, which signaled a general decline in health, and probably why she felt so determined to settle her final affairs with Ted Lentz in Sturgeon Bay.

Carl Hardee would later recall that it was to Ted Lentz that Curtis had sold Ferda Lokin, "over a period of time," around 1970. Furthermore, Carl attested that "Ted Lentz was a great friend to Kay, watching out for her interests, and assuring that she had a place to call home. Ted always kept me informed on her doings and progress, and he cared about her very much."[32]

Curtis's legal will was finally signed and notarized on February 12, 1978:

I do hereby give and bequeath all of my said estate to my godson, Wolf-Christian Dullo, […] to be his absolutely. […] I nominate, constitute and appoint Theodore A. Lentz […] as personal representative of this will, […and] he is, upon liquidation of the estate, to forward the proceeds (along with an accounting of the liquidation) to the beneficiary. […] I have hereunto subscribed my name and affixed my seal to this […] in the presence of witnesses at Washington Island, [signed] Katharine W. Curtis.[33]

The letter-writing campaign to ISHOF succeeded by August 22, 1978, when *The Door County Advocate* published a heartwarming feature titled, "Washington Island's Kay Curtis Becoming a Legend in Her Time." To explain the history behind Curtis's timely induction, this article quoted some of her more charming anecdotes for a general retelling of her early swimming career, while also summarizing her time with the ARC and Special Services. The reporter made sure to emphasize her unique personality, and humorously noted, "During her hectic but satisfying years abroad, Kay met almost all of America's four and five-star generals, and managed to have at least one argument with all of them." She was further characterized as a perennial traveler, who often gets itchy feet and "just packs up and leaves; [while the question of] where to go is no problem, [because] Kay's friends, like her interests, are legion." And despite Curtis being initially quoted as saying, "I'm at home everywhere, but don't belong anywhere," the reporter concluded by also quoting an "insurance" card (that Curtis kept on the dashboard of her car): "In case of injury or death, notify the CAP office on Washington Island [to bring me home]."[34]

Curtis soon also received a hand-written note from Margaret "Peg" Seller, who helped to innovate water ballet in Canada as Curtis was perfecting her own hybrid in Chicago. Seller graciously wrote, on September 29, 1978, "I was just thrilled when Beulah [Gundling] wrote me that you were going to be inducted into ISHOF. About time! You should have been one of the first in there. I'm just so glad, and so happy for you. I know we both appreciate these honors, but what really mattered to both of us was the joy and pleasure we gave to others, and, along the way, to ourselves."[35]

Curtis was expected to receive the full "royal treatment" with her fellow inductees at ISHOF, including "their footprints in cement [like] Hollywood stars," and a dinner cruise aboard a luxury yacht. She wrote to ISHOF on February 26, 1979, about the final details of this ceremony (scheduled for April 30), and the following is regarded as her last known surviving letter:

> I am sincerely sorry that I seem to be such a nuisance, and I will try to answer some of the problems that we seem to be facing.
> First, the package that I sent you was received by your office, and I did receive a receipt of the same. As to the contents, please try to picture me, at eighty-two years, trying to hunt up any "memorabilia" of any kind, particularly since I was out the US from 1943 to 1962 (having practically nothing to do with swimming). I included all that I could "unbury" in the line of "water" memorabilia. But since I have never been part of "competitive swimming," other than in the form of an "official," I have no "awards" except one (from the IAAA), which is so heavy that I cannot afford to mail it to you. I am having enough trouble finding enough cash to get myself to you, but I will try to bring this award to you if you want it. [...] I also made a great effort to include pictures of the synchronized swimming show that I staged in Caserta, Italy, during [WWII]. The postcard of the Kay Curtis Modern Mermaids at the Chicago World's Fair has me in a swimsuit, in the middle of the entire group, [...but] I am sorry to report that, as a coach, I had very few pictures taken.
> And now, at eighty-two years, I am in no physical condition to make swimsuit appearances. In fact, last May [1978], I joined the long list of "cancer patients," and I have dropped from weighing 160 lbs. to 120—just a sack of bones! And I doubt that many old friends will recognize me.
> [...] Marge Turner, who will be wherever I am, is helping to defray my travelling expenses, and is one of my most faithful swimming pupils of long standing.
> [...] I will, of course, expect to attend the banquet on Monday eve; [the] luncheon [on] Tuesday, after the "footprints in cement," and the cruise [later] that night, providing that I am not worn to a shadow![36]

After Curtis's induction into ISHOF, *The Door County Advocate* published a follow-up article on July 24 with the summary, "Kay Whitney Curtis Richly Deserves Her Niche in Swimming Hall of Fame." In fact, Curtis's particular niche in the ISHOF museum had been uniquely adorned with her World War II portrait (from Capri) hanging front and center. And some of her accompanying friends reported that her acceptance speech was both eloquent and delightfully humorous, including this disclosure:

> Those of you who wondered why I ever monkeyed around with synchronized swimming in the first place will be surprised to know it was because [I figured] there had to be something more artistic to swimming than a big [old fatty] plunging head first into a pool.

Curtis modestly explained to the reporter, back home, that she didn't mind waiting so long for this immensely gratifying honor, but that it would have been preferable to be named as the "creator" of synchronized swimming, instead of just a "coach" (as inscribed on her ISHOF memorial). More importantly, and as a fitting testament to her future-orientation, she made sure to mention (for this article's readership), "Her all-consuming goal, at present, is to find 'some rich person' to build a municipal pool on Washington Island. 'And it doesn't have to be fancy,' she smiled, 'just good-sized.'"[37]

A month after the ISHOF ceremony, Curtis also appeared at the twenty-fifth IAAA festival, starting on May 24, 1979, in Park Ridge, Illinois. She stayed with Bernice Lorber Hayes in Chicago during that time, and Cathy Goodwin later wrote about this event:

> This was the second time [that Curtis and I had] met, as she was one of the special guests attending the anniversary event. [...] And a moment from that evening that I will always cherish is when [my mentor], Bernice Lorber Hayes, spoke about Kay and presented her with a white rose, in honor of her vision for and dedication to synchronized swimming. I can still hear the roar of applause from our standing ovation.[38]

About a year later, Curtis made her last known public appearance at the March (1980) IAAA "Midwest Symposium" in Evansville, Indiana. Bernice Lorber Hayes was originally scheduled to give a coed workshop (with live swimming demonstrations), but later delegated this to Cathy Goodwin, who continued writing about this interaction with Curtis:

> While we were talking, I shared that I had a few "butterflies" about presenting, [and], ever the teacher, Kay gave me a few speaking points, a great deal of encouragement, and then sat in the front row during the presentation (providing that boost in confidence that I sorely needed). I am happy to say that the "butterflies" flew away, and the presentation was a success.
>
> In conversation, after the workshop, I asked her how she felt about synchronized swimming being added to the [1984] Olympic Games. I was surprised at her answer. While Kay was very happy that synchro had been recognized and would debut at the [Olympics] in Los Angeles, she said that her [original intention] was a (co-ed) activity to be enjoyed by swimmers of all skill levels and their families, not just the elite swimmers.
>
> My impression was that she was very proud of the fact that her vision had been realized in the many "grass-roots" clubs that formed over the years, providing the opportunity for swimmers to enjoy synchro and participate in events like this symposium.

One of the last known photos of Katharine Whitney Curtis, by Carl Hardee, during the IAAA Midwest Symposium in Evansville, Indiana (March 1980).

And, while none of them would be Olympic-bound, their accomplishments (great or small) would be just as rewarding.[39]

This testimony serves as an important historical record for Curtis's final thoughts on synchronized swimming, while it also uniquely confirms, at the "last minute," that she was aware of its upcoming acceptance at the 1984 Olympics. She was staying with Carl Hardee during that 1980 symposium in Evansville, and Carl later recalled that Curtis "was frail, but she didn't let on about the seriousness of her illness."[40]

When the Whitney family received word that Curtis had been hospitalized in Sturgeon Bay, they didn't have much time. Her younger brother, George, hurried from Florida to Ohio, and departed with Gaylord for Wisconsin. They fatefully arrived on July 6, 1980, with only moments to spare. The day was hot, and, as the two men entered the hospital to be directed along its corridors, George's emotions swelled upon the final doorway. He was so overwhelmed by the tragic sight of his "unstoppable" big sister just lying there, made pale and powerless by disease, that he immediately left the room and sat down quietly in the hall. Gaylord gently pulled a chair closer to what remained of his larger-than-life "Aunt Kate," who was thinner now than he'd ever seen her before. She couldn't speak, and she barely seemed awake until Gaylord greeted her and held her hand. Kate's fingers squeezed Gaylord's in return, and, while her eyes remained closed for most of her final moments, she could feel now that she wasn't alone.

It always seemed like a fleeting moment before Aunt Kate departed again on some grand new adventure, and Gaylord would just have to wait to hear about the glorious details afterwards. She was always destined to belong to the wider world that she so often dedicated herself, but it was most important, at the end, that she was with family. When the time came, she tried to speak with some motions of desperation, but Gaylord couldn't understand. He apologized earnestly as he leaned closer, feeling her final breaths against his ear. He got up to call for the nurse, but it was upon their immediate return that Katharine Whitney Curtis was already gone.[41]

Perhaps the mother of synchronized swimming was dreaming about her past in those final moments, about the intrinsic beauty of life, or the nostalgia of how life could have been. But it's more fitting to think that her heart was focused, as always, on her hopes and dreams for the future. It's more fitting to think that she was already there.

Legacy

Just after Gaylord consoled his father and departed for Ohio, a younger man arrived at Sturgeon Bay Hospital in search of Curtis. Many years later, Carl Hardee would mournfully recount that he always thought he was the last person to see her, lying on the loading dock, as she was about to be taken away by the mortuary. Carl described that he was so overcome by emotion, "I went into the field across from the hospital and cried. Ted Lentz came to pick me up [after I expressed my anguish] and we went to the island." Carl would always claim Curtis as the uppermost influence in his life, and that the world could never appreciate her enough.[42]

The news of Curtis's death quickly spread to her many other friends, and her memorial was overseen by Marge Turner and Bernice Lorber Hayes, both of whom wrote intimate tributes, including this IAAA bulletin:

Gaylord Lee Whitney holding Katharine's portrait at ISHOF (February 2014).

Katharine Whitney Curtis
by Bernice L. Hayes

Katharine Whitney Curtis, our good friend, died July 6 (1980). At her request, she was cremated and buried beside her mother, Anne Whitney, in the lovely old cemetery on Washington Island, Wisconsin.

A graveside service, conducted by the Episcopalian priest, was held on Monday, July 14 (1980). Kay did not want a funeral service, so the priest departed from tradition and asked that anyone who wished to say something should speak. So, many did! These island friends told about good friendship; help and inspiration given; love of the Island and how much she did for it; her talent for organization; her need for beauty and the ability to create it; her great influence as a teacher, and her delight in being chosen an honoree of ISHOF.

[…] It was Kay's dream to foster a form of swimming for all swimmers—beginners to the highly skilled—who might not be interested in speed competition, but who could find a creative outlet in swimming. She worried that competition might spoil it, but felt that it was one way to introduce it to many people. Her preface in [her book] says, "[Synchronized swimming is] for those who are interested in the grace and rhythm of swimming."

Called "Synchro's First Lady," Kay was a 1979 honoree of ISHOF. It meant so much to her that she requested the award be placed on her tombstone [during the memorial].

How lucky we were to have Kay with us for our (twenty-fifth) IAAA anniversary celebration. We owe her so much![43]

Marge Turner's obituary for Curtis was published in the autumn of 1980, with these additional reflections:

Katherine Whitney Curtis, The Mother of Synchronized Swimming (and ISHOF honoree), passed away, July 6 (1980), at the age of eighty-three. Kay was affectionately known to her students as "Auntie Kay." Her ashes are buried on Washington Island.

> [...] Kay will be remembered by all who knew her as a warm, cheerful, outgoing, helpful, and interesting person—always ready to tackle new ideas. She remained cheerful and positive in mental attitude, and unsinkable to the end. She was the kind of person that one hopes will go on forever. And she will, through the many people whose lives she touched and influenced.[44]

Marge Turner was later remembered (by Gaylord) as the woman whom Curtis always claimed to be the female half in synchronized swimming's first duet—paired with Willard Congreve, who also happened to be Gaylord's high school choir teacher in Chicago. Marge would arrange various other memorial tributes in 1980, while also making important provisions for preserving Curtis's legacy by donating nearly 2,000 pages of Curtis's original correspondence (with other documents) to the Chicago Historical Society in 1981.

A month after synchronized swimming made its official Olympic debut in 1984, Washington Island's Bethel Evangelical Free Church published this commentary in its (September 9) newsletter:

> It was thrilling to hear that, [...] at the opening ceremony, the sport was introduced as being developed by Katherine (Kay) Curtis. We all remember Kay, and I'm sure [that we] did not give her the honor due her as she lived among us for many years. Kay [first] came to the Island in 1916 as a swimming instructor, [and] she bought [Ferda Lokin in 1936] with the funds received from her water ballet show, the Kay Curtis Modern Mermaids, at the Chicago Century of Progress in 1934 [where synchronized swimming first received its name].[45]

It's also worth noting that, unsurprisingly, Washington Island now has a simple, "good-sized" municipal pool, with Marge Turner's bas-relief sculpture of Curtis on the wall nearby.

Ever since 1984, competitive synchronized swimming has continued to replace its more "artistic" counterpart—epitomized by the (now discontinued) IAAA festivals—which even Curtis once described as looking "more like dancing than swimming." And, although the American and Canadian synchronized swimming teams would initially dominate the Olympic stage through 1992 and the end of the Cold War, an unbroken championship streak has since risen out of Russia that remains virtually guaranteed by their institutional government support (lacking in the west). And for various other reasons, Olympic synchronized swimming has now become more popular and successful in countries that have no specific claim to its historical origins, such as Japan, Spain, and the People's Republic of China.

In the modern culture of the United States, this idiosyncratic sport has remained in perpetual danger of becoming even more niche, as its general rate of participation remains static at best. Furthermore, America's unique claim to the sport—Curtis's history and why everyone in the world says "synchronized swimming"—seems to be diminishing with FINA's 2017 decision to rename the sport "artistic swimming." Ironically, those in favor of this decision think it will both clarify and popularize the creative nature of the sport, while those arguing against it, such as Russia, prefer "synchronized swimming" largely because of its previously athletic (or competitive) emphasis. In truth, a more ideal balance can be achieved by not only keeping the original name, but also by simply rediscovering its history in the life of Katharine Whitney Curtis, who always made sure to counterbalance the current trend.

And while it doesn't currently seem necessary to emphasize the benefits of healthy competition, it must indeed be restated here that Curtis's final dreaming was not spent on the exceptional wonders of Olympic glory, but a more common (and more noble) participation by average swimmers coming together as a family. After all, true nobility was never achieved by being better than other people, but by choosing to help other people for the better—for strength to be shared, for beauty to inspire, and for love to bind everything that we build in this world—until the end.

True nobility was never meant to be exceptional.

True nobility was meant to be common.

Chapter Notes

Abbreviations

AFN   American Forces Network
ARC   American Red Cross
ATW   Anne Townsend Whitney
CHS   Chicago Historical Society: Katharine Whitney Curtis Papers
EA   Estelle Angier
GLW   Gaylord Lee Whitney
ISHOF International Swimming Hall of Fame: Fort Lauderdale, Florida
JW   Jane Whitney
KWC   Katharine Whitney Curtis
LRW   Lee Rankin Whitney
VV   Victoria Vacha
WFP   Whitney Family Papers

Chapter 1

1. "This Is Your Life," script, c. April 1962, CHS.
2. "Wins Postal Fight," clipping, c. December 1923, CHS.
3. "Sailor Comes Back ... Him," clipping, undated, CHS.
4. Kronshage, "Around the Town," clipping, undated, WFP.
5. "Lee Whitney Says 'Never Again,'" clipping, c. June 1911, WFP.
6. "He Remembers Milwaukee," clipping (L. C. Whitney scrapbook), undated, CHS.
7. Whitney Research Group: http://wiki.whitneygen.org/wrg/index.php/Family:Whitney,_Leroy_Chester_(1846-1910)
8. Rankin Genealogy Chart, undated, CHS.
9. Wright, Francis Hamilton Rankin Diary Excerpts, 1848–1863, private collection.
10. Newton, "'Send Sweetheart Onion' ... Descendant," *Milwaukee Journal*, January 6, 1945.

Chapter 2

1. Gilbert, "Vet ... Drummer Boy at 11," *The Chicago Sun*, May 30, 1944.
2. Frank, *The Medical History of Milwaukee: 1834–1914*, p. 24.
3. ATW, letters to parents, 1883, CHS.
4. KWC, "The Saga ... Worker," speech, undated, CHS.
5. "Young Girl ... Records," clipping, August 1912, CHS.
6. *Ibid.*
7. Hawkins, "Follow Your Heart's Desire," *Wisconsin Alumnus*, February 1941, p. 102.
8. Steebs, "Washington Island's ... Time," *The Door County Advocate*, June 1977, p. 7 (II).
9. *Ibid.*
10. "University Happenings ... Office," *Wisconsin State Journal*, clipping, undated, WFP.
11. Hawkins.
12. "Joe C. Steinauer ... Figure," clipping, March 1974, p. 4, CHS.
13. KWC, *Rhythmic Swimming*, 1942, p. 1.
14. Steebs.
15. "Madison Girl ... Home Lover," *Sunday State Journal*, December 1916, p. 6.
16. Hawkins.
17. "Somewhere in France," letter to KWC, June 2, 1918, WFP.

Chapter 3

1. Steebs, "Washington Island's ... Time," *The Door County Advocate*, June 1977, p. 7 (II).
2. Middleton, "Physical Fitness ... Girls," *Physical Culture*, February 1920, p. 35, CHS.
3. Steebs.
4. KWC, *Rhythmic Swimming*, 1942, p. 1.
5. Bell, "Open Union ... Occasion," clipping, c. 1925, CHS.
6. "Record Swim by Pinemere Lady," *Minocqua Times*, August 20, 1926, p. 1.
7. "Woman ... Death's Door," clipping, 1927, CHS.
8. "Aquatic Carnival ... Out," clipping, December 1927, CHS.
9. "Shows How ... Person," *Chicago Journal*, February 13, 1928, CHS.
10. "Instructors Plan Channel Swim," *Normalite*, February 14, 1928, CHS.
11. "Aquatic Playlet ... Costumes," *Normalite*, May 29, 1928, p. 4, CHS.
12. "Pick Teams ... Qualify," clipping, December 1928, CHS.
13. KWC, "Competitive SS," *Journal of Health & Physical Education*, January 1941.
14. Bean, *Synchronized Swimming*, 2005, p. 9.

15. "Neptune Walks the Plank ... Pageant," *Chicago Tribune*, 1929, p. 10, CHS.
16. George Whitney, letter to Marion Baker, December 1932, WFP.
17. KWC, travel notes, July 1932, CHS.
18. KWC, travel notes, August 1932, CHS.
19. Hawkins, "Follow Your Heart's Desire," *Wisconsin Alumnus*, February 1941, p. 103.
20. "Sport Session for Women," *University of Michigan*, February 8, 1933.
21. Magnusson, "In Athletic Hall of Fame," clipping, CHS.
22. Vacha, letter to ISHOF, November 28, 1977, ISHOF.
23. KWC, letter fragment, c. 1934, CHS.
24. Bean, p. 11.
25. *Ibid.*, p. 10.
26. *Ibid.*, p. 11.
27. *Ibid.* p. 10.
28. *Ibid.* p. 11.
29. Lyddane, letter to KWC, March 21, 1935, CHS.
30. LRW, letter to Marion and George, April 2, 1935, WFP.
31. Hawkins.

Chapter 4

1. GLW, unpublished interview, December 31, 2013.
2. GLW, "The Promise," unpublished essay, undated, WFP.
3. KWC, travel notes, December 1937, p. 1, CHS.
4. *Ibid.*, p. 2.
5. Vacha, letter to ISHOF, November 28, 1977, ISHOF.
6. "Royalty Statements," Burgess Publishing, CHS.
7. Havlicek, letter to ISHOF, November 29, 1977, ISHOF.
8. Wales, letter to ISHOF, undated, ISHOF.
9. Havlicek.
10. Hayes, letter to ISHOF, December 9, 1977, ISHOF.
11. Havlicek.
12. Hayes.
13. Bean, *Synchronized Swimming*, 2005, p. 15–16.
14. Mueller, letter to ISHOF, November 23, 1977, ISHOF.
15. Hayes.
16. Havlicek.
17. Hawkins, "Follow Your Heart's Desire," *Wisconsin Alumnus*, February 1941, p. 101.
18. Wales.
19. Hawkins.
20. KWC, *Rhythmic Swimming*, 1942, p. 2.

Chapter 5

1. KWC, letter to EA, October 13, 1942, CHS.
2. KWC, letter to EA, October 15, 1942, CHS.
3. KWC, letter to EA, January 24, 1943, CHS.
4. KWC, letter to ATW, January 27, 1943, CHS.
5. KWC, letter to JW, January 27, 1943, CHS.
6. KWC, newsletter, February 1943, CHS.
7. KWC, letter to ATW, February 10, 1943, CHS.
8. Cross, "Glad to Report ... North Africa," telegram to JW, February 24, 1943, CHS.
9. KWC, newsletter, March 2, 1943, CHS.
10. KWC, letter to JW, March 22, 1943, CHS.
11. *Ibid.* (Censorship insert).
12. KWC, narrative report, March 1, 1943, CHS.
13. KWC, letter to ATW, March 31, 1943, CHS.
14. KWC, letter to JW, April 2, 1943, CHS.
15. KWC, letter to ATW, April 11, 1943, CHS.
16. KWC, letter to JW, April 25, 1943, CHS.
17. KWC, newsletter, April 25, 1943, CHS.
18. Bradley, *A General's Life*, p. 156.
19. KWC, letter to JW, April 26, 1943, CHS.
20. KWC, letter to ATW, April 30, 1943, CHS.
21. KWC, letter to JW, May 3, 1943, CHS.
22. KWC, letter to ATW, May 6, 1943, CHS.
23. KWC, letter to ATW, May 12, 1943 CHS.
24. KWC, letter to ATW, June 20, 1943, CHS.
25. KWC, letter to JW, June 24, 1943, CHS.
26. KWC, letter to ATW, July 1, 1943, CHS.
27. "Army & Navy: The 513th Comes Home," *Time*, April 26, 1943.
28. KWC, letter to EA, August 5, 1943, CHS.
29. KWC, newsletter, August 6, 1943, CHS.

Chapter 6

1. GLW, unpublished interview, December 31, 2013.
2. Hirshon, *General Patton*, p. 403.
3. KWC, letter to ATW, September 8, 1943, CHS.
4. Hirshon, p. 404.
5. KWC, newsletter, September 26, 1943, CHS.
6. KWC, letters to ATW, JW and LRW, September 29, 1943, CHS.
7. *Ibid.*
8. KWC, letter to ATW, October 10, 1943, CHS.
9. KWC, letter to Estelle, October 12, 1943, CHS.
10. KWC, letter to ATW, October 29, 1943, CHS.
11. KWC, letter to JW, November 11, 1943, CHS.
12. KWC, letter to ATW, December 12, 1943, CHS.
13. KWC, newsletter, January 12, 1944, CHS.
14. Newton, "Milwaukeean's ... Patton," *Milwaukee Journal*, September 26, 1944.
15. KWC, newsletter (continued), January 12, 1944, CHS.
16. "I guess ... myself," *The Chicago Tribune*, clipping, CHS.
17. KWC, letter to ATW, March 1, 1944, CHS.
18. KWC, letter to JW, March 1, 1944, CHS.
19. KWC, letter to EA, March 4, 1944, CHS.
20. KWC, letter to ATW, March 28, 1944, CHS.
21. KWC, letter to JW, April 2, 1944, CHS.
22. "To Kay Curtis," poem, 1944, CHS.

Chapter 7

1. "Whitey," letter to KWC, June 12, 1944, CHS.
2. KWC, letter to EA, July 8, 1944, CHS.

3. KWC, letter to EA, August 2, 1944, CHS.
4. Newton, "Milwaukeean's ... Patton," *Milwaukee Journal*, September 26, 1944.
5. "Whitey," letter to KWC, September 27, 1944, CHS.
6. KWC, letter to EA, October 21, 1944, CHS.
7. KWC, newsletter, December 13, 1944, CHS.
8. KWC, newsletter, January 1, 1945, CHS.
9. KWC, letter to ATW, February 21, 1945, CHS.
10. KWC, letter to ATW, February 26, 1945, CHS.
11. KWC, letter to Marge Turner, March 25, 1945, CHS.
12. Hirshon, *General Patton*, p. 618.
13. KWC, newsletter, April 2, 1945, CHS.
14. KWC, letter to ATW, April 24, 1945, CHS.
15. "Caserta Aquacade," *Stars & Stripes*, clipping, May 24, 1945, CHS.
16. "Additional Swimmers ... Aquacade," clipping, CHS.
17. "Aquacade to Be Presented ... Kind," *The Chronicle*, May 27, 1945, CHS.
18. "Aquacade Postponed ... Saturday," *The Chronicle*, June 3, 1945, CHS.
19. KWC, letter to ATW, June 10, 1945, CHS.
20. "Aquacade Continues Today," *The Chronicle*, June 10, 1945, CHS.
21. KWC, letter to EA, June 16, 1945, CHS.
22. KWC, letter to ATW, June 19, 1945, CHS.
23. KWC, newsletter, June 24, 1945, CHS.
24. "Kay Curtis Produced AFHQ Aquacade," *Newsbrief (ARC)*, July 1945, p. 3, CHS.
25. Swensen, letter to ARC, June 25, 1945, CHS.
26. Christenberry, commendation, June 20, 1945, CHS.
27. Hausner, letter to KWC, undated, CHS.

Chapter 8

1. LRW, letter to GLW, July 24, 1945, WFP.
2. KWC, letter to ATW, July 3, 1945, CHS.
3. KWC, letter to ATW, July 4, 1945, CHS.
4. KWC, letter to ATW, July 8, 1945, CHS.
5. KWC, letter to ATW, July 11, 1945, CHS.
6. KWC, letter to ATW, July 22, 1945, CHS.
7. KWC, letter to ATW, August 10, 1945, CHS.
8. KWC, letter to ATW, August 26, 1945, CHS.
9. KWC, letter to ATW, August 31, 1945, CHS.
10. KWC, letter to ATW, September 11, 1945, CHS.
11. Potts, letter to KWC, September 23, 1945, CHS.
12. "Directions ... 'Chateau Beauvallon,'" leaflet, undated, CHS.
13. KWC, newsletter, October 6, 1945, CHS.
14. KWC, letter to ATW, October 7, 1945, CHS.
15. KWC, letter to ATW, October 28, 1945, CHS.
16. KWC, letter to ATW, November 14, 1945, CHS.
17. George Whitney, letter to KWC, November 20, 1945, CHS.
18. KWC, letter to EA, December 1, 1945, CHS.
19. KWC, letter to ATW, January 12, 1946, CHS.
20. KWC, newsletter, January 27, 1946, CHS.
21. KWC, letter to EA, March 15, 1946, CHS.
22. KWC, letter to ATW, March 27, 1946, CHS.
23. KWC, letter to ATW, April 9, 1946, CHS.
24. KWC, letter to EA, June 10, 1946, CHS.
25. "Whitey," letter to KWC, August 16, 1946, CHS.
26. KWC, letter to Caroline Rankin, August 23, 1946, WFP.
27. KWC, letter to EA, August 31, 1946, CHS.
28. KWC, letter to EA, October 21, 1946, CHS.

Chapter 9

1. "Court Leaves ... Crimes," *Stars & Stripes*, September 30, 1946.
2. KWC, newsletter, December 16, 1946, CHS.
3. "Office of Chief of Counsel ... 0929," identification card, November 28, 1946, CHS.
4. KWC, letter to EA, January 11, 1947, CHS.
5. "Letter from Gretl," January 13, 1947, CHS.
6. KWC, letter to ATW, February 12, 1947, CHS.
7. KWC, letter to ATW, August 5, 1947, CHS.
8. KWC, letter to ATW, September 8, 1947, CHS.
9. KWC, newsletter, October 3, 1947, CHS.
10. KWC, letter to ATW, October 23, 1947, CHS.
11. KWC, letter to David Clark Leach, December 9, 1947, CHS.
12. KWC, letter to Avery Brundage, January 27, 1948, CHS.
13. Brundage, letter to KWC, March 6, 1948, CHS.
14. Williams, *The Million Dollar Mermaid*, p. 395–396.
15. KWC, letter to ATW, February 22, 1948, CHS.
16. KWC, letter to ATW, March 4, 1948, CHS.
17. KWC, letter to ATW, April 16, 1948, CHS.
18. KWC, letter to EA, May 5, 1948, CHS.
19. KWC, travel notes, June 1948, CHS.
20. KWC, letter to EA, July 4, 1948, CHS.
21. KWC, newsletter, October 1948, CHS.
22. KWC, letter to ATW, November 2, 1948, CHS.
23. KWC, letter to ATW, November 22, 1948, CHS.
24. KWC, letter to ATW, December 12, 1948, CHS.
25. KWC, newsletter, January 1949, CHS.
26. KWC, letter to ATW, January 24, 1949, CHS.
27. KWC, letter to EA, March 8, 1949, CHS.
28. KWC, letter to ATW, March 13, 1949, CHS.
29. KWC, letter to EA, April 6, 1949, CHS.
30. KWC, letter to ATW, May 11, 1949, CHS.
31. KWC, letter to ATW, May 29, 1949, CHS.
32. KWC, newsletter, May 31, 1949, CHS.
33. KWC, letter to ATW, July 15, 1949, CHS.
34. KWC, letter to ATW, July 22, 1949, CHS.
35. KWC, letter to ATW, August 12, 1949, CHS.
36. KWC, letter to EA, September 3, 1949, CHS.
37. KWC, letter to Fredrick H. Cords, October 5, 1949, CHS.
38. KWC, letter to EA, January 15, 1950, CHS.
39. KWC, letter to EA, February 10, 1950, CHS.
40. KWC, letter to ATW, April 18, 1950, CHS.
41. Wolf-Christian Dullo, email correspondence, 2015.

42. KWC, letter to ATW, August 21, 1950, CHS.
43. KWC, letter to EA, August 25, 1950, CHS.
44. KWC, letter to ATW, October 22, 1950, CHS.
45. KWC, letter to ATW, October 29, 1950, CHS.
46. KWC, letter to ATW, November 19, 1950, CHS.
47. KWC, letter to ATW, January 4, 1951, CHS.
48. KWC, telegram to JW (for ATW), January 8, 1951, CHS.

Chapter 10

1. KWC, newsletter, March 1951, CHS.
2. *Ibid.*
3. *Ibid.*
4. "Letters to the Editor ... Agency," *The Albina Advertiser*, September 1951, WFP.
5. KWC, letter to ATW, September 9, 1951, CHS.
6. KWC, letter to ATW, July 31, 1951, CHS.
7. KWC, newsletter, October 1951, CHS.
8. "Tatler's Leader Page Parade," *Irish Independent*, November 5, 1951, CHS.
9. KWC, newsletter, October 1951, CHS.
10. KWC, letter to ATW, February 2, 1952, CHS.
11. KWC, letter to EA, February 11, 1952, CHS.
12. "For Immediate Release ... 'Spotlight,'" *Public Information Office*, February 13, 1952, CHS.
13. KWC, letter to ATW, March 9, 1952, CHS.
14. KWC, newsletter, April 1952, CHS.
15. KWC, letter to ATW, May 11, 1952, CHS.
16. KWC, letter to ATW, June 30, 1952, CHS.
17. KWC, newsletter, August 9, 1952, CHS.
18. KWC, letter to EA, September 25, 1952, CHS.
19. KWC, letter to ATW, October 31, 1952, CHS.
20. KWC, letter to EA, December 14, 1952, CHS.
21. KWC, letter to EA, December 30, 1952, CHS.
22. KWC, letter to ATW, January 20, 1953, CHS.
23. KWC, letter to ATW, January 27, 1953, CHS.
24. KWC, letter to EA, April 29, 1953, CHS.
25. KWC, travel notes, May 1953, CHS.
26. KWC, letter to ATW, June 9, 1953, CHS.
27. KWC, letter to Marge Turner, August 20, 1953, CHS.
28. KWC, letter to EA, October 9, 1953, CHS.
29. KWC, letter to ATW, October 11, 1953, CHS.
30. KWC, letter to ATW, October 19, 1953, CHS.
31. KWC, letter to VV, February 23, 1954, CHS.
32. KWC, letter to EA, March 2, 1954, CHS.
33. KWC, letter to EA, March 14, 1954, CHS.
34. "Mrs. Anne Whitney ... 78," clipping, CHS.
35. ATW, letter to KWC, c. 1942, CHS.
36. KWC, letter to EA, April 11, 1954, CHS.
37. KWC, letter to EA, October 20, 1954, CHS.
38. KWC, letter to VV, August 8, 1954, CHS.
39. KWC, letter to EA, November 18, 1954, CHS.
40. KWC, letter to VV, January 30, 1955, CHS.
41. KWC, letter to VV, March 15, 1955, CHS.
42. KWC, letter to EA, April 4, 1955, CHS.
43. KWC, letter fragment, c. June 1955, CHS.
44. KWC, letter to EA, September 27, 1955, CHS.
45. KWC, letter to JW, December 31, 1955, CHS.
46. KWC, letter to JW, January 10, 1956, CHS.
47. KWC, letter to EA, May 13, 1956, CHS.
48. KWC, letter to EA, July 18, 1956, CHS.
49. KWC, letter to VV, November 18, 1956, CHS.
50. KWC, letter to EA, December 31, 1956, CHS.
51. KWC, letter to EA, January 14, 1957, CHS.
52. KWC, letter to EA, March 17, 1957, CHS.
53. KWC, letter to EA, October 7, 1957, CHS.
54. KWC, letter to EA, October 30, 1957, CHS.
55. KWC, letter to VV, November 4, 1957, CHS.
56. KWC, letter to VV, November 20, 1957, CHS.
57. Wolf-Christian Dullo, email correspondence, 2015.
58. KWC, letter to VV, December 11, 1957, CHS.
59. KWC, letter to VV, December 30, 1957, CHS.
60. KWC, letter to EA, January 7, 1958, CHS.
61. KWC, letter to VV, February 13, 1958, CHS.
62. KWC, letter to VV, March 14, 1958, CHS.
63. "Employee Performance Appraisal ... 1958," CHS.
64. KWC, letter to VV, June 20, 1958, CHS.
65. KWC, letter to Norma J. Olsen, October 22, 1958, CHS.
66. KWC, letter to VV, November 22, 1958, CHS.
67. KWC, letter to VV, December 24, 1958, CHS.
68. KWC, letter to VV, January 8, 1959, CHS.
69. KWC, letter to Yohanan Beham, January 22, 1959, CHS.
70. KWC, letter to Yohanan Beham, July 13, 1959, CHS.
71. KWC, "Reader's Letter: Synchronized Swimming," *The Jerusalem Post*, July 13, 1959, CHS.
72. Wirz, letter to KWC, July 27, 1959, CHS.
73. Gil, letter to KWC, September 14, 1959, CHS.
74. KWC, letter to Bella Wirz, September 16, 1959, CHS.
75. KWC, letter to VV, November 18, 1959, CHS.
76. KWC, letter to VV, March 30, 1960, CHS.
77. KWC, letter to VV, April 12, 1960, CHS.
78. KWC, letter to Guthmeier (Air India), April 25, 1960, CHS.
79. KWC, letter to Christian Signorell, April 29, 1960, CHS.
80. KWC, letter to VV, May 18, 1960, CHS.
81. KWC, letter to VV, May 28, 1960, CHS.
82. KWC, travel notes, June 20, 1960, CHS.
83. KWC, letter to VV, July 16, 1960, CHS.
84. KWC, letter to VV, August 16, 1960, CHS.
85. KWC, letter to VV, September 14, 1960, CHS.
86. KWC, letter to VV, October 10, 1960, CHS.
87. KWC, letter to VV, October 26, 1960, CHS.
88. KWC, letter to VV, November 14, 1960, CHS.
89. KWC, AFN radio script, January 6, 1961, CHS.
90. *Ibid.*
91. KWC, letter to VV, April 22, 1961, CHS.
92. KWC, letter to EA, September 30, 1961, CHS.
93. KWC, letter to VV, October 19, 1961, CHS.
94. KWC, letter to VV, October 24, 1961, CHS.
95. KWC, letter to VV, November 6, 1961, CHS.
96. KWC, AFN radio script, February 11, 1962, CHS.
97. KWC, letter to EA January 15, 1962, CHS.
98. "This Is Your Life," script, c. April 1962, CHS.

Chapter 11

1. GLW and Caroline Whitney, unpublished interview, April 29, 2018, CHS.
2. KWC, newsletter, December 1963, CHS.
3. KWC, newsletter, August 1963, CHS.
4. Hardee, email correspondence, 2014–2019.
5. *Ibid.*
6. *Ibid.*
7. KWC, letter to VV, July 16, 1960, CHS.
8. KWC, newsletter, November 1964, CHS.
9. KWC, newsletter, April 1965, CHS.
10. KWC, newsletter, January 1966, CHS.
11. KWC, newsletter, December 1966, CHS.
12. KWC, newsletter, May 1, 1967, CHS.
13. KWC, newsletter, June 20, 1968, CHS.
14. KWC, newsletter, August 1969, CHS.
15. Jepsen, "Kay Curtis ... Projects," *The Door County Advocate*, September 17, 1970, p. 2 (I), CHS.
16. KWC, newsletter, December 1970, CHS.
17. Nixon, letter to KWC, March 23, 1971, WFP.
18. Wolf-Christian Dullo, letter to KWC, May 2, 1971, CHS.
19. Renate Dullo, letter to KWC, January 4, 1972, CHS.
20. Goodwin, unpublished essays, 2018.
21. KWC, "Comments ... Festival," *The Aquatic Artist*, July–December 1973, p. 10.
22. Magnusson, "Islanders ... Party," *The Door County Advocate*, July 1973, CHS.
23. KWC, newsletter, December 1973, CHS.
24. Dykeman, "Enthusiastic, Jane Whitney," *Knoxville News-Sentinel*, undated, WFP.
25. Morrison, "Swim Queen Now in Polk," *The Ledger Local*, November 15, 1974, p. 3A.
26. KWC, newsletter, c. July 1975, CHS.
27. Owen, KWC medical file, March 17, 1976, CHS.
28. KWC, newsletter, December 1977, CHS.
29. *Ibid.*
30. Hayes, letter to ISHOF, December 9, 1977, ISHOF.
31. KWC, letter to GLW, January 28, 1978, WFP.
32. Hardee.
33. KWC, Last Will and Testament, February 12, 1978, CHS.
34. Steebs, "Washington Island's ... Time," *The Door County Advocate*, June 1977, p. 7 (II).
35. Seller, letter to KWC, September 29, 1978, CHS.
36. KWC, letter to ISHOF (Mary), February 26, 1979, CHS.
37. Steebs, "Kay Whitney Curtis Richly ... Fame," *The Door County Advocate*, July 24, 1979, CHS.
38. Goodwin.
39. *Ibid.*
40. Hardee.
41. GLW, unpublished interview, December 31, 2013.
42. Hardee.
43. Hayes, "In Memory," IAAA bulletin, 1980.
44. Turner, KWC Obituary, clipping, September-October, 1980, CHS.
45. Warren, "Community News," *Bethel Church Tidings*, September 9, 1984, WFP.

Bibliography

"Additional Swimmers Needed for Aquacade." Clipping (scrapbook). Chicago Historical Society: Katharine Whitney Curtis Papers.

"Aquacade Continues Today." *The Chronicle*. June 10, 1945. Chicago Historical Society: Katharine Whitney Curtis Papers.

"Aquacade Postponed; to be Coming Saturday." *The Chronicle*. June 3, 1945. Chicago Historical Society: Katharine Whitney Curtis Papers.

"Aquacade to Be Presented This Coming Weekend: Spectacle First of Its Kind." *The Chronicle*. May 27, 1945. Chicago Historical Society: Katharine Whitney Curtis Papers.

"Aquatic Carnival Tuesday; All Out: Novel Program and Unusual Costumes Arranged for Christmas Pageant." Clipping. December 1927. Chicago Historical Society: Katharine Whitney Curtis Papers.

"Aquatic Playlet a Four-Day Success: Frogs, Tadpoles, Crabs and Lilies Display Unique Costumes." *Normalite*. May 29, 1928. Chicago Historical Society: Katharine Whitney Curtis Papers.

"Army & Navy: The 513th Comes Home." *Time*. April 26, 1943.

Baker, Jean-Claude, and Chris Chase. *Josephine: The Hungry Heart*. New York: Cooper Square Press, 2001. Print.

Bean, Dawn Pawson. *Synchronized Swimming: An American History*. Jefferson, NC: McFarland., 2005. Print.

Bell, S. S. "Open Union League Tank Tomorrow: Swimming Director Prepares Program of Water Games for the Occasion." Clipping. c. 1925. Chicago Historical Society: Katharine Whitney Curtis Papers.

Bradley, Omar N., and Clay Blair. *A General's Life: An Autobiography by General of the Army*. New York: Simon & Schuster, 1983. Print.

Brundage, Avery. Letter to Katharine Whitney Curtis. March 6, 1948. Chicago Historical Society: Katharine Whitney Curtis Papers.

"Caserta Aquacade." *Stars & Stripes*. Clipping (scrapbook). May 24, 1945. Chicago Historical Society: Katharine Whitney Curtis Papers.

Christenberry, Col. C. W. Commendation. June 20, 1945. Chicago Historical Society: Katharine Whitney Curtis Papers.

"Court Leaves Faint Hope for 21 Nazis: Judgement Blames All for Crimes." *The Stars & Stripes (European Edition)*. September 30, 1946.

Cross, Col. Will. "Glad to Report Safe Arrival Katharine Whitney Curtis, North Africa." Telegram to Jane Whitney. February 24, 1943. Chicago Historical Society: Katharine Whitney Curtis Papers.

Curtis, Katharine Whitney. American Forces Network Radio Scripts. 1961–1962. Chicago Historical Society: Katharine Whitney Curtis Papers.

_____. "Comments on the 1973 International Festival." *The Aquatic Artist*. July-December 1973.

_____. "Competitive Synchronized Swimming." *Journal of Health & Physical Education*. January 1941.

_____. Last Will and Testament. February 12, 1978. Chicago Historical Society: Katharine Whitney Curtis Papers.

_____. Letter fragment. c. June 1955. Chicago Historical Society: Katharine Whitney Curtis Papers.

_____. Letter to Avery Brundage. January 27, 1948. Chicago Historical Society: Katharine Whitney Curtis Papers.

_____. Letter to Bella Wirz. September 16, 1959. Chicago Historical Society: Katharine Whitney Curtis Papers.

_____. Letter to Caroline Rankin. August 23, 1946. Whitney Family Papers.

_____. Letter to Christian Signorell. April 29, 1960. Chicago Historical Society: Katharine Whitney Curtis Papers.

_____. Letter to David Clark Leach. December 9, 1947. Chicago Historical Society: Katharine Whitney Curtis Papers.

_____. Letter to Fredrick H. Cords. October 5, 1949. Chicago Historical Society: Katharine Whitney Curtis Papers.

_____. Letter to Gaylord Lee Whitney. January 28, 1978. Whitney Family Papers.

_____. Letter to Guthmeier (Air India). April 25, 1960. Chicago Historical Society: Katharine Whitney Curtis Papers.

_____. Letter to International Swimming Hall of Fame. February 26, 1979. Chicago Historical Society: Katharine Whitney Curtis Papers.

_____. Letter to Norma J. Olsen. October 22, 1958. Chicago Historical Society: Katharine Whitney Curtis Papers.

_____. Letters to Anne Townsend Whitney, 1943–1953. Chicago Historical Society: Katharine Whitney Curtis Papers.

_____. Letters to Estelle Angier, 1942–1962. Chicago Historical Society: Katharine Whitney Curtis Papers.

_____. Letters to Jane Whitney, 1943–1959. Chicago Historical Society: Katharine Whitney Curtis Papers.

_____. Letters to Marge Turner, 1945–1953. Chicago Historical Society: Katharine Whitney Curtis Papers.

_____. Letters to Victoria Vacha, 1943–1961. Chicago Historical Society: Katharine Whitney Curtis Papers.

_____. Letters to Yohanan Beham. 1959. Chicago Historical Society: Katharine Whitney Curtis Papers.

_____. Narrative reports (American Red Cross), 1943–1945. Chicago Historical Society: Katharine Whitney Curtis Papers.

_____. Newsletters, 1943–1977. Chicago Historical Society: Katharine Whitney Curtis Papers.

_____. "Reader's Letter: Synchronized Swimming." *The Jerusalem Post*. July 13, 1959. Chicago Historical Society: Katharine Whitney Curtis Papers.

_____. *Rhythmic Swimming: A Source Book of Synchronized Swimming and Water Pageantry*. Minneapolis: Burgess Publishing, 1942. Print.

_____. "The Saga of an Untrained Recreation Worker." Speech. Undated. Chicago Historical Society: Katharine Whitney Curtis Papers.

_____. Telegram to Jane Whitney. January 8, 1951. Chicago Historical Society: Katharine Whitney Curtis Papers.

_____. Travel Notes, 1932–1960. Chicago Historical Society: Katharine Whitney Curtis Papers.

"Directions for Finding Kay Curtis and Col. John Brock: at 'Chateau Beauvallon.'" Leaflet. Undated. Chicago Historical Society: Katharine Whitney Curtis Papers.

Dullo, Renate. Letter to Katharine Whitney Curtis. January 4, 1972. Chicago Historical Society: Katharine Whitney Curtis Papers.

Dullo, Wolf-Christian. Email correspondence. 2015–2018.

_____. Letter to Katharine Whitney Curtis. May 2, 1971. Chicago Historical Society: Katharine Whitney Curtis Papers.

Dykeman, Wilma. "Enthusiastic, Jane Whitney." *Knoxville News-Sentinel*. Undated. Whitney Family Papers.

Eisenhower, David. *Eisenhower: At War, 1943–1945*. New York: Random House, 1986. Print.

"Employee Performance Appraisal: USAEUR Special Activities Division, June 1957 to June 1958." Chicago Historical Society: Katharine Whitney Curtis Papers.

"For Immediate Release: From EUCOM Special Activities Division, 'Spotlight.'" *Public Information Office*. February 13, 1952. Chicago Historical Society: Katharine Whitney Curtis Papers.

Frank, Louis Frederick. *The Medical History of Milwaukee: 1834–1914*. Milwaukee: Germania Publishing Co., 1915. Print.

Gil, E. Letter to Katharine Whitney Curtis. September 14, 1959. Chicago Historical Society: Katharine Whitney Curtis Papers.

Gilbert, Paul T. "Vet, Now 94, Was Drummer Boy at 11." *The Chicago Sun*. May 30, 1944.

Goodwin, Cathy. Unpublished essays. 2018.

Hardee, Carl. Email correspondence. 2014–2019.

Hausner, Peter. Letter to Katharine Whitney Curtis. Undated. Chicago Historical Society: Katharine Whitney Curtis Papers.

Havlicek, Frank. Letter to Selection Committee. November 29, 1977. International Swimming Hall of Fame: Fort Lauderdale, Florida.

Hawkins, Lucy R. "Follow Your Heart's Desire: And Have Fun Out of Living as These Three Alumnae Have Done." *The Wisconsin Alumnus*. February 1941.

Hayes, Bernice Lorber. "In Memory." IAAA Bulletin. 1980.

_____. Letter to Selection Committee. December 9, 1977. International Swimming Hall of Fame: Fort Lauderdale, Florida.

"He Remembers Milwaukee." Clipping (L. C. Whitney scrapbook). Undated. Chicago Historical Society: Katharine Whitney Curtis Papers.

Hirshon, Stanley P. *General Patton: A Soldier's Life*. New York: HarperCollins, 2002. Print.

"I Guess I Am a Character Myself." *The Chicago Tribune*. Clipping. Chicago Historical Society: Katharine Whitney Curtis Papers.

"Instructors Plan Channel Swim." *Normalite*. February 14, 1928. Chicago Historical Society: Katharine Whitney Curtis Papers.

Jepsen, Gladys. "Kay Curtis Spearheaded Host of Island Projects." *The Door County Advocate*. September 17, 1970. Chicago Historical Society: Katharine Whitney Curtis Papers.

"Joe C. Steinauer Dies: Key UW Athletic Figure." Clipping. March 1974. Chicago Historical Society: Katharine Whitney Curtis Papers.

"Kay Curtis Produced AFHQ Aquacade." *Newsbrief (American Red Cross): Mediterranean Theater*. July 1945. Chicago Historical Society: Katharine Whitney Curtis Papers.

Kronshage, E. H. "Around the Town." Clipping. Undated. Whitney Family Papers.

"Lee Whitney Says 'Never Again.'" Clipping. c. June 1911. Whitney Family Papers.

"Letter from Gretl." January 13, 1947. Chicago Historical Society: Katharine Whitney Curtis Papers.

"Letters to the Editor: The Arab Tourist Agency." *The Albina Advertiser*. September 1951. Whitney Family Papers.

Lyddane, R. J. Letter to Katharine Whitney Curtis. March 21, 1935. Chicago Historical Society: Katharine Whitney Curtis Papers.

"Madison Girl Near to the 'New Woman': She Plays Nearly Everything the Madison Boy Does and at the Same Time Is a Home Lover." *The Sunday State Journal*. December 3, 1916.

Magnusson, Sarah. "In Athletic Hall of Fame." Clipping. Chicago Historical Society: Katharine Whitney Curtis Papers.

_____. "Islanders Honor Kay Curtis at Special Community Party." *The Door County Advocate*. July

1973. Chicago Historical Society: Katharine Whitney Curtis Papers.
Middleton, Ethelyn. "Physical Fitness for Business Girls." *Physical Culture*. February 1920. Chicago Historical Society: Katharine Whitney Curtis Papers.
Morrison, Sally. "Swim Queen Now in Polk." *The Ledger Local*. November 15, 1974.
"Mrs. Anne Whitney Is Dead at 78." Clipping. Chicago Historical Society: Katharine Whitney Curtis Papers.
Mueller, Edward B. Letter to Selection Committee. November 23, 1977. International Swimming Hall of Fame: Fort Lauderdale, Florida.
"Neptune Walks the Plank at Chicago Normal College Pageant." *Chicago Tribune*. 1929. Chicago Historical Society: Katharine Whitney Curtis Papers.
Newton, Antoinette. "Milwaukeean's Vivid Pictures of Generals Eisenhower, Patton." *Milwaukee Journal*. September 26, 1944.
_____. "'Send Sweetheart Onion,' Was a Civil War Slogan: Story of Arabella, and Early 'Red Cross,' Owned by Milwaukee Descendant." *Milwaukee Journal*. January 6, 1945.
Nixon, Richard. Letter to Katharine Whitney Curtis. March 23, 1971. Whitney Family Papers.
"Office of Chief of Counsel for War Crimes: Pass No. 0929." Identification card. November 28, 1946. Chicago Historical Society: Katharine Whitney Curtis Papers.
Owen, Dr. Edward E. Katharine Whitney Curtis Medical File. March 17, 1976. Chicago Historical Society: Katharine Whitney Curtis Papers.
"Pick Teams to Swim at Crane; Many Qualify." Clipping. December 1928. Chicago Historical Society: Katharine Whitney Curtis Papers.
Potts, Allan. Letter to Katharine Whitney Curtis. September 23, 1945. Chicago Historical Society: Katharine Whitney Curtis Papers.
Rankin Genealogy Chart. Undated. Chicago Historical Society: Katharine Whitney Curtis Papers.
"Record Swim by Pinemere Lady." Minocqua Times. August 20, 1926. Chicago Historical Society: Katharine Whitney Curtis Papers.
"Royalty Statements." Minneapolis: Burgess Publishing. Chicago Historical Society: Katharine Whitney Curtis Papers.
"Sailor Comes Back to Repay Dollar That 'Staked' Him." Clipping. Undated. Chicago Historical Society: Katharine Whitney Curtis Papers.
Seller, Peg. Letter to Katharine Whitney Curtis. September 29, 1978. Chicago Historical Society: Katharine Whitney Curtis Papers.
"Shows How to Save Drowning Person." *Chicago Journal*. February 13, 1928. Chicago Historical Society: Katharine Whitney Curtis Papers.
"Somewhere in France." Letter to Katharine Whitney Curtis. June 2, 1918. Whitney Family Papers.
"Sport Session for Women." *The University of Michigan: School of Education*. Vol. 34, No. 26. February 8, 1933.
Steebs, Keta. "Kay Whitney Curtis Richly Deserves Her Niche in Swimming Hall of Fame." *The Door County Advocate*. July 24, 1979. Chicago Historical Society: Katharine Whitney Curtis Papers.
_____. "Washington Island's Kay Curtis Becoming a Legend in Her Time." *The Door County Advocate*. June 14, 1977. p. 7 (II).
Swensen, Helga D. Letter to American Red Cross. June 25, 1945. Chicago Historical Society: Katharine Whitney Curtis Papers.
"Tatler's Leader Page Parade." *Irish Independent*. November 5, 1951. Chicago Historical Society: Katharine Whitney Curtis Papers.
"This Is Your Life." Script. c. April 1962. Chicago Historical Society: Katharine Whitney Curtis Papers.
"To Kay Curtis." Poem. 1944. Chicago Historical Society: Katharine Whitney Curtis Papers.
Turner, Marge. Katharine Whitney Curtis Obituary. Clipping. September-October, 1980. Chicago Historical Society: Katharine Whitney Curtis Papers.
"University Happenings of Interest: Olsen Seeks Office." *Wisconsin State Journal*. Clipping. Undated. Whitney Family Papers.
Vacha, Victoria. Letter to Selection Committee. November 28, 1977. International Swimming Hall of Fame: Fort Lauderdale, Florida.
Wales, Ellen D. Letter to Selection Committee. Undated. International Swimming Hall of Fame: Fort Lauderdale, Florida.
Warren, Rev. James B. "Community News." *Bethel Church Tidings*. September 9, 1984. Whitney Family Papers.
"Whitey." Letters to Katharine Whitney Curtis, 1944–1946. Chicago Historical Society: Katharine Whitney Curtis Papers.
Whitney, Anne T. *Let's Talk About "Washington Island," 1850–1950*. Washington Island: Town of Washington, 1995. Print.
_____. Letter to Katharine Whitney Curtis. c. 1942. Chicago Historical Society: Katharine Whitney Curtis Papers.
_____. Letters to Parents. 1883. Chicago Historical Society: Katharine Whitney Curtis Papers.
Whitney, Gaylord Lee. "The Promise." Unpublished essay. Undated. Whitney Family Papers.
_____. Unpublished interview. December 31, 2013.
_____, and Caroline Whitney. Unpublished Interview. April 29, 2018.
Whitney, George. Letter to Katharine Whitney Curtis. November 20, 1945. Chicago Historical Society: Katharine Whitney Curtis Papers.
_____. Letters to Marion. 1932. Whitney Family Papers.
Whitney, Lee Rankin. Letter to Gaylord Lee Whitney. July 24, 1945. Whitney Family Papers.
_____. Letter to Marion and George. April 2, 1935. Whitney Family Papers.
Whitney Research Group: http://wiki.whitneygen.org/wrg/index.php/Family:Whitney,_Leroy_Chester_(1846-1910)
Williams, Esther, and Digby Diehl. *The Million Dollar Mermaid*. New York: Simon & Schuster, 1999. Print.

"Wins Postal Fight." Clipping. c. December 1923. Chicago Historical Society: Katharine Whitney Curtis Papers.

Wirz, Bella. Letter to Katharine Whitney Curtis. July 27, 1959. Chicago Historical Society: Katharine Whitney Curtis Papers.

"Woman Will Try Swimming Feat at Death's Door." Clipping. 1927. Chicago Historical Society: Katharine Whitney Curtis Papers.

Wright, Elizabeth A. Francis Hamilton Rankin Diary Excerpts, 1848–1863. Private collection.

"Young Girl Swims Across the Lake; Breaks Records." Clipping. August 1912. Chicago Historical Society: Katharine Whitney Curtis Papers.

Index

Addis Ababa, Ethiopia 163
Agadir, Morocco 56–61, 64–65, 67, 79
Air India 157, 159
Albany, New York 12
Alexander, Gen. Harold 84, 86, 88
Allied Force Headquarters *see* Caserta, Italy
The Amateur Athletic Union 27, 31, 36, 45–48, 123, 174
The American Civil War 14, 16
The American Expeditionary Force 24
The American Forces Network 153–154, 161–163
The American Red Cross 7–8, 15, 30, 35, 50, 54–121
American Samoa 167
Amsterdam, Netherlands 154
Angier, Estelle 53, 143, 147–148, 167
Annapolis Hotel 53
Ansbach, Germany 117
Antico Stabilimento Balneare di Mondello 68–72
Anzio, Italy 80
Aquatic Artist 174
The Arab Tourist Agency 137–138
Armour & Company 26–27, 31
"artistic swimming" 184
The Asian Flu Pandemic 151
The Audubon Society 173, 176, 179
"Auld Lang Syne" 85, 128
Australia 167
Austria 153

Baalbek, Lebanon 166
bachelor's degree 27
Bad Nauheim, Germany 122–128
Bailey, Alma 120–121
Baker, Josephine 62, 130
Bangkok, Thailand 167
Bari, Italy 80, **108**
Bartholomei, Victor 64
Barton, Clara 15
Bastogne, Belgium 84

The Battle of Bull Run 14
The Battle of Monte Cassino 78
The Battle of Perryville 16
The Battle of the Bulge 84
The Battle of Wadi Akarit 60
The Bay of Pigs Crisis 162
Bean, Dawn Pawson 31, 45
Beham, Yohanan 155–156
Beirut, Lebanon 166
Benny, Jack 71
The Berlin Wall 162
Biarritz, France 106
Biedenkopf, Germany 126–130, 163
birth 7, 19
Bizerte, Tunisia 63, 68–69
The Black Forest, Germany 132
The Black Hills Gold Rush 17
black market 117, 119
"Black Thursday" 31
The Blarney Stone 144
Bologna, Italy 126
Bolzano, Italy 126, 128, 135
Bora Bora 167
Bradley, Gen. Omar N. 62, 69, 87
Bremerhaven, Germany 116
Brenner Pass, Italy 135
"Bridge of Spies" 163
Brock, Col. John A. 29, 82–83, 85–86, 88–89, 97–108, 118, 128, 169
Brundage, Avery 123–124
Budapest, Hungary 149
Buffalo, New York 12
Busseti Travel Agency 126, 136

Cairo, Egypt 163
Calas, France 102–106
Camp Chocoroa 26
Camp Kilmer 116
Camp Meade 53
Camp Minewonka 26–27
Camp Pinemere **20**, 29
Canada 31, 174, 184
cancer 132, 171, 180, 182
Cannes, France 98, 101, 106, 123
Capri, Italy 72–78, 126, 140, 145
Casablanca, Morocco 55–57, 60–64

Caserta, Italy 83–101
The Caserta Aquacade 85–95
Cashel, Ireland 11, 144
The Central Amateur Athletic Union 27, 36, 45, 47
Chateau Beauvallon 101–105
Chicago, Illinois 10, 16–17, 26–27, 30–31, 35–41, 44–48, 80–83, 111, 133, 144, 169
The Chicago Historical Society 1, 184
Chicago Normal College *see* Chicago Teacher's College
Chicago State University *see* Chicago Teacher's College
Chicago Teacher's College 30–32, 40, 44–47, 71, 174
The Chicago Teacher's Day Program 45
The Chicago World's Fair (1933–1934) 8, 32, 34–38
Chico State Teachers College 26
China 113, 167, 184
Christenberry, Col. C.W. 94
Churchill, Winston 53, 55, 138
Cleveland, Ohio 111
Clubmobile 77
Coburg, Germany 117
Cody, "Buffalo" Bill 18
The Cold War 6, 113–184
Cologne, Germany 127
"The Colonel" *see* Brock, Col. John A.
The Colony Club 53
Columbus, Ohio 6, 170–171, 182
communism 113, 115, 125–126
The Community Action Program 171, 180
Congreve, Willard 184
Coolidge, Calvin 9–10
Copenhagen, Denmark 123, 129, 132
Crane College 31–32, 35
The Cross Florida Barge Canal 173
Crugom, James, Jr. 16–17
Crugom, Dr. James, Sr. 16–17

Index

The Cuban Missile Crisis 6, 166–167
Curtis, George W. 28, 169
Curzi, Cesare 154, 156
Czechoslovakia 125, 160–161

"D-Day" *see* The Normandy Invasion Landings
death 182
Death's Door, Wisconsin 29, 43
Delafield, Wisconsin 10, 19
DePaul University 32, 35
Derosier, Mary 141
displaced children *see* orphans
divorce 10, 19, 28
The Dolomites 135
The Door County Memorial Hospital 179
Dressler, Marie 76
Dublin, Ireland 11, 138
Dullo, Renate 115–116, 135, 138, 141, 145, 147, 149–153, 161, 163, 171–174
Dullo, Wolf-Christian 147–153, 162–163, 171–174
Dullo, Wolfgang 141, 147, 151–152, 161, 163, 171–172
The Dust Bowl 33

Eisenhower, Dwight D. "Ike" 8, 64, 68–69, 74–75, 87, 139, 143–144, 180
Erlangen, Germany 117
Evansville, Indiana 181–182

Fairbanks, Douglas, Jr. 69, 71
"Fedhaven," Florida **159**, 173–177
Ferda Lokin *see* Washington Island, Wisconsin
FICPAC 165
Fiji 167
FINA 124, 141, 184
Fisher Cave 32
513th Squadron 64
Flint, Michigan 13–14
Florence, Italy 126
Flying Fortresses 64
Foggia, Italy 80
Forbes, Pansy 158
Ford, Gerald 175–176
Ford Island, Hawaii 166
Fountain of Three Dolphins 90, 92
France 98, 101–108
Frankfurt, Germany 163, 166
Fürth, Germany 117

Gagarin, Yuri 162
Gandhi, Mahatma 124
Garden of Gethsemane 137
Gatlinburg, Tennessee 147
German POWs 103, 105–106
Gilbert, Paul T. 16
Gill's Rock Ferry 41–42, 171

Giza, Egypt 136–138
Glienicke Bridge 163
Goodwin, Cathy 174, 181–182
Gottfried, Annemarie 127–130, 163
Gottfried, Heinz 127–130, 163
Gottfried, Katharina 129–130, 148, 152, 163
Gouch, Gladys 7–8
gravestone 6, 146, 183
The Great Depression 31
Greece 136, 138, 140
Green Bay, Wisconsin 171, 179
Greenwich Village, New York 145
"Gretl" 119
El Guettar Valley 58–59
Gundling, Beulah 141–142, 155–158, 174, 180
Gundling, Henry 141–142, 155, 158, 174
Gustav Line 72, 78

Hamburg, Germany 117, 119
Hardee, Carl 168–169, 179, 181–182
Harkins, Gen. Paul 71
Hashim, Gov. Ihsan Bey 137
Hausner, Peter 91, 94–95
Havlicek, Frank 45, 47
Hayes, Bernice Lorber 45, 158, 174–175, 178, 181–183
Hayward, Wisconsin 108
Hearn, Daniel 11, 144
Hearn, Lafcadio 11
Heidelberg, Germany 127, 159, 161–163
The Helms Hall of Fame 8, 21, 154, 157
Herzogenaurach, Germany 117
"Hill 609" 62
The Himalayas 167
Hitler, Adolf 87, 115, 128
Hoade, Father Eugene 137
Holm, Amy 108
Holm, Eleanor 124
honeymoon **28**, 31
Hong Kong 167
Honolulu, Hawaii 166
Horsetail Falls 34
The Hungarian Revolution 149
Husseini, Dr. Musa 137–137
hysterectomy 132

IAAA **116**, 157–159, 174, 180–184
Ida Noyes Hall 27, 96
Illinois Athletic Club 37–38
In Harm's Way 165, 170
India 166–167
Indonesia 166–167
InterContinental Hotel *see* Medinah Athletic Club
Ireland 10–11, 138–139, 144
The Irish Independent 138–139

The Irish Potato Famine 10
ISHOF 78, 178–181, 183
"Isle of Capri" (song) 77
Israel 137–138, 154–157

Japan 184
Jericho, Palestine 137–138
The Jerusalem Post 156
John, Bill 29, 56, 60–61, 63–64, 69, 71–72, 76, 82, 98, 118, 169
Jolson, Al 69, 71
Jordan, Kingdom of 137–138

Kartzow, Olga 74, 126, 140, 145
Kasserine Pass, Tunisia 55, 64
Katmandu, Nepal 167
Kellerman, Annette 8, 20–21
Kennedy, John F. 161–162
Khartoum, Sudan 163
King Abdullah I of Jordan 137–138
King Paul of Greece 140, 168
Kiphuth, Robert 47–48, 155–156, 174

The Lady's Aid Society 14
Lake Mendota 20–21
Lake Michigan 37, 39
Lanikai-Kailua, Hawaii 166
Lansing, Michigan 14
Lapeer, Michigan 12
last will & testament 179
Lazise, Italy 161
Leach, David Clark 27, 45–47, 122–123
The Leave Activities Office 8
Lecce, Italy 80
Leipzig, Germany 17
Lentz, Theodore A. 178–179, 182
Let's Talk About Washington Island 5, 131
LGBTQ+ 28–29, 145, 168–169
Libbey, Maj. Walt 128
The Liberty Club 62
Lincoln, Abraham 13–14
The Lincoln Club 117
The Linde Stadium Club 117
London, United Kingdom 138
Los Angeles, California 167
The Louvre 107
Luxembourg 123, 129

Madison, Wisconsin 10, 16, 19–21, 25, 171
Malta 163
The Man Who Came to Dinner 167
The Manhattan Project 96, 99
Manitowoc, Wisconsin 41
marriage 28, 124
Marseilles, France 89, 97–107
The Marshall Plan 115, 120, 125–126, 128, 141
Matthews, Francis P. 138

Index

McCarthy, Sen. Joseph 143
McCormick, Pat 141
McNarney, Gen. Joseph T. 88, 91
Medenine, Tunisia 58
Medinah Athletic Club 37
Meredith, Burgess 165
"The Merry Widow Waltz" 27
Mexico 33–35, 44
Milwaukee, Wisconsin 7, 9–10, 17–19, 38, 80, 109–110, 144
The Modern Mermaids 8, 31, 35–38, 45, 48, 156, 174
Mondello, Sicily *see* Palermo, Sicily
Mount of Olives 137
Mount Vernon, Virginia 53
Mount Vesuvius 75
Munich, Germany 126, 154, 166, 172
Mussolini, Benito 64

Nairobi, Kenya 163
Naples, Italy 71, 80, 84, 126, 140
Neal, Patricia 165
"Negro" American soldiers 56, 62, 106, 117, 120–121, 127
New York, New York 11, 53, 116, 133, 144–145, 149
New Zealand 166–167
NFFE 9
Nice, France 101, 106–107
Nixon, Richard M. 161–162, 173, 175, 177
The Normandy Invasion Landings 16, 79, 88
North Africa 55–65, 81
Notre Dame Cathedral 107
Nuremberg, Germany 8, 115–122, 128–161, 163, 172
The Nuremberg War Crimes Trials 111, 115–116

Oak Park, Illinois 32
Oakley, Wiley 147
Ohrdruf, Germany 86–87
Oklahoma migrants 32–33
Olsen, Norma J. 154
The Olympic Games 19, 123–124, 154, 181–182, 184; Helsinki 139–142
orphans 74–75, 80, 117, 119

Pakistan 166
The Palace of Justice, Nuremberg 115–117, 148
Palermo, Sicily 66–72
Panama 170
"Panorama" *see* The American Forces Network
"Paradise" *see* Agadir, Morocco
Paris, France 17, 100–101, 107–108, 130, 138
Park Ridge, Illinois 181
Patton, Gen. George S., Jr. 55, 58–60, 64–70, 80, 83–85, 87, 104, 180
Pearl Harbor, Hawaii 48, 96, 165
Pershing, Gen. John J. 25
physical education 19, 21, 24, 26–27, 29
Pompeii, Italy 77
Pontiac, Michigan 12–13
Pope Pius XII 126
Port Le Havre 107–109
portrait 78, 100, 180, **183**
Portugal 136
Potts, Allan 100–101
Powers, Francis Gary 159–160, 163
Preminger, Otto 165
Prentiss, Paula 165
Prince Philip of Edinburgh 141
Princess Elizabeth von Wittgenstein 74, 126, 140, 145
Principia 26
Prohibition 33–35
The Provost Marshal Building *see* The Palace of Justice, Nuremberg

Rabat, Morocco 56
Rangoon, Burma 167
Rankin, Arabella 11–14, 139
Rankin, Charles 13–14
Rankin, Francis 11–14, 139
Regensburg, Germany 118
Renk, Renate *see* Dullo, Renate
Rhythmic Swimming 1, 7, 27, 44, 48, 91
Ritter, R.M. 124
Robles, Marco Aurelio 170
Rome, Italy 80, 126, 166
Roosevelt, Franklin D. 49–50, 53–55
Roosevelt, Theodore 10
Rose, Billy 48, 93
Ross, Norman 37
Rotterdam, Netherlands 154
Rubinstein, Arthur 71
Russia 113, 130, 159–161, 184

St. Louis, Missouri 26
St. Moritz, Switzerland 123
St. Paul, Minnesota 26
St. Peter's Basilica 126
St. Stephen's Gate 137
Santa Cesarea, Italy 87
Schakel, Virginia "Ginny" 86, 90
Schwabach, Germany 117
Schwarzwald see The Black Forest, Germany
Selassie, Emperor Haile 168
Seller, Margaret "Peg" 180
The Shwedagon Pagoda 167
Sicily 64–72, 76–77
Singapore 167
The Soldier's Aid Society 14
Spain 136, 184
The Special Services 7–9, 121–164
Spider Lake 108–109
Stars & Stripes 87, 115–117, 140
Steinauer, Joe C. 23
Stevens, Milton 64
Stockholm, Sweden 123
The Story of San Michele 75
Strasbourg, France 127
stunt swimming 23, 27
Sturgeon Bay, Wisconsin 29, 179; hospital 182; radio station 172
Sullivan, Missouri 32
The Summit School 26
Swensen, Helga D. 93–94
Switzerland 107, 128, 138
synchronized swimming 6–8, 19, 21, 27, 31, 35–39, 44–48, 65, 85–95, 122–124, 129, 132, 139, 141–142, 153–154, 156–159

Tallahassee, Florida 157–159
Tamworth, New Hampshire 26
The Tarpon Club 27, 36
"This Is Your Life" 6–9, 163–164
Three Lakes, Wisconsin 26
Townsend, Akerly 17–18
Townsend, Ellen Crugom 17–18, 22
"Travel Time" *see* The American Forces Network
The Tritons 45
Truman, Harry S. 120, 125, 143
Tryon, Tom 165
Tulsa, Oklahoma 24
Tunis, Tunisia 68–69
Turkey 138
Turner, Marge 158, 182–184
Tyler, S. Roger, Jr. 137
Tyrrhenian Sea 72

The U-2 Incident 159–160
"U.S. Route 66" 32–33
The U.S. Rubber Company 36
The U.S. Sanitary Commission 14–15
The University of Alabama 29
The University of Chicago 8, 23, 26–27, 29–30, 35, 96
The University of Manitoba, Canada 174
The University of Michigan 29, 35
The University of Wisconsin 21, 23

Vaasa Leader 166
Vacha, Victoria 32–36, 38, 45, 111, 145, 149, 151, 171, 175
"V-E" Day 87
Verona, Italy 126
"V-J" Day 99

Wales, Ellen Murphy 129
Warsaw, Poland 160

Washington, D.C. 9, 14, 50, 53, 83, 111, 146
Washington Island, Wisconsin 5–6, 29, 39–40, 43, 96, 99, 108, 121–122, 125, 131, 133–135, 142–148, 166–173, 175, 177–184
The Watergate scandal 175–176
Waukesha, Wisconsin 18
WAVES 103–104
Wayne, John 165, 170
West Germany 6–9, 115–164
"Whitey" 51, 79–82, 109–111
Whitney, Andrea 171
Whitney, Anne Townsend 5, 10, 17–20, 22, 26, 40–44, 49–50, 96, 104, 121, 130–135, 142–148, 168, 179, 183
Whitney, Caroline 161–163, 165–166, 169–171
Whitney, Christopher 162, 165–166, 175, 178
Whitney, Edna 10, 19
Whitney, Gaylord Lee 1, 5–6, 32, 38–44, 49–50, 54–55, 66–67, 96, 103, 111, 122, 134, 147, 157, 161–163, 165–166, 169–170, 178, 182–184
Whitney, George 19, 22, 31–32, 38, 40–41, 103–104, 162, 182
Whitney, Jane Ellen 19, 22, 103–104, 146–147, 171–172, 175, 177
Whitney, Jane Rankin 10–11, 13
Whitney, Lee Rankin 9–10, *13*–15, 18–19, 38–39, 50, 96–97, 104, 108–111
Whitney, Lenore 165
Whitney, Leroy Chester 10
Whitney, Marion Baker 31–32, 38, 40, 162
Whitney, Meredith 171
Whitney, Robert Lee 19, 21–22, 96–97, 102, 111, 125, 169
Wiesbaden, Germany 117
Wilbur Wright Junior College 39, 44–46, 71, 108, 111, 174
Williams, Esther 48, 123
Wilmette, Illinois 47
Wirz (Thannhauser), Dr. Bella 156–157
The Wisconsin Alumnus 23, 48
World War I 21, 24–26, 68
World War II 14, 16, 29, 48–100, 146–147

www.ingramcontent.com/pod-product-compliance
Lightning Source LLC
Chambersburg PA
CBHW060344010526
44117CB00017B/2953